ARTILLERY
AT THE
GOLDEN GATE

The Harbor Defenses of San Francisco in World War II

By Brian B. Chin

PICTORIAL HISTORIES PUBLISHING COMPANY INC.
Missoula, Montana 59801

LIBRARY OF CONGRESS
CATALOG CARD NO. 94-65848
ISBN 0-929521-85-4

First Printing March 1994

Partial Funding For This Book Was Provided By
The Fort MacArthur Museum Association, San Pedro, California

PICTORIAL HISTORIES PUBLISHING COMPANY, INC.
713 SOUTH THIRD STREET
MISSOULA, MONTANA 59801

Introduction

A cool, damp summer fog drifted over the hills of Fort Cronkhite in August 1964. I stood on the hillside facing a huge concrete entrance and peered down the cavernous chamber towards the far opening where the fog rolled past. As I walked into the tunnel, my footsteps echoed. Emerging on the other side, I looked up and saw a massive concrete awning over the opening. I turned and climbed up the earthen hill into which the tunnel had been burrowed. The fog-shrouded scrub landscape of the Marin headlands stretched below. Atop the hill, I found rusted strands of barbed wire surrounding crumbled-in foxholes. Shards of rotting timbers stuck out of the ground, the remains of wood framing used in some other time to shore up the dugouts. I looked again at the thick fog and the scrub hills of Fort Cronkhite, and wondered who had been here before me, and why they had built these old military structures. Somewhere in the mist, clanging bell buoys and sonorous fog horns sounded. If this were a clear summer day, I would have seen the Pacific Ocean below, and across the Golden Gate, I would have seen San Francisco.

Between the two world wars, the U.S. Army emplaced huge coastal defense guns on these barren hills overlooking the Golden Gate and the "concrete soldiers" waited for the attack of enemy battleships that never came. This much was clear to the weekend visitors of post-war generations. The sightseers came to the abandoned Army forts and clambered atop the old gun positions in search of incomparable Pacific vistas. On anniversaries of the December 7th Pearl Harbor attack, television news crews from the city also trekked out to the forts at the Golden Gate. As the video cameras rolled, the news reporter would stand before an old emplacement, and in a condescending tone, talk of the war jitters that supposedly overtook San Franciscans on that date of infamy. Smiling smugly, the reporter relished the irony that the Army had prepared its artillery defenses at great effort without ever having the occasion to fire a shot against the enemy fleet that never showed up.

On a September evening in the early autumn of 1991, in a small town on the eastern fringes of Ohio, I sat talking with an old Army colonel in his little mansion. I had known him for a few years, and visited him occasionally. There was always some wartime story he dredged up from the past about his adventures overseas in North Africa and Europe. The colonel's wartime photographs showed a dashing officer with a Clark Gable moustache and insouciant wrinkle of the brow be he astride a camel in the North African desert or sitting down to his dejeuner at a sidewalk Parisian bistro. The colonel served at various Allied headquarters with some notable military leaders of the period. But during the earlier days of World War II, this West Point officer had commanded some of the big guns and mine defenses at the Golden Gate. Fifty years later, on a September afternoon, with the autumn leaves just starting to turn red, I informed the colonel of my latest project. "So you're writing a book about Fort Scott," he replied. "Well, it's a big job. At San Francisco, I had my own coast artillery regiment," he reminded me. Then I leaned closer, eager to hear the real story about the San Francisco harbor defenses from one who had been in high command. "We were ready for the Japanese battleships," began the West Point colonel with a wry smile, "but they never showed up."

Brian B. Chin
San Francisco, November 1993

Acknowledgements

Artillery at the Golden Gate had its genesis in the summer of 1991 when the U.S. Government proposed the closing of Army bases in San Francisco and Marin County, notably the Presidio, Fort Winfield Scott, and the five sub-posts that made up the harbor defenses of the Golden Gate in World War II. The announced base-closings provided the impetus to publish a collection of vintage photographs culled from the files of the Presidio Army Museum. Modest intentions soon gave way to a full-blown historical treatment of the subject. The story of the big-gun defenses of San Francisco Bay in the mid-Twentieth Century was too fascinating a tale not to be told completely. The National Park Service, which had been charged with converting the abandoned Army property into public park lands, had done studies of the harbor defense posts on the bay. These studies concerned themselves largely with military archeology and engineering. But details were scarce on harbor defense operations and activities of Army coast artillery units stationed at the forts. This book hopes to fill that void by explaining the Golden Gate harbor defenses---their operations, armament, and organization---and how the defenses fit into the bigger picture of the Bay Area during World War II. The resulting book not only gives the "war history" of the Harbor Defenses of San Francisco, but imparts a mood and feeling for the colorful wartime city which these defenses protected.

Without the following individuals who gave to this project their time, knowledge, memories, photographs, and sometimes writing and proof-reading abilities, this book would not have been possible: Dale Barnhart, Preston B. Cannady, Calvin S.K. Chin, Daniel G. Cook, Ralph DeMoisy, Edward W. Fitzgerald, Harry N. Freeman, John Freeman, Rose Gyn, Lee Kanof, Arthur Kramer, Jack R. Lehmkuhl, Frank A. Liwski, Frank W. Mahoney, Richard R. Moorman, Leo Murphy, Rudy Palihnich, Mario Paolini, Harrison S. Payne, Tom Scally, John Schonher, Willis E. Spitzer, Charles J. Sullivan, John J. Taheny, Felix M. Usis, George B. Webster, and Fred C. Weyand.

The following individuals gave access to records and photographs from their respective institutions: Patricia Akre, San Francisco Archives of the S.F. Public Library, Mark Berhow, Sam Stokes, and Tom Thomas of the Fort MacArthur Museum, Richard Boyden of the Pacific Sierra Region of the National Archives, Steven Gammons of the U.S. Army Center of Military History, Mary Gentry of the Treasure Island Museum, Steven A. Haller and Irene Stachura of the S.F. Maritime National Historical Park, Maria T. Hanna of the Suitland Reference Branch, National Archives, John Martini of the Golden Gate National Recreation Area, Kevin Turner and Lynn Fonfa of Fort Point, Herbert Garcia and J. Edward Green of the Presidio Army Museum, Wendy Swenson of Fairmont Hotel Public Relations, Jean Thevierge and Jean Cloud of the Redwood City Public Library, Robert W. Parkinson and Ernest A. Tordsen of the Golden Gate Chapter, S.S. Historical Society.

In addition, the following individuals supplied documents, photographs, or lent their areas of expertise in the cause of this book: Charles Bogart, Kenneth Cooper, Jr., Dixon Greenwood, David H. Grover, Mary Louise Usis, and Felix Usis, Jr. Eliot M. Louie provided photographic services.

TABLE OF CONTENTS

Introduction- iii

Acknowledgements- iv

Chapter 1: Gold in Peace, Iron in War/page 1

Chapter 2: Last Year of the Regulars/page 11

Chapter 3: From Rookies to Concrete Soldiers/page 25

Chapter 4: "An Enemy Will Attack
                    the Golden Gate Bridge"/page 43

Chapter 5: High Tide of Danger/page59

Chapter 6: Buoyant Mines and Cracked Crab/page 77

Chapter 7: They Shall Not Pass/page 85

Chapter 8: War City on the Bay/page 105

Chapter 9: Wide Awake and on the Job/page 127

Chapter 10: Victory and Beyond/page 143

Chapter 11: Operation Blowtorch/page 159

Bibliography

Index

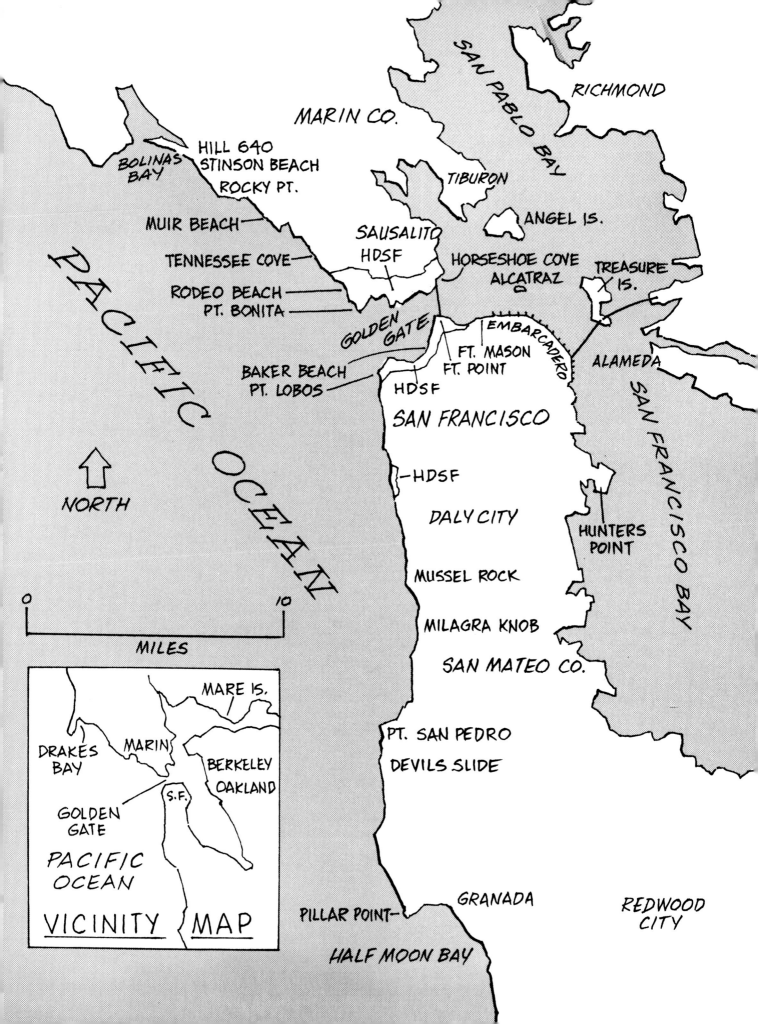

Chapter 1:

Gold in Peace, Iron in War

"Usis," ordered Brigadier General Edward A. Stockton into the phone, "come over right away." Across the bay in his Berkeley hills home, Lieutenant Colonel Felix M. Usis hung up the telephone and got ready to drive over to Fort Winfield Scott, the main post for the Harbor Defenses of San Francisco. This Sunday morning, there was no rest for Usis, the HDSF Mine Commander. After four months at the Command and General Staff School at Fort Leavenworth, Kansas, Lieutenant Colonel Usis had arrived back in the Bay Area by train on December 7, 1941 to be greeted with the news of the Pearl Harbor attack.

Usis drove west across the San Francisco-Oakland Bay Bridge. Interurban trains operated on the lower deck of the silver span. The top deck carried six lanes of two-way vehicle traffic. The veteran coast artillery officer noticed few other autos traveling with him toward San Francisco. But the oncoming traffic going east seemed unusually heavy. Perhaps the eastbound cars were trying to escape the coastal areas, Usis thought to himself. After the surprise

air attack on Hawaii, the Japanese threat to San Francisco could not be discounted. With this in mind, Lieutenant Colonel Usis continued driving toward the city, which was to become for a time, the front line of America's war in the Pacific.

Stunned by the Japanese surprise attack at Pearl Harbor, West Coast residents worried that a follow-up strike might hit America's Pacific shore. To self-assured San Franciscans who long considered their harbor the most important on the Pacific coast, there was no question which target enemy battleships and air fleets would chose next. After all, San Francisco Bay, with its network of industries, naval yards, and military bases, was too important for the Japanese not to attack. As San Franciscans stood on Ocean Beach, nervously scanning the western horizon for Japanese battleships or carrier aircraft, they had only to recall the interwar years when Bay Area governments and commercial interests enthusiastically encouraged the building of military bases in the region. By 1941, with military and industrial activity at high pitch around the bay, San Francisco was on the bull's eye---the tempting target for a Japanese fleet. Perhaps the city could now assure itself just how important it was.

Lieutenant Colonel Felix M. Usis beside ceremonial cannon at Fort Scott parade ground. (Presidio Army Museum)

The specter of hostile vessels sailing through the Golden Gate dogged San Francisco from its earliest history. In the late 1700's when the town was but a languishing Spanish colonial settlement on the shores of a splendid natural harbor, the local military garrison constructed an adobe and brick fort at the top of the rocky bluff on the south side of the Gate. Completed in 1794, this small fortification mounted about a dozen light cannon. By all accounts unimpressive, the Castillo de San Joaquin, as the Spaniards named the fort, never had to stand the test of combat. But the progression of San Francisco harbor fortifications had begun. When California joined the United States, and the U.S. Army assumed responsibility for guarding the Golden Gate, the site of this early fort became the starting point for the American defenses.

During the War of 1812, few American coastal defenses opposed the British forces along the Atlantic coast. After that war, the U.S. Congress saw the immediate need for large forts at strategic points and passed legislation to build them. The fortifications were costly and the appropriations for construction came slowly, with forts along the Eastern seaboard having priority. Fort Point at San Francisco was the first and only classic casemated coastal fort of this period constructed on the Pacific coast. Between 1854 and 1861, Army engineers built Fort Point where the Castillo de San Joaquin once stood. The massive brick and granite structure supported a large concentration of guns on its four tiers. Army engineers also established individual gun batteries on Alcatraz Island to protect the inner harbor. During the Civil War, the San Francisco defenses were augmented by new batteries at Angel Island and at Point San Jose on the shore of the city itself, at the site of today's Fort Mason. Civil War combat on the East Coast revealed the weakness of brick forts that were subjected to continuous bombardment. But individual gun batteries, dug-in and well-dispersed, proved more resilient under fire. After the Civil War, Army engineers constructed such emplacements on both sides of the Golden Gate armed with large-caliber, smooth-bore, muzzle-loading Rodman cannon But American harbor defenses like those at

San Francisco were soon out-gunned and out-ranged by iron battleships, powerful breech-loading rifled cannon, and effective propellant charges then being developed by world powers.

In 1885, an act of Congress created the Endicott Board to develop a national harbor defense policy. Named after its chairman, Secretary of War William C. Endicott, the board consisted of American military experts in the fields of ordnance and engineering. After a thorough review of American coast defenses in light of recent advances in artillery and warships, the Endicott Board issued proposals for a new generation of seacoast armament. New harbor defenses were to include armored gun turrets, machine guns, underwater mines, and electric searchlights. The Board listed twenty-two American ports to be fortified. They put New York first on the list--followed by San Francisco in second place. The Board proposed 110 guns and 128 mortars for the defense of the latter city. The recommendations of the Endicott Board resulted in coastal defense construction at many American harbors, including San Francisco Bay. These turn-of-the-century fortifications, together with some notable future additions, comprised the defenses guarding the Golden Gate during World War II. Like the B-52 jet bombers of a more recent national defense system, the big guns of the Coast Artillery would be older than most of the World War II GI's who manned them.

In 1891, Army Engineers emplaced the first new batteries at Fort Winfield Scott on the seaward end of the Presidio. Sited on the crest of high bluffs overlooking Fort Point, Batteries Miller and Godfrey mounted three 10-inch and three 12-inch rifles respectively. The War Department named emplacements for distinguished Army officers. Then Batteries Cranston (two 10-inch guns,) Lancaster (three 12-inch guns,) and Boutelle (three 5-inch guns) joined the first two on this promontory. Soon after, engineers installed Battery Howe-Wagner (sixteen 12-inch mortars) several hundred yards southeast of this gun line.

Next, the battery builders worked their way south along the San Francisco shoreline. Emplacements with names like Saffold (two

12-inch guns,) Stotsenburg-McKinnon (sixteen 12-inch mortars,) Crosby (two 6-inch guns,) and Chamberlin (four 6-inch guns) hunkered into the bluffs and sand dunes all the way to Baker Beach. The last of these batteries was completed in 1904. Farther south, above Lands End, the Army established Fort Miley in 1900 and emplaced sixteen 12-inch seacoast mortars of Battery Springer-Livingston. Battery Chester, further west at Miley, pointed three 12-inch rifles directly over Lands End.

The Army concurrently fortified the Marin shore of the Golden Gate, starting at Fort Baker. Battery Spencer sited three 12-inch guns at Lime Point, 450 feet above the narrows of the Gate. By 1904, Batteries Kirby (two 12-inch guns,) Wagner (two 5-inch guns,) Duncan (two 8-inch guns,) and Yates (six 3-inch guns) took vantage points from Kirby Beach to Horseshoe Cove. Even before they proof-fired Fort Baker's armament, Army engineers planned gun batteries on the seaward end of the Marin shore. To bring enemy vessels under fire well forward of the Golden Gate, the Army created Fort Barry in 1901. On its barren headlands were emplaced Batteries Mendell (two 12-inch guns) and Alexander (eight 12-inch mortars.) Soon followed Batteries Guthrie and Rathbone, with four 6-inch guns apiece; and finally, Battery O'Rorke with four 3-inch guns. The smaller rifles were intended to fire on fast, lightly armored vessels like destroyers and minesweepers, while heavy guns and mortars engaged battleships.

The typical American seacoast battery mounted guns in an open concrete emplacement. The gun barrels, nearly invisible from the sea, poked slightly over the parapet. Some seacoast rifles, mounted on disappearing carriages, remained behind the parapet until their muzzles rose over the crest to fire. The resulting recoil knocked the guns back into

the pits, ready for reloading. Safely behind the parapet, gunners turned cranks and loaded shells and powder into the armament. Other crews worked in the power, ammunition, and fire-control rooms sheltered under the reinforced-concrete structure. In addition to gun batteries, Army engineers established electrical searchlight stations and mine facilities. Concrete mine casemates (from which mines were electrically detonated) were built at Baker Beach and Fort Barry. The Army constructed docks and storage buildings for mine operations at Forts Baker, Scott, and Yerba Buena Island.

Approximately six companies of artillerymen manned the new armament. These artillery companies were first formed in 1901 and some of the units saw service in the Philippines. The troops lived at the Presidio and went up the hill to Fort Scott for artillery drill and target practice on the big guns. During the 1906 fire and earthquake, these soldiers created good will for the Army in San Francisco when they helped civil authorities restore order in the ravaged city. In 1912, handsome Mission Revival barracks surrounding a central parade ground were built at Fort Scott, and this post became headquarters for the Coast Defenses of San Francisco. The artillery companies from the Presidio then moved to the new barracks.

The Golden Gate defenses were manned during World War I. But by then, several new foreign dreadnoughts out-ranged

1910 artillery gun crew of Battery Lancaster at Fort Scott. (Presidio Army Museum)

American seacoast artillery; the new battleships carried turrets with high firing angles, which increased the range of shipboard guns. This development worried the U.S. Army. In theory, an enemy battleship ten miles south of San Francisco at San Pedro Point, staying just outside range of the batteries at Fort Miley, could bombard the greater part of the city with impunity. To counter this threat, the Chief of Coast Artillery in Washington D.C. suggested installing 16-inch guns on a military reservation just south of Ocean Beach. The Army had purchased this sandy area between the sea and Lake Merced in 1900 for coast defenses. Nothing was built there until 1917, when the Army named the property Fort Funston and emplaced Battery Walter Howe with four 12-inch mortars to cover the southern approach to the harbor entrance. Too late for World War I, Battery Howe was not completed until 1919. As for the 16-inch Funston battery proposed by the Chief of Coast Artillery, the Army held off construction for now.

The Army succeeded in emplacing more modern long-range armament on the Marin side of the Golden Gate during World War I. In 1915, the Ordnance Department introduced a seacoast gun carriage which permitted a higher angle of elevation for the standard 12-inch barrel, which dramatically increased its range from eight to seventeen miles. The War Department included San Francisco on the short list to receive one of the new installations. Thus Battery Wallace, sporting a pair of these improved weapons, was constructed at Fort Barry during World War I. To keep construction rapid, simple, and inexpensive, Battery Wallace was built with no overhead cover or protective parapets. The two guns stood on circular concrete pads. Only a five hundred-foot dispersion of the guns and magazines offered some protection against a direct hit. A concrete structure between and to the rear of the armament housed the power plant, plotting room, and ammunition magazines. This part of the installation did have a protective covering of concrete and earth. The Army built Battery Wallace as a stop-gap fortification that filled the need for long-range seacoast artillery at the Golden Gate. Overhead protection, now especially required because of the airplane, waited for another day.

No enemy warships appeared off the California coast to challenge the defenses during World War I. The German fleet was bottled up in Europe. Japan was an ally of the Western Powers. Life was quiet enough at the Coast Defenses of San Francisco to enable a number of artillery companies to depart for France where they manned antiaircraft weapons. Meanwhile in San Francisco, a healthy war economy flourished. Many factories and most shipyards switched to war production. Existing yards expanded and new ones were built. They all operated twenty-four hours a day. The demand for workers drew job seekers to San Francisco, resulting in a housing shortage and over-crowding in shops, restaurants, and public

Target practice with 12-inch gun of Battery Wallace at Fort Barry after World War I. (Presidio Army Museum)

transportation. The population of San Francisco increased from 417,000 in 1910 to 507,000 in 1920, due largely to workers and ex-servicemen who came to the city in wartime and decided afterwards to stay. The San Francisco Bay Area proved its strategic value in the Great War and civic boosters would use that theme again in the coming decades.

San Francisco shared in the national prosperity of the 1920's. A phalanx of new commercial buildings rose in the financial district and the downtown shopping area around Union Square and Market Street from 3rd to 8th Streets prospered with new hotels, stores, and movie theaters. Along the bay front from the Embarcadero to Hunters Point, the city's main industrial zone filled to capacity. Then new industries expanded down the peninsula, beyond the city limits. On the sandy hills in the western part of town, vast residential housing tracts became San Francisco's version of the suburbs. These were the Richmond and Sunset Districts, "with long rows of almost identical cottages, each with a lawn in front and with garage doors beneath the living room bay window." On the craggy hills west of Market Street, in the Mission and Potrero districts, new residential areas sprouted on the rocky heights. Burrowing under these hills, the Twin Peaks Tunnel, finished in 1917, brought streetcar lines to the southwestern part of town, where developers began transformation of pastures, vegetable gardens, and sand dunes into suburban areas. Forts Miley and Funston, once isolated on the undeveloped ocean side of the city, found San Francisco's new housing tracts

nearly at their front gates.

Despite local prosperity, San Franciscans feared they could not match the material success of their southern rival, Los Angeles . The 1920 Census showed that upstart Los Angeles, now awash in oil wells and movies, surpassed San Francisco in population and commercial growth. As the ultimate indignity, Hollywood film stars in their expensive roadsters flocked to San Francisco for weekend parties at the city's most elegant hotels. "Hollywood Must Stop Using San Francisco for a Garbage Can," editorialized the *San Francisco Examiner* when rotund film comedian Roscoe "Fatty" Arbuckle faced manslaughter charges in 1921 for the death of a minor starlet during a weekend binge in his 12th floor suite at the St. Francis Hotel.

To maintain San Francisco's preeminence, if not in the commercial realm, at least in the minds of her citizens, civic leaders turned to the theme of the Bay Area as a strategic military center. In the 1920's, city newspapers wrote often of San Francisco as the "American Singapore," a magnificent harbor for the U.S. Navy's Pacific Fleet. "We do not need the fleet to protect us from anybody," proclaimed the *San Francisco Chronicle* in 1919. "What we want of the fleet is to sell it supplies, do the necessary repair work, and enjoy the company of the uniforms at our society hops." Civic boosters, wary of further industrialization and the labor chaos it brought, felt tourism and military bases made

"San Francisco's version of the suburbs"---new homes for sale in the Sunset District, April 24, 1926. (San Francisco Archives, S.F. Public Library)

The beginning of Sunset District housing tracts leading to the sea as viewed from Funston Avenue and Pacheco Street, January 16, 1928. Fort Funston is off the photo left. (San Francisco Archives, S.F. Public Library)

better foundations for the bay region's economy.

San Francisco courted the military services with a variety of civic tributes; Army Day, Navy Day, Harbor Day, Armistice Day, and Defense Week were publicized and celebrated enthusiastically each year during the interwar period. Coast Artillery bands and marching units from Fort Scott participated regularly in parades marking these occasions. In 1932, the city built the War Memorial Opera House and Veteran's Building at the Civic Center to honor the war dead of the First World War. Veterans received preference in hiring for civil service jobs. When the Pacific Fleet visited port, sailors rode free on the Municipal Railway. In 1933, the new heavy cruiser USS *San Francisco* was christened in its namesake city.

The U.S. Navy encouraged San Francisco's enthusiasm for increased military activity in the bay. Diminished by the naval building freeze (Washington Naval Treaty, 1922) and peacetime cutbacks, the Navy wanted allies in the U.S. Congress to help fight its budget battles. The admirals found eager friends in the San Francisco civic establishment and the Bay Area congressional delegation. San Francisco Mayor Angelo J. Rossi and the *San Francisco Chronicle* created the Bay Cities Naval Affairs Committee to bring navy facilities and repair yards to the Bay Area.

The Navy did what it could to demonstrate why San Francisco should become the "American Singapore." Coinciding with the inauguration of President Franklin D. Roosevelt, naval units maneuvered off the California coast in 1933. By designating San Francisco the main target of an attack, the Navy hoped to convince the new president to maintain a strong naval presence in the bay. After the war games, the Navy declared San Francisco "destroyed" by the mock attack. Local newspapers duly reported the event, publicizing the need for naval bases and rearmament.

Lobbying efforts by the U.S. Navy and local interests eventually paid dividends. The Navy got its funding and San Francisco got its military development and the resulting commercial rewards. The federal government spent one billion dollars on naval projects in the Bay Area before Pearl Harbor; $650 million went to shipbuilding alone. The naval buildup was accomplished in stages, as one writer termed the Navy's "strategy of overload" in getting President Roosevelt and the Congress to dispense more money; first, the fleet was built up, swamping Bay Area facilities. This justified construction of further facilities, which required the protection of additional naval forces, naval bases, and Army harbor defenses.

In 1923, an Army War Plans Division study declared the San Francisco defenses outmoded. No antiaircraft batteries protected the forts against air attack, and with the exception of Battery Wallace, the shore batteries were out-ranged by modern shipboard guns. The War Plans Division urged construction of

Army Day ceremonies at Crissy Field in the Presidio during the early 1930's. (San Francisco Archives, S.F. Public Library)

new long-range batteries. But during peace-time, the Army shelved improvement plans for lack of funds. After World War I, small care-taker detachments maintained the existing armament and guarded the military posts. In 1924, the old Coast Defenses gave way to a new Army command---the Harbor Defenses of San Francisco, and its accompanying tactical unit, the 6th Coast Artillery Regiment. The regiment was made up of batteries bearing letter designations (Battery A, B, C, etc.) During the interwar period, the Harbor Defenses of San Francisco and the 6th Coast Artillery were paper organizations, with only enough troops to garrison the harbor forts. Occasionally, reservists or ROTC cadets fired the seacoast guns during summer training.

When Japan invaded China in the 1930's, San Francisco loomed prominently as a naval base should the U.S. be drawn into a conflict with the Japanese. The U.S. Navy counted on the harbor defenses to protect seaward approaches to San Francisco Bay, so Navy ships could safely sortie out to meet the enemy. In late 1934, Japan renounced the Five Power Naval Treaty which limited construction of heavy battleships. Soon, Japan re-sumed building warships equipped with armament able to out-range seacoast guns at the Golden Gate. With in-creased naval activity on the bay, the Navy wished to safeguard its installations and insist-ed the Army's aging harbor defenses be strengthened. During an inspection tour of Pa-cific coast military installations in the summer of 1935, a Congressional House Appropriations Committee approved the immediate construction of the long-planned 16-inch gun battery at Fort Funston and a sim-ilar installation on the Marin headlands.

Work proceeded rapidly. The San Francisco District Office of the Army Corps of Engineers dusted off its old plans for the Fun-ston battery. Chief of Engineering Design George F. Crowe devised casemates for two

The Golden Gate Bridge had not yet been built when these Navy four-stack destroyers laid down a smoke-screen in maneuvers past old Fort Point. (Presidio Army Museum)

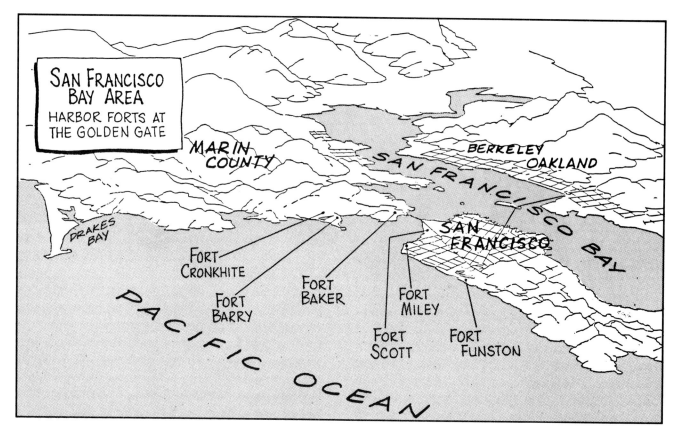

16-inch guns separated by six hundred feet of galleries, power rooms, and ammunition magazines. The ground work for Battery Davis began on a sandy ridge at Fort Funston in October 1936. 16-inch gun barrels, which the Army obtained from canceled Navy battlecruisers, came from the Aberdeen Army Proving Grounds in Maryland. The Watertown Arsenal in Massachusetts manufactured the Army-designed gun carriages. In March 1937, the armament arrived at Mare Island aboard the Army transport *Ludington*. The shipment moved by flatcar to Fort Funston's nearest rail terminus, where the gigantic gun tubes transferred onto long flat-bed trailers. This unusual caravan caused a stir as it drove through the sparsely settled part of town.

At Funston, after mounting the 16-inch naval guns on their modified Model 1919 carriages, the Corps of Engineers test fired the armament to settle their concrete foundations in the sand. Then eight and one-half foot thick concrete casemates reinforced with steel rod and mesh were constructed around the guns. Twenty feet of earth covered the casemates and the long connecting tunnel. The engineers

embedded a two-foot thick concrete burster course under the top surface of the soil to explode shells before they could penetrate to the main work. When completed in February 1939, Battery Davis appeared as an earthen ridge with two openings for the guns six hundred feet apart at either end. The Corps of Engineers also built separate casemates for radio, plotting, and switchboard rooms, and a battery commander's station. All were dispersed at some distance from the guns. The engineers camouflaged the installations with a covering of trees, grasses, and ice plant. The emplacements at Funston cost $860,440. Each16-inch gun carried a separate price of $1,130,940.

During construction of the Funston battery, the Army established Fort Cronkhite on the Marin headlands north of Fort Barry. The new post encompassed Elk Valley, Tennessee Point, and the eight-hundred foot heights of Wolf Ridge. The Army also acquired several small parcels of land overlooking Stinson Beach and Drakes Bay for artillery observation posts. At Fort Cronkhite, the Corps of Engineers built Battery Townsley, mounting

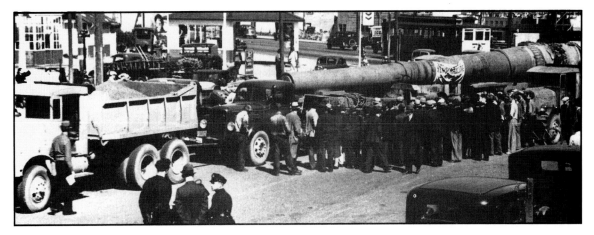

(Above) Prime mover taking16-inch gun barrel to Fort Funston stops on street to untangle a cable as crowd gathers to observe, April 1, 1937. (San Francisco Archives, S.F. Public Library)
(Below) Fort Funston 16-incher on concrete foundation prior to overhead casemating, February 24, 1938. (Presidio Army Museum)

two casemated 16-inch rifles. The emplacement was similar to the Funston battery. But rather than mounting the guns first, engineers finished the casemates, then brought the 16-inch barrels in through the openings. Popular myth has the massive gun tubes, on their way to Cronkhite, becoming jammed in the long Fort Barry tunnel.

The two 16-inch batteries provided the Harbor Defenses of San Francisco with armament capable of shooting a 2100-pound armor-piercing projectile some 44,000 yards (twenty-five miles) to sea. The casemates protected the long-range rifles from air attack and naval gunfire. Batteries Davis and Townsley were the first heavy caliber casemated batteries emplaced at any American port. The honor of having the first two of these powerful batteries symbolized the strategic importance of the Bay Area. By September 1, 1939, when war broke out in Europe with Germany's invasion of Poland, the Harbor Defenses of San Francisco contained a variety of armament, from the aging guns and mortars of 1890 to the modern 16-inch casemated batteries of the future. The soldiers needed to man these defenses would come later.

In 1939, writer-photographer Edwin

Wooden forms for pouring concrete casemates of 16-inch Battery Townsley at Fort Cronkhite. Point Bonita of Fort Barry can be seen in middle distance, with Fort Miley and San Francisco across the Gate. (Presidio Army Museum)

Rosskam described the export of U.S. scrap metal through San Francisco's harbor to Japan: "Eastward, through the port of San Francisco, the most industrialized nation in the world sends out its manufactures . . . Japan is one of the largest customers. During the last few years, America's broken machinery, rusted rails, and junked automobiles have been leaving San Francisco in a steady stream to become guns, shells, bombs, and bullets." San Francisco's municipal flag carries the city's official motto: *Oro en Paz, Fierro en Guerra---Gold in Peace, Iron in War.*

Moving the 16-inch gun barrels into the completed Battery Townsley casemates, July 27, 1939. (Presidio Army Museum)

Chapter 2:
Last Year of the Regulars

April 6, 1940, Army Day at the Presidio of San Francisco: The local Junior Chamber of Commerce sponsored this annual commemoration of the United States' entry into World War I. Throughout the afternoon on that spring day, six thousand civilians milled about Crissy Field and the Presidio parade ground, marveling at the display of military equipment from all combat branches. Bands from the Presidio and the 6th Coast Artillery Regiment circulated through the crowd, providing a military atmosphere with their music. Then at four o'clock, a fifteen-gun salute fired by a coast artillery detachment heralded the arrival to the reviewing stand of Lieutenant General John L. DeWitt and his 4th Army staff. Battalions from San Francisco-based Army regiments paraded past; the 30th Infantry, 6th Coast Artillery, and 65th Coast Artillery Regiments of the regular Army, and the 159th Infantry and 250th Coast Artillery Regiments of the California National Guard.

As officers on the reviewing stand returned the salute of the last battalion to march past, the Crissy Field crowd began to disperse. The Jaycees had orchestrated another

Prewar public display of coast artillery projectiles at Presidio main parade ground. (Presidio Army Museum)

successful San Francisco Army Day. But world conflicts overshadowed this year's remembrance of the Great War. The soldiers and civilians who participated in Army Day 1940 did so with the current events of Europe fresh in mind. The German Army had conquered Poland the past September and now lined up against French and British forces in Western Europe . Newspapers reported German naval units on the move for the invasion of Norway.

Also on the reviewing stand for this Army Day in the spring of 1940 was Major

General Henry T. Burgin, commanding the 9th Coast Artillery District. Headquartered at the Presidio, the 9th Coast Artillery District controlled all regular and reserve coast artillery troops in California and other Western states. The Harbor Defenses of San Francisco (HDSF) came within the 9th CA District's jurisdiction. A harbor defense, consisting of a number of forts, was the U.S. Army command charged with guarding a harbor or other water area, chiefly with shore batteries and submarine minefields. Like many Army commands in peacetime, HDSF was not fully operational. In 1939, coast artillerymen in the entire Army numbered only 4,200. The American Army was emerging from "the lean years of the thirties," historian Lee Kennett wrote. As late as 1939, the Army's meager budget allotted only 1.2 percent of its funds for research and development. A small cadre of regulars, many with no other prospects during the Depression, joined the service and dreamed of "a corporal's stripes and five more dollars a month." And then there were the officers, many of them West Pointers, who remained first lieutenants and captains in a small peacetime Army with little room for advancement.

The headquarters building of the Harbor Defenses of San Francisco was located on the bend of the horseshoe-shaped barracks row encircling the parade ground at Fort Winfield Scott. From the windows of HDSF Headquarters, officers looked across the grassy parade, past the stately Mission Revival enlisted men's barracks on either side, and saw the graceful towers of the new Golden Gate Bridge not too far distant. In the spring of 1940, Brigadier General Thomas A. Terry, the HDSF commander, operated from this office with his harbor defense staff, carrying on the routine of running Fort Scott and the sub-posts on both sides of the Golden Gate. General Terry's staff drafted a new program of harbor defense improvements and prepared troop training plans in response to conflicts overseas. HDSF shared the Fort Scott building with the headquarters of the 6th Coast Artillery Regiment.

The regiment's Battery C occupied the barracks next to the HDSF headquarters building. When the original battery commander was transferred to the Marin side, Second Lieutenant George B. Webster took over the unit. Webster, a reserve officer on active duty, remained the only commissioned officer in the battery until mid-1940. Battery C manned 155mm guns and 3-inch antiaircraft guns at Fort Funston. The three-gun AA battery stood on concrete pads. The men drilled on the fixed guns, but did not fire them. But service target practice, in which live ammunition was fired on moving waterborne targets, was conducted several times with Battery C's four 155mm seacoast guns positioned on a ridge near the San Francisco Police Department pistol range at Funston.

Each 155mm gun traversed on a Panama mount, a steel and concrete circular ring set into the ground. Before the annual target shoot,

1938 view of Fort Scott barracks and parade ground with Golden Gate Bridge in the distance at right.

Battery C fired excaliber gun drills using 37mm guns sited near the 155's. When target practice with the 155mm guns was about to take place, the San Francisco crab fleet appeared in the Funston battery's field of fire. The Coast Guard tried to chase the crabbers away, but the fishermen kept coming back. An exasperated safety officer assigned to the target practice turned to Second Lieutenant Webster and said, "Go ahead and shoot." Webster gave the order to commence firing. "When we let the first rounds go out," he later remembered, "all the crabbers picked up and headed for the Golden Gate." The Harbor Defenses ordered Webster to pull one of his 155mm guns out of position, strip the artillery piece down, and remove the old paint. Battery C repainted the gun with automotive lacquer to give it a new glossy finish. "We entered a high-shine 155 in the world's fair," as George Webster recalled the Army's display at the 1940 Golden Gate International Exposition at Treasure Island.

During national holidays, harbor defense troops marched in civic parades down San Francisco's Market Street. When the coast artillerymen marched in East Bay events, they went to Oakland aboard the *El Aquario*, an Army Quartermaster water lighter which serviced Alcatraz and Angel Island. Once, while the troops paraded in Oakland, the *El Aquario's* civilian skipper waited in a bar and had too much to drink. When the *El Aquario*, loaded with soldiers, returned to the Fort Scott mine dock, the skipper's unsure boat handling caused the vessel to strike and shatter the longitudinal timbers at the end of the wharf. The troops had a hard time getting off the ship that day.

In early 1940, the 6th Coast Artillery Regiment existed at one-third of its allotted wartime strength. Its active batteries included the Regimental Headquarters Battery and Batteries A, B, and C at Fort Scott. Batteries E and K resided across the water at Fort Baker. The 6th Coast Artillery activated a further battery in 1940, but events in Europe soon made inevitable a harbor defense buildup to full force.

During September 1939, First Lieutenant Arthur Kramer, a West Point graduate who had served two years at the Harbor De-

fenses of Pearl Harbor, attended the regular course at the Coast Artillery School in Fort Monroe, Virginia. But his attendance was cut short in February 1940 "because of the situation in Europe," and Kramer was dispatched to the Harbor Defenses of San Francisco. In April, he arrived at Fort Scott where he was appointed HDSF Ordnance Officer, commanding officer of the 6th CA Headquarters Battery, and commanding officer of HQ Battery, 1st Battalion of the same regiment. Commanding two separate batteries simultaneously led to unusual situations, especially for paperwork. As Kramer recalled years later: "I was required to write to myself and to 'request acknowledgment by indorsement hereon' which I duly indorsed back to myself. My signature was properly and legally on three successive pieces of correspondence!"

At Fort Funston, the 16-inch rifles of Battery Davis had not fired since emplacement in 1937. By summer 1940, with the completion of Battery Townsley at Cronkhite, the Army desired to fire one of its 16-inch casemated guns to verify the sturdiness of the mounts and concrete structure. Thus the newer of the two 16-inch batteries was chosen for the test, with First Lieutenant Arthur Kramer, as HDSF Ordnance Officer in charge of the firing. "We were going into unexplored territory," Kramer remembered, since this was to be the first firing of a 16-inch casemated battery in the U.S.

Certain test results were sought, like the maximum pressure inside the barrel when a round was fired. Kramer also wanted to see how far the seacoast rifles could shoot projectiles with more than the normal charge of gunpowder. Consulting a firing table, Kramer estimated that 16-inch guns might attain fifty-three thousand yards at their furthest range, meaning the projectiles would hit the water 30.11 miles out to sea, about five miles farther than the Farallon Islands. In order to discern the splashes, Kramer waited for a day when the Farallones were visible through the summer haze. "That, in July, took a lot of waiting," he later said.

The historic moment arrived on July 1, 1940. Since a casemated 16-incher had never before fired, First Lieutenant Kramer took all

July 1, 1940 proof-firing of Battery Townsley 16-inch guns. Fort Barry and Bird Island visible in background. (Presidio Army Museum)

precautions. The guns were to be fired with electric primers connected to a regular blasting machine outside the emplacement. Before each round, the gun crew and observing officers vacated the emplacement upon Kramer's order. As the officer in charge of the test firing, even as a "rather junior first lieutenant," Kramer had authority to tell senior field-grade officers that firing would not commence until they had cleared the battery.

On this sunny first day of July, the two 16-inch guns fired five rounds apiece. Before firing each round, Kramer placed small tubular copper deformation gauges in the gun chamber. After a salvo, the crushed copper cylinders were retrieved from the chamber and compared with a chart to determine the internal maximum pressure of the 16-inch gun's discharge. With the standard charge of 660-pounds of powder, the deformation gauges registered pressures of thirty-nine thousand pounds per square inch. Kramer also conducted tests for maximum range. Having picked a clear day for that reason, he attempted to spot

the projectiles' splash 30.11 miles out to sea, five miles beyond the Farallones. Each Townsley gun fired a round with a standard powder charge plus ten percent. Then with barrels fully elevated, the guns fired with fifteen percent more than the normal charge. The projectiles went farther than Kramer expected; he never saw their splashes.

The sergeant who looked after Battery Townsley during its construction, asked Kramer if he could watch the firing of the last round from within the emplacement. The Ordnance Officer thought it would be safe and gave his permission. While everyone else remained outside, the caretaker sergeant had a close look as Gun No. 2 fired its fifth round. He suffered no injuries from the mighty blast, but reported the hasp of a steel magazine door behind him had been ruptured by the shock.

The July 1st test firing revealed no problems with the 16-inch guns or their concrete casemates. The official Army Corps of Engineers report noted only minor damage to non-vital fittings on the gun carriages. On July

27, 1940, the Army's Harbor Defense Board launched plans to construct twenty-seven new 16-inch casemated batteries and add concrete protection over twenty-three existing big-gun emplacements. Because the German navy now had clear access to the Atlantic through captured French ports, the Harbor Defense Board wanted to modernize American seacoast defenses. New and powerful armament meant fewer troops would be needed for harbor defense, freeing soldiers for other duty. HDSF, with two new 16-inch batteries, served as the model for the modernization program. Shortly after the test firing, the 6th Coast Artillery assigned Battery E to the 16-inch guns at Cronkhite, and Battery C to the big guns at Fort Funston.

"It was a hell of a privilege" to command the 16-inch guns, recalled George B. Webster, who, as a second lieutenant in command of Battery C in the summer of 1940, accepted the new battery's two hundred rounds of war reserve ammunition. Battery C turned their 3-inch antiaircraft guns over to neighboring Battery B, but kept their 155mm guns as secondary armament. The official transfer of the Funston 16-inch battery from the Corps of Engineers to the Harbor Defenses would not occur until September 1940, but Battery C took early custody of the big guns to prepare for the proof-firing and target practice to take place later in the year. General Terry, the HDSF commander, brought a special visitor to the new Funston emplacement. Second Lieutenant Webster was introduced to a retired Army officer named Davis. He was the son of the late Brigadier General Richmond P. Davis, a prominent coast artillery officer for whom the Funston

battery was named.

Second Lieutenant Webster felt elation in taking command of this new and important seacoast battery. "I reveled in it," he remembered. Webster checked the war reserve ammunition which resided in two bays at the emplacement. His count turned up 199 rounds---one projectile short of the full complement. Further investigation could not reveal how and why a 2100-pound projectile had disappeared. A short time later, Webster went to the Treasure Island fair where his battery's specially lacquered 155mm gun was on display. Next to the shiny artillery piece stood the 16-inch shell missing from Webster's inventory. The HDSF Ordnance Officer, without telling the Battery C commander, had moved the projectile out of the ammunition magazine and put it on public view at Treasure Island.

The expanding Army needed more officers. Congress had earlier passed the Thomason Act which offered qualifying ROTC college graduates one-year commissions as second lieutenants in the Regular Army. The Reserve Officers' Training Corps program on college campuses included a "branch-specific" senior ROTC unit. Large schools like the University of California at Berkeley had several senior units; infantry, engineers, field artillery, and coast artillery. Smaller colleges like the University of Santa Clara or the University of San Francisco had only one Army branch represented. At Santa Clara, this senior unit was

12-inch seacoast mortar of Battery Howe at Fort Funston as fired by ROTC cadets on July 12, 1938. (Presidio Army Museum)

field artillery, at USF, coast artillery. During six weeks in the summer between their junior and senior years, cadets camped near Battery Mendell at Fort Barry or went to Fort Funston. In 1940, some Funston ROTC cadets nearly shot down a target-towing aircraft with a blast from a 12-inch seacoast mortar and peppered shrapnel in the vicinity of a target-towing vessel with the 3-inch antiaircraft guns.

At the close of UC Berkeley's school year in 1940, the ROTC commandant recommended cadet Harrison Payne for a Thomason Act commission on the basis of his grade point average. Payne had not planned on joining the Army. He had already found work as a chemist at the Shell Oil Company in the East Bay. But Harry Payne's father figured that war was coming and persuaded his cadet son to seize the opportunity. Payne came to Fort Scott as one of the Thomason Act officers of 1940, receiving his commission as a second lieutenant in the Coast Artillery. The terms of commission were simple: The Thomason Act officer had to be a citizen, between the ages of 21 and 30, single, not previously married, and a college graduate or one who could demonstrate equivalent knowledge through special examination. Going into the Regular Army, Thomason Act lieutenants were automatically six weeks junior to West Pointers of the same graduating year.

Alabama contributed at least five Thomason Act officers in 1940 to the Golden Gate defenses. After taking a one-month refresher course at Fort Monroe, the five piled into one sedan and drove out to San Francisco that summer. The new officers heard that a former ROTC instructor from the University of Alabama was there ahead of them. Daniel G. Cook, Preston B. Cannady, Kenneth Cooper, and two others arrived at Fort Scott on an August weekend. Two of the young officers found assignment to batteries on the San Francisco side. Cook and the rest went on to Fort Baker. The newly minted lieutenants walked into the post adjutant's office at Baker to announce themselves, and found their old instructor standing there. "I've been looking for you boys," he said with a smile, "I saw you on orders coming out." Two of the new officers drew assignments to Batteries E and K of the

6th Coast Artillery, while Daniel Cook joined recently activated Battery F.

In the routine of the peacetime Army, new officers on post paid courtesy calls on senior commanding officers. The thought of such an obligation made more than one nervous second lieutenant swallow hard. "In those days, you stayed away from the colonels and generals and you got along better. I was just tongue-tied with generals," remembered one junior lieutenant at HDSF. The courtesy call was carried out in a prescribed manner: The young officer making the call rang the doorbell of the general's residence and waited. If there was no answer, the young man pushed his engraved calling card under the door, straightened up, and felt relieved his obligation had been fulfilled. However, if the general was at home, the caller would enter to "visit." The duration of smoking one cigarette was the suggested length of the stay. Bidding farewell, the visitor slipped his calling card into the card bowl in the foyer, unnoticed if possible, and departed.

Second Lieutenant Daniel Cook thought he had the ideal situation. His fellow officers had assured him the Fort Scott post commander was "a real nice guy" and would be at home. On the other hand, General Burgin, the 9th Coast Artillery District commander, could be a difficult character, but was supposed to be out of town. Cook decided the time was right to make his calls. At the post commander's house, Cook received no answer at the door. He slipped his calling card under the door and left. His second stop would be easy, Cook thought; General Burgin was not supposed to be at home. The second lieutenant pressed the doorbell and waited. Suddenly, to Cook's surprise, the door opened; the General was home! Cook steeled himself, anticipating the worst. Instead of the cantankerous senior officer Cook expected, General Burgin grinned affably, exclaiming, "Hello, son. Won't you come in?"

The one officer a newly assigned second lieutenant dealt with on a daily basis was his battery commander, normally a captain. The battery was the basic administrative and tactical unit within the Harbor Defenses. Generally having over one hundred non-

Observer sights through Swasey Depression Position Finder which measured range and azimuth of target. Reader wearing telephone headset transmits aiming data to distant plotting room. Ship recognition charts adorn wall of station. (Presidio Army Museum)

commissioned officers and men led by five or six officers, the typical battery manned a group of guns firing on a single target. Within this unit, the battery commander reigned supreme. His responsibility extended beyond armament to the training, feeding, housing, and welfare of all men under his command.

When Harrison Payne joined the 6th Coast Artillery, he reported to Battery B at Fort Scott. On the first morning, Payne walked into the battery commander's office to meet his captain, a six-foot four-inch West Pointer who had been with the Harbor Defenses since September 1939. "Oh, you' re the genius they sent me," said Captain Richard R. Moorman, peering down at his new second lieutenant, who stood five-feet seven-inches tall. Payne's scholastic achievements which won him his Thomason Act appointment, destined him for great responsibilities in Battery B. On the spot, Captain Moorman made Harry Payne the range, supply, and engineering officer of the unit.

In the summer of 1940, Battery B resided at the Scott barracks. Every morning after breakfast, the unit scrambled aboard trucks for the commute to Fort Funston. On the way, a crew was dropped off at the Sutro Heights observation station. The trucks continued along the Great Highway, past Ocean Beach to Fort Funston, where the unit manned Battery Walter Howe with its four 12-inch seacoast mortars. On these weapons of 1890 vintage, Battery B conducted gun drills and practiced plotting targets. The firing of seacoast artillery against moving targets was a technical skill that required constant practice by all battery personnel. Actual firings were rare, usually limited to the annual service target practice. Large-caliber projectiles were costly and the Army expended them slowly; also, barrels of the big guns could wear down after firing as few as one hundred rounds. Gun drills conscientiously pursued, were considered adequate to keep the crews sharp. Army technical manuals gave detailed procedures for firing each type of seacoast armament, assigning tasks to each man and section within the battery.

At the vision slit of the battery commander's station on the left flank of the mortars, Captain Moorman scanned the ocean with a high-powered spotting scope, looking for a fishing boat or some other local craft to serve as the practice target. When a target was found, the commander, through the battery telephone net, ordered the observation stations to begin tracking it. From the Sutro Heights station, and from another one next to the command post, the observers slowly cranked their azimuth instruments, keeping the cross-hairs on the moving fishing boat.

At twenty second intervals, bells rang at the stations. The azimuth reading as indicated at that moment on the scale at the base of the scope was noted by the observers and relayed by phone to the battery plotting room. The plotting detail, supervised by Lieutenant Payne as range officer, huddled around the 110-degree M1915 plotting board. This was a semicircular table, marked out as a graphic

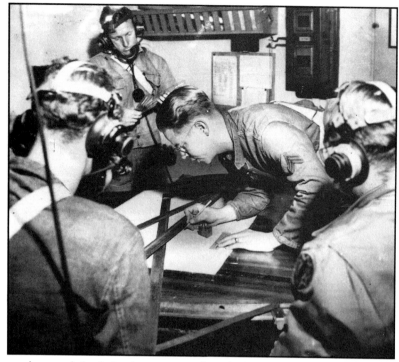

At the plotting room, the plotter marks the position of the observed target at the intersection of two metal arms representing lines of sight from reporting base-end stations. (San Francisco Archives, S.F. Public Library)

scale model of the battery and its field of fire in relation to the observing stations. As the observers reported azimuth readings, the range crew pivoted two steel arms on the plotting board. The arms represented angles of sight from the two observing stations to the target. Where the arms intersected, a mark was made. At further twenty second intervals, the steel arms were moved to new readings phoned in by the observers, and new plot points were marked. From three or more plot points, the speed and direction of the moving target was clear; its position, when the following twenty second interval bell rang, could be accurately predicted.

Based on the target's movement on the board, the plotting detail continuously transmitted aiming data to the gun pit. Here, the azimuth setter and elevation setter of each 12-inch mortar cranked their piece

to the numbers given, keeping the weapon trained on the moving target. When the battery commander felt the range section had accurately tracked the target, he ordered "commence firing." At the mortars, the crews rammed shells and powder bags into the breeches. The mortars traversed and elevated onto their final coordinates. When the time interval bell rang again, the mortars fired. In actual target practice, several 1046-pound shells would be plunging down on the spot where the target was expected to be passing on the ring of the next bell. If gun drills using dummy projectiles and powder bags were anticlimactic, experience had shown this sort of training to be sufficient in yielding good results when the time came to fire live ammunition during the annual service target practice.

Battery B's alternate assignment were three 3-inch M1917 antiaircraft guns mounted on a small knoll twelve hundred feet southeast of the mortars. The range crew tracked targets with a long, tubular height-finder instrument. Readings were electrically transmitted by cable to the director, a large rotating box which housed a Sperry mechanical computer. Oper-

Range crew practices tracking targets on stereoscopic height finder at Fort Funston AA battery. The instrument seems to be pointed at the horizon rather than skyward. (Presidio Army Museum)

ators peered through the director's telescopic sights and tracked the flying target. The director's Sperry computer sent a steady pulse of data through the transmission cable to the gun's azimuth and elevation dials. As the dials rotated, the gun setter and elevation setter

U.S. Army Mineplanter Ellery W. Niles. (D. Grover)

kept matching arrows trained on this rotation by cranking the wheels that kept the gun moving with the target. Matching dials also enabled the mechanical fuse setter to cut the projectile's fuse to explode so many seconds later. With fuse cut, the thirteen-pound shell was quickly slammed into the breech and fired. Ideally, the climbing projectile would explode at the spot where the target was predicted to be. Flying shrapnel from the exploding shell might also hit the target on a near miss.

At three o'clock in the afternoon Battery B ceased gun drills and boarded their trucks for the ride back to Fort Scott. At the five o'clock evening formation, the men donned Class A uniforms and trooped the colors on the parade ground with other batteries stationed on the post. In late 1940, Battery B moved into old Civilian Conservation Corps barracks at Fort Funston. Captain Moorman judged the housing "rather primitive, but adequate."

In August, First Lieutenant Frank A. Liwski came to San Francisco after duty at the Panama Canal where he was mine property officer of a submarine mine battery at Fort Amador. The West Pointer took part in mining the Pacific entrance of the canal as the U.S. responded to war in Europe. When he got to HDSF, First Lieutenant Liwski took command of Battery A, one of two mine batteries with the 6th Coast Artillery. "Employed for the installation, maintenance and operation of a controlled minefield," as described in the ROTC Manual for Coast Artillery, the mine battery planted and cared for mines, explo-

sives, and mineplanting equipment. Mine facilities ashore included warehouses where empty mine cases were kept, loading rooms for filling mines with TNT, and cable storage warehouses, where in darkened rooms coiled electric mine cable lay immersed in huge tanks of salt water to prevent cable deterioration. At Scott, storehouses and a mine dock stood on the shoreline road leading to Fort Point. At Baker, similar buildings faced Horseshoe Cove.

In the late summer of 1940, the U.S. Army Mineplanter *Lt. Col. Ellery W. Niles*, returned to San Francisco from Panama. The sleek 185-foot *Niles* belonged to HDSF. Shipbuilders Pusey and Jones of Wilmington, Delaware built the vessel in 1937 with a 35-foot wide steel hull and twin propellers driven by a 1,120-horsepower diesel engine. On deck, davits and power hoists equipped the planter for lifting mines and cable. In 1940, the *Ellery W. Niles* was the newest of eight Army planters in service. The others were built before 1920. The Army designed the *Niles* as the prototype for a new class of planters---but the heavy diesel engine reduced the ship's maneuverability for mineplanting work. Due to this weakness, the Army commissioned no more like her.

The Harbor Defenses did not maintain minefields at the harbor entrance in peacetime, but batteries practiced minelaying. Once, the planting crew from Battery A went out with the *Niles* to recover an experimental mine group of empty mines planted the previous year. This was valuable training for the ship's crew and the mine planting detail from the battery---and good experience in cooperation for the officers involved. Captain Frank Liwski, commander of Battery A, considered Chief Warrant Officer Richard T. Carlsen of the *Niles* a "top-notch skipper." According to Army policy, the battery commander deferred to the mineplanter skipper aboard ship. The Army officers and men involved with submarine mines often referred to themselves as "the Army's navy."

During Navy war games in the summer of 1940, an old S-class submarine entered San Francisco Bay at periscope depth. The vessel remained undetected until it surfaced inside the harbor. This exercise showed that rough currents and the narrow passage of the Golden Gate could not hinder the entry of enemy submarines. The U.S. Navy commissioned the Tiburon Net Depot on August 4, 1940. Located on the site of an old naval coaling station on quiet northern waters of the bay, the depot's mission involved developing and installing a submerged steel fence across the Golden Gate to prevent enemy submarines from entering the harbor.

In the autumn of 1940, the Chief of Naval Operations ordered the Tiburon depot to test the installation of a submarine net. The

Portion of gallery at Battery Davis, Fort Funston. (Presidio Army Museum)

Navy laid three sections of old World War I netting in the waters off the depot. Two Navy tugs, the *Eider* and the *Dreadnought,* served as gate vessels. Opening and closing the movable gate took four minutes. While the net experiment succeeded in the slow two and one-half knot current off Tiburon, Navy men knew the real net would be facing currents of five to six knots across the Golden Gate. A civilian expert, Charles Rice of the Smith-Rice Salvage Company, recommended heavy ground tackle for anchoring net and gate vessels in fast current. For years, Bay Area salvage firms operated successfully at the harbor entrance using heavy anchors. Navy Captain Stanley M. Haight, the net depot commander, hoped the new class of gate vessels under construction would be "reasonably habitable" because of the "stormy weather . . . in the Golden Gate during the fall and winter seasons."

When Battery C, 6th Coast Artillery was ready to conduct an informal

Camouflaged entrance to plotting and switchboard room for Funston 16-inch guns in separate casemate at some distance to rear of battery. (Presidio Army Museum)

proof-firing of the Funston 16-inch guns, Second Lieutenant George Webster, the battery commander, posted men to the outlying base-end stations. Communications between stations and the battery had been installed by the artillery engineers, but observing instruments from the Ordnance Department were not yet in place. The range crews brought in portable azimuth instruments normally used with their 155mm guns. But on this proof-firing, the scopes were not employed for fire-control. For the test, the 16-inch rifles of Battery Davis fired cast-iron slugs that broke apart after they left the muzzle. Battery commander Webster put men in the observing stations to watch the water area for any boats that might be hit by shrapnel from the proof-firing slugs.

Battery Davis fired in the fall of 1940. The test slugs were shaped like ash cans with copper rotating bands on the back ends to provide a gas-seal in the 16-inch gun breech. The cast-iron slugs had no hitting power---they served to place a load on the gun barrel and gun carriage to test durability of the artillery piece when it fired. The slug emerged from the

16-inch muzzle with a powerful centrifugal spin that caused it to shatter into many pieces over the water. Battery C conducted the informal proof-firing during the local crabbing season. The Coast Guard tried to clear the crab boats from the firing area. When the authorities had moved one crab boat to safety and went after another one, the original crabber would sail back to the same spot from where he was chased. But after the first salvo erupted from the Funston battery, all the crab boats scattered. George Webster, the battery commander, reported that he sensed, rather than heard, the 16-inch gun when it fired. Standing on the gun platform, Webster felt as if a railroad train was going by as the huge rifle fired and recoiled. Those standing under and in front of the muzzle reported a thundering crack, a "supersonic boom" in the age of propeller planes.

The test-firing sequence lasted several days, but no more than seven rounds were fired from either gun. The gunners tried a variety of powder loads, including reduced charge, full charge, and 150-percent charge. Once the proof-firing was completed, Second

Casemated 16-inch battery under camouflage paint and ground cover at Fort Funston, September 21, 1940. (Presidio Army Museum)

Kobbe Avenue---the main entrance to Fort Winfield Scott under ramp to Golden Gate Bridge.

Lieutenant Webster had Battery C preparing for a service target practice. Excaliber firing with the unit's 155mm guns occurred frequently. These smaller seacoast rifles had plenty of shells, which allowed for much excaliber target practice during a time when ammunition was scarce. Webster looked forward to firing the 16-inch guns against moving targets, but he was transferred to Panama before that happened.

The fall of 1940 brought successive command changes at HDSF. Brigadier General Thomas A. Terry left the Harbor Defenses to head the 1st Coast Artillery District in Boston. On September 17th, as the 6th Coast Artillery band played "appropriate airs," General Terry inspected 6th and 65th Coast Artillery honor guards lining Kobbe Avenue. After bidding farewell to his staff, General and Mrs. Terry left the post by car. Colonel Rollin L. Tilton, commander of the 6th Coast Artillery, assumed command of the defenses while retaining his regimental post. A month later, on October 18th, Colonel Tilton also departed San Francisco for another command. He in turn was replaced at HDSF and 6th Coast Artillery by Colonel Edward A. Stockton, Jr., destined to become the first wartime commander of the Golden Gate defenses.

On September 16th, Congress passed the Selective Service Bill, permitting the com-

pulsory induction of men aged twenty-one to thirty-five. A month later, registration for the draft began. The first recruits would arrive at San Francisco in January to fill HDSF ranks. Meanwhile, the Army began activating reserve officers. A number of West Coast reservists came to the Harbor Defenses of San Francisco. During the call-ups, the Army kept the regular officers of long service from being outranked by incoming reservists. In October 1940, regular officers with at least three years in service and the rank of first lieutenant received temporary, or "jawbone" promotions to the grade of captain. The eligible regulars took the higher rank "in all respects except pay," one of them remembered. "There we were," the West Pointer continued, "senior to the newly recalled with all the responsibilities of rank except pay." They would not receive a captain's pay until the war started.

One reserve officer called to active duty with HDSF found the going rough at the start. Captain Charles L. Bell, a Los Angeles utility company executive in civilian life, inherited Battery F, 6th Coast Artillery from an easygoing West Point officer who sometimes shot pool with the enlisted men in the battery dayroom. Bell, however, was a stickler for discipline. "Coming in behind an easy guy, he had everybody up in arms," recalled Daniel Cook, one of Bell's lieutenants in the Fort Baker mine battery. Captain Bell wanted to get along better with the men. Cook suggested the captain attend the inter-regimental basketball games in which the battery competed. Captain Bell said he would think it over.

On Saturdays, the batteries stationed at Fort Baker marched on the parade ground. Each week, the best marching unit won a prize. The snappy military bearing of guidon bearer Sergeant Williams, often brought the award to Battery F. "He'd prance up there and the way he'd go around that parade ground, we'd win every time," recalled Daniel Cook

Sausalito---the main drag. (San Francisco Archives, S.F. Public Library)

proudly. Sergeant Williams was a popular NCO in the battery. Off-duty, he frequented the Four Winds, a bar in nearby Sausalito favored by the enlisted men. One evening, the sergeant got into a fight with a civilian customer and ended up in jail. Lieutenant Cook had him released. The next morning, Captain Bell discussed Sergeant Williams' punishment with Lieutenant Cook. Restrict him to post for a week, suggested Cook. Rejecting that as too lenient, Bell insisted on demoting Sergeant Williams. "If you bust him," Lieutenant Cook thought, "you'll have to bust every sergeant in the battery."

That afternoon, when Cook returned to the office, the first sergeant called him over, pointing to a pile of torn paper in the wastebasket. Captain Bell had the first sergeant type orders that morning demoting Sergeant Williams. Bell later had second thoughts, and tore up the papers before they could be issued. After this incident, the captain began attending the basketball games his men played at the Fort Baker gymnasium against the other batteries. And he bought the beer for his team when they won. Captain Bell even held Lieutenant Cook's pistol and holster when Cook had to leave during a game to pick up his date in Sausalito.

To give his men some training in local defense, Captain Bell ordered a mock attack on the Fort Baker mine storehouse. He planned to defend the installation with most of the battery while Lieutenant Cook led a band of infiltrators in attack. In preparation, Cook obtained a supply of small paper sacks from Perry's Market in Sausalito, where the battery mess did business. The mess sergeant filled the bags with white flour. Cook then asked a fellow Thomason Act officer, Lieutenant Ralph Courtney of Battery A, to bring his men to join the small attack force. The raiders gathered on the hills

Headquarters, Harbor Defenses of San Francisco---also HQ for 6th Coast Artillery Regiment.

above Fort Baker. After distributing the flour-filled sacks, the two junior officers led the charge down the wooded hillside. The attackers threw flour bags at buildings all the way down the hill, hitting especially hard the object of the raid, the mine storehouse. Captain Bell was upset at this turn of events, expecting only a small infiltration party. He did not imagine Cook would enlist the help of a larger force. But the attack succeeded, and Bell could not argue with that.

Unmarried young lieutenants stationed at the northern sub-posts lived at the Fort Baker Bachelor Officers' Quarters. When not on duty with their batteries, the tenants of the BOQ led a care-free life, sometimes with loud parties and boisterous singing into the night. One Sunday afternoon, the young men faced the close of an autumn weekend with little to do. One lieutenant announced he was going to Hazel's Sweet Shop in Sausalito for a hamburger and milkshake. He promptly got in his car and left the base. Soon, another young man decided to do the same thing. Then one by one, the other lieutenants jumped into their automobiles and drove off. When Daniel Cook finally decided to join them, he found everybody else had gone. Driving into Sausalito, Lieutenant Cook realized that he "was the green, innocent one." In fact, none of his fellow officers went to the Sweet Shop; Lieutenant Cook found all of them at the Four Winds, the bar where Sergeant Williams had a fight with the civilian. "I didn't do anything," Cook recalled, "so it ended up that I had to bring them all back." Being the only sober

Front entrance of HDSF Headquarters at Fort Scott in 1941.

one, Cook drove the other officers back to Fort Baker in his own car. Later that night, the obliging lieutenant ferried drivers to Sausalito to pick up all the stranded automobiles his BOQ mates had left behind.

Chapter 3:

From Rookies to Concrete Soldiers

In January 1941, Bay Area newspapers devoted their front pages to the world war in which America was not yet a participant. The German Air Force continued their aerial bombardment against England, with London, Bristol, Cardiff, and Portsmouth being the targets that month. The Italian Army, having crossed the Greek frontier by way of Albania, fell back the same way when the Greeks counterattacked. On the Mediterranean Sea, Axis and British forces clashed in sharp air and naval actions. The ongoing Japanese invasion of China further fueled American concern that the widening world conflict might spread to the Western Hemisphere.

President Roosevelt tried to prepare Americans militarily and psychologically for war. Some Americans opposed Roosevelt's defense preparations, yet the president had managed to obtain congressional approval for military conscription the previous October. On January 2, 1941, Roosevelt announced a new defense program; the production of two hundred 7100-ton freighters built to a standard design, soon to be known as the Liberty ships. Four days later, in his State of the Union message, Roosevelt proposed the four freedoms; the freedoms of speech and worship and the freedoms against fear and want. In the historic address, the President called once again for the United States to serve as the arsenal of democracy. On January 8th, the president submitted his proposed 1942 budget

to Congress. Defense spending, $10.5 billion, made up more than half of the total. Bay Area industries and military bases took a share of the defense expenditure. And at the end of this chain, the Harbor Defenses received an infusion of men and materiel.

As part of the federal budget, the U.S. Army appropriations bill earmarked $92 million for coast artillery modernization. Major General Joseph A. Green, the Chief of Coast Artillery, testified before a congressional committee in early January. The congressmen asked General Green to justify Army coast artillery modernization, since the U.S. Navy, upon which much money had already been spent, was supposedly the country's main coastal defender. "The Navy is the greatest advocate of modernizing our harbor defenses," General Green responded. "It wanted assurances that our harbors cannot be captured by an enemy. Our Navy wants to be left free so that it can get out and seek the enemy."

The Army had its own reason for spending $92 million on defense modernization. As General Green spoke to the committee, the Army War Plans Division completed a study entitled: "Harbor Defenses, Their Purpose, Composition, and Organization." Harbor defenses made residents of coastal cities feel secure, the study concluded. In wartime, the defenses acted as a deterrent to enemy attack. Without adequate harbor defenses, even a nuisance raid on a coastal city might cause authorities to demand military protection. The Army did not wish to disperse more than the minimum strength in ground and air forces on static home defense when it felt the route to victory lay in taking the war to the enemy.

The 65th Coast Artillery Regiment, based at Fort Scott since 1938, was an antiaircraft artillery unit. On January 6, 1941, the 65th took its AA guns south to the Antiaircraft Training Center at Camp Haan in Riverside, California. Their departure cleared the barracks at Fort Scott for the first wave of drafted recruits soon to begin training at HDSF. In the coming months, the sound of marching feet and martial music on the drill fields, and the faint boom of seacoast artillery on the distant headlands would make the forts of the Golden Gate bustling centers of harbor defense activity.

On the evening of January 16th, a day after HDSF announced activation of new battalions, the San Francisco chapter of the Reserve Officers Association met at Fort Scott. Through the courtesy of Captain Arthur Kramer, the gathering convened in the mess hall of the 6th Coast Artillery Headquarters Battery. As guest speaker, HDSF commander Colonel Edward A. Stockton explained "The Anti-Aircraft and Seacoast Defenses of the Panama Canal Department." This topic had nothing to do with San Francisco, but many of the reserve

officers listening to Colonel Stockton would shortly return to active duty under his command at the Harbor Defenses.

"The history of the 18th Coast Artillery is an item for histories of the future, not of the present or the past," recalled the 1941 HDSF yearbook, "as it is the baby of the Coast Artillery branch of the United States Army." On January 15th, the 2nd Battalion of the 18th Coast Artillery Regiment was activated at San Francisco. The initial staff consisted of nineteen officers, mostly reservists, and approximately sixty-five non-commissioned officers, many drawn from the experienced ranks of the 6th Coast Artillery. The officers and NCO's had eleven days to prepare for command. On the 25th of January, a train carrying new inductees to the 18th Coast Artillery rolled onto the Crissy Field spur track at the Presidio. Out came 437 Midwestern draftees, conscripted from the 6th Corps Area, which included Illinois, Wisconsin, and Michigan. In January 1941, training camps and replacement centers did not yet exist. These recruits came directly from induction centers to the Harbor Defenses. The men were allotted to the 2nd Battalion's four batteries; the Headquarters Battery and Batteries D, E, and F. They occupied vacated barracks at Fort Scott.

Another train to Crissy Field delivered Southern and Midwestern recruits to the 6th Coast Artillery's 4th Battalion, which was also activated in January. The draftees were "duly impressed with the Golden Gate, and are buckling down to the task of defending it," reported the *Coast Artillery Journal*, the official publication of the Coast Artillery Officers' Association. Morale was no problem, the magazine continued, due to the "excellent barracks,

New recruits for 2nd Battalion, 18th Coast Artillery given orientation by Captain William R. Nodder, battalion executive and plans and training officer. Fort Scott barracks, January 25, 1941. (San Francisco Archives, S.F. Public Library)

Battery E, 18th CA gun crew at gun drill on 6-inch armament at Baker Beach, Fort Scott. Note sandbags and camouflage netting in place. (San Francisco Archives, S.F. Public Library)

fine climate, and nearby ultra friendly City of San Francisco."

"The regiment as now constituted . . . will initiate unit training January 27, 1941, and will be proficient therein by April 26, 1941," stated a training memorandum issued by Lieutenant Colonel William F. LaFrenz, Plans and Training Officer of the defenses. Each day started with reveille at 6 a.m. The men did calisthenics and policed the grounds before breakfast. By 7:45 a.m., recruits began morning drills; they learned the manual of arms and learned to march by squad and platoon, instructed according to the training manual by a corporal or sergeant. At Fort Baker, a call went out for help in drilling recruits from Arkansas. The drill sergeants could not understand the drawling accents of the Southern recruits. A special Arkansas recruit detachment was formed and Lieutenant Daniel Cook from Battery F helped train them. Since Cook was from Alabama, so the theory went, he would be more successful in communicating with the Arkansans. After lunch, between 1:00

and 4:30 p.m., recruits gathered around the battery's assigned armament as NCO's explained the working parts of the big guns. The trainees practiced aiming, loading, and firing procedures, drilling with dummy powder bags and projectiles.

In the 2nd Battalion of the 18th Coast Artillery, Battery D manned two 6-inch disappearing guns at Fort Scott above Baker Beach, while on the beach, Battery E drilled with two 6-inch rifles of Battery Chamberlin. Two 12-inch barbette guns southwest of the Scott parade ground went to Battery F. The Headquarters Battery of the 2nd Battalion trained to operate command posts assigned to it by HDSF. Of the newly activated 6th Coast Artillery units, Battery M manned antiaircraft searchlights and Battery N, seacoast searchlights; Batteries D and L drilled on the old 12-inch disappearing rifles of Battery Mendell at Fort Barry. "During peacetime, there was not much money allotted to training. To do a lot of firing of those large caliber guns was expensive

Battery F, 18th CA drills on 12-inch barbette rifle of Battery Saffold, Fort Scott.

and caused erosion of the gun barrels," recalled John Schonher, the Battery D, 6th CA commander whose men trained on Mendell.

Training included monthly War Conditioning Periods when recruits bivouacked in the field. Hikes of varying length by day or night built stamina. Once a week, the men took a 25-mile night hike with full pack, rifle, and sidearm. The 2nd Battalion of the 18th Coast Artillery sometimes marched as a unit from Fort Scott down to Half Moon Bay and back again with the battalion commander, 52-year old Lieutenant Colonel F.H. Holden leading the way, carrying his own 25-pound field pack like everyone else in the command. Charles Sullivan, an 18th CA recruit from Chicago remembered the strain of the return trip, as the battalion ascended the steady incline of the scenic coast road leading to the back gate of Fort Scott.

Marching and parade ground ceremony played an important role transforming recruits into harbor defensemen. "Advantage will be taken of all formations in which precision and exactness are required," stated Training Memorandum Number 6, "to inculcate pride of organizations and discipline in the troops." When the men had trained sufficiently, batteries participated in two retreat formations each week; one preceded by an inspection in ranks, the other as part of a battalion or regimental parade. A formal guard mounting took place weekly at Fort Scott. Each month, harbor defense commander Colonel Stockton re-

viewed the batteries at each fort, followed by inspection of troops and quarters. The 6th Coast Artillery Band provided military music for all ceremonies. Several of the bandsmen were draftees from a Detroit symphony orchestra. John Schonher, an officer in the 6th CA Regiment, remembered hearing the flute solo from Tchaikovsky's "Peter and the Wolf" rising out of the musical cacophony as the band tuned their instruments on the parade ground.

Training such a number of conscripts proved challenging to the NCO's and reserve officers. Unless they possessed World War I experience in training men, or had experience with the Civilian Conservation Corps, none of the officers had ever done anything like this before. "We did a lot of training with fresh troops in 1941," John Schonher explained. "These men were sent to us directly from induction centers and had no basic training. Therefore, basic military training had to be conducted along with the specialized training necessary for coast artillery." For Second Lieutenant Tom Scally, an activated reserve officer, the duty was "better than a downtown job." A graduate of University of San Francisco ROTC, Scally rode to work every morning, driven by his father to Fort Scott from their Richmond District home. Dropped off at the parade ground in time for the eight o'clock formation, Scally did his daytime duties until the five o'clock retreat ceremony. His father waited at the parade ground with the car, "and by 5:20 I was home," Scally recalled.

Drawn from the same reserve unit as Scally, Lieutenant Colonel Felix M. Usis commuted to HDSF from his house in the Berkeley hills. A West Pointer who arrived in France shortly after World War I ended, Usis left his job as personnel manager at the Ford Motor Company in the East Bay, returning to active duty in February 1941 at Fort Scott. "I went in as a battalion

6th Coast Artillery regimental band at Fort Scott parade ground. (Presidio Army Museum)

commander," Usis recalled. "My intent was the mines." Assigned to the 6th Coast Artillery's Mine Command, Usis found his unit, which included Batteries A and F, already up and running. "But everything was very secret," he noted. "The command post was already built. They prepared for it because they knew something was going to happen."

As more officers and their families joined the Harbor Defenses, a housing shortage developed. Most families lived at the Presidio or Fort Scott. Many others had to rent apartments in the surrounding civilian neighborhoods. To provide additional quarters for HDSF members, the Army built Camp Spurr on the site of former Civilian Conservation Corps buildings at Fort Barry. Named after Lieutenant Colonel John P. Spurr, a local coast artillery officer in the 1920's, the new camp consisted of houses for married non-commissioned officers and their families, as well as a two-story barracks for bachelor officers. This BOQ stood on a slight rise above the houses, prompting it to be dubbed the "Castle on the Hill." The messhall in the BOQ featured a jukebox. Many young officers from Fort Baker moved to Camp Spurr in 1941.

"San Francisco was born out of gold-hunger and nursed on catastrophes. Today it lives a little more sedately on lettuce and ships, peas and silk, wine and scrap iron," wrote Edwin Rosskam in a 1939 essay. The financial clearing house and banking center on the tributary of "one of the richest agricultural lowlands of the world," San Francisco sat "with its face toward the Pacific." That "American Singapore" refrain of civic boosters in the 1920's came to life with the frantic tempo of Bay Area military development of the 1940's. A guide book, *Army Posts and Towns: The Baedeker of the Army*, described the charms of the region to officers and military families. San Francisco was "a city much larger than the population of 635,000 indicates; a city with tradition and personality." As for the famed San Francisco weather, "After you get used to it," the Army guide book went on, "the best climate in the world; about the same all year. You can play tennis or golf almost every day, but you'll want an overcoat at night."

"The stranger coming to San Francisco has no alternative but to be an adventurer," observed novelist William Saroyan shortly before the war. Harry Freeman, who commanded an antiaircraft battery, remembered his men's initial reaction to the city as being "typical of the tourist." They were "all kids from Minnesota. Many had not even been out of the state before they came to California in the National Guard. Coming up to a very romantic city, whatever time they had off, they went to it." For Freeman himself, reflecting years later, it seemed the city "was smaller and more glamorous in those days." The hills and the Bay Bridge held their attractions. On a captain's pay, Freeman went to the top of the Mark Hopkins Hotel and considered it "the height of living."

"Chinatown was by far the first place most of us visited," Freeman recalled. Guide books mentioned this city attraction without fail: "Provocative, elusive, fascinating, the mecca for all San Francisco's tourists." Apart from the exotic atmosphere and souvenir shops, the central lure for the servicemen was "the food, of course." Chinatown restaurant fare was inexpensive and plentiful. The young soldiers, hailing from less "exotic" parts of the country, marveled at the "food markets that tumble out on the avenue with their hanging displays of queer cuts of meat and fowl and very different Chinese vegetables." Even Chinese-American GI's stationed at Fort Ord in Monterey drove up to Chinatown for the weekend. "Everything was cheap," claimed Calvin Chin of the 7th Infantry Division. "You'd get a Scotch and Soda. It'd only cost you 25-cents."

Those wanting entertainment with their drink took a short stroll from Chinatown to a one block stretch of Pacific Street at Columbus Avenue. An iron sign arching across the intersection proclaimed in big white letters, "International Settlement." Known from an earlier time of the city's history as the Barbary Coast, the city renamed the zone to tidy its reputation. But soldiers knew the nightclubs there were distinct from any others in town. "It was concentrated," one HDSF officer remembered, "Every place was a bar." The block "filled with drunks and socialites and ex-cons and good entertainers and lousy entertainers and cops and stool pigeons," wrote city newspaper columnist Herb Caen, "everything . . . but public dancing because this is indecent and might lead to a return of the Barbary Coast." In 1941, coast artillery recruit Dale Barnhart saw "a lot of bar hopping, learning how to drink, and sightseeing."

Army Day, April 6, 1941 featured the new recruits of January, who had twenty days to go in completing their first round of training. The vanguard of the "citizen soldiers" coming to San Francisco in the momentous years to follow, these troops would get a chance to show the public and the press what they had learned in four months of Army training. The San Francisco Junior Chamber of Commerce devised clever promotions for the Sunday event. A photograph in the April 6th edition of the *San Francisco Chronicle* showed a Dodge four-door sedan on the firing platform next to the breech end of a 12-inch barbette gun at Fort Scott. In the picture, a man in fedora hat and sport jacket stood by the car, talking with an Army officer. The civilian was Mr. J.O. "Ollie" Pfeiffer, Northern California division manager for the Gilmore Oil Company. He led a company junket, the "Gilmore-Dodge Scout Party," down the California coast, and paid a call at Fort Scott to chat with an "executive officer in charge of one of Fort Scott's huge long-range coast guns." But the newspaper did not explain how the Dodge sedan got all the way up to the firing platform. Most likely, HDSF post engineers hoisted the car next to the 12-inch gun, as the Army cooperated with the Jaycees in publicizing the coming celebration.

Army Day 1941 found curious citizens inspecting the coast artillery equipment on display at Fort Scott. The *Chronicle* noted that "soldiers, who a few months ago were civilians, put the equipment through its paces for the crowds." But curious visitors asked questions about the military exhibits. "Reasonable questions were answered," a *Chronicle* scribe wrote, "but after all, there are

Summer day along Grant Avenue, San Francisco Chinatown, August 10, 1940. (San Francisco Archives, S.F. Public Library)

secrets." When a civilian asked about the effective range of a particular gun or searchlight on display, the attending HDSF soldier replied, "pretty far." One elderly woman asked a lieutenant, "Where are the big guns on the Marin side?" The young officer casually motioned in the air "with a sweep of his arms that took in the horizon from Alcatraz to the Cliff House." In the late afternoon, the exhibition of Army harbor defense prowess closed with a regimental parade. The *Chronicle* noted the entire event would be restaged at the Golden Gate Park Polo Grounds the following Saturday.

Lieutenant Daniel Cook's platoon represented Battery F of the 6th CA in the Army Day tent pitching contest. As a stopwatch ran, tents were to be erected and struck, then put back in their packs. But a week of heavy April rain prevented the troops from practicing for the event. Doing the next best thing, Cook brought his platoon into the Fort Baker gymnasium where "they never pitched and struck tents so many times in their lives."

On Saturday, the rains stopped in time for the repeat Army Day celebration at Golden Gate Park. A crowd of several thousand came to the Polo Grounds to see an array of seacoast mines, ammunition, searchlights, sound detectors, antiaircraft machine guns, and a military encampment. In the tent pitching contest, Lieutenant Cook's platoon from Battery F won, with "the tents coming down before they got up." Units of the 6th and 18th Coast Artillery marched in review and Major General Henry T. Burgin of the 9th Coast Artillery District inspected the honor guard. The 2nd Battalion of the 18th then performed a battalion drill demonstration. The *Chronicle* stressed that ninety percent of the soldiers were inductees from the East and Midwest with only three months in service.

After completing their initial training on

April 26th, batteries learned to operate within their assigned battalions and groups until July 19th, when regimental and groupment training began. From the start, HDSF's Training Memorandum Number 6 told the officers and recruits what was expected of them: "The regiments, groupments, and the Harbor Defenses of San Francisco will be proficient by the end of the 29th week, Aug. 16, 1941."

While the Harbor Defenses of San Francisco improved its capability to protect the Golden Gate, the U.S. Navy spent one billion dollars establishing bases and shipyards around the bay. The Navy purchased Hunters Point from Bethlehem Steel and added four dry-docks and 250 acres of landfill to the giant repair center. Treasure Island, site of the memorable 1939 Golden Gate International Exposition, became a naval base. A huge navy arsenal was built at Port Chicago. Naval air stations were established at Alameda and Sunnyvale. As previously mentioned, the Navy set up a submarine net depot at Tiburon. The burgeoning war economy affected most Bay Area communities. When the Navy stepped up operations at Mare Island Naval Shipyard and began to hire men "at the rate of 1000 per month," the population of nearby Vallejo increased quickly from 20,000 to 60,000. Cars carrying job seekers to town were claimed to "bear the names of 20 states." Hotels and rooming houses became crowded; housewives rented spare bedrooms to "two or three men who work different shifts and can share the bed in eight hour turns." The federal government was reported to be building 4000 units of housing in nearby swamp basins to accommodate some of the 19,000 Mare Island workers. Vallejo's biggest concern was vice, the *San Francisco Chronicle* reported. The law moved in to clean up the town, which "gave relief to churchmen, headaches to owners of the 34 liquor stores and bars that greet workmen" as they emerged from Mare Island after their shifts.

As national defense and defense industries dominated Bay Area life, a threatened strike in the shipyards made front page news. San Francisco had the reputation of being a union town, a reputation earned most recently from the violent waterfront strike of 1934. In the spring of 1941, American Federation of Labor machinists, represented by the Bay Cities Metal Trades Council threatened a shipyard walkout over wages. As the deadline for a May 9th strike vote neared, Navy Secretary Frank Knox and Rear Admiral Emory S. Land of the U.S. Maritime Commission sent an urgent appeal to the Metal Trades Council asking them to avert the strike. It "will not be a strike against the shipbuilders," Navy Secretary Knox stressed, "as it will be a strike against our country's program of national defense."

On Friday May 9th, the machinists voted to strike anyway, claiming not to have previously ratified a master's agreement prohibiting strikes and lockouts for the duration of the national emergency. The strike went into effect the following Monday morning with 2,000 machinists walking picket lines at shipyards on both sides of the bay. The lockout was not total, but enough workers refused to cross the lines, causing the Navy to speculate the strike might affect construction of four cruisers, twenty-four destroyers, and forty-three auxiliary vessels. The strike would last two months and would nearly involve troops of the Harbor Defenses. But for now, new HDSF batteries completed the initial training phase and prepared for scheduled target practice.

"Warning on Target Practice Thursday," announced the *Chronicle*. "Warning of major caliber seacoast artillery target practice to start at 9 a.m. Thursday for an indefinite period was issued yesterday from the plans and training office of Colonel W.F. LaFrenz at Fort Scott. Fishermen, airmen, and trans-pacific mariners were told that the danger zone is the 'south long range'." Local newspapers and radio stations issued such warnings whenever harbor defense guns fired in peacetime. In 1941, record target practice took place all summer during battalion and group training at the Golden Gate.

Three batteries of the 6th Coast Artillery practiced in May. From Fort Funston, Battery B fired its 12-inch mortars. At Fort Barry, Battery D fired 12-inch disappearing guns and Battery K fired the two 12-inch Wallace rifles in a practice well covered by Army photographers. Record Target Practice was an important event

*Workers refuse to cross union machinists'
picket line at East Bay shipyard, morning
of May 12, 1941. (Presidio Army Museum)*

practice conducted on the 8th and 9th of May went well. The *Coast Artillery Journal* reported the firing produced "results that may bring a red E on all cuffs" of the enlisted men. Officially, the practice shoot garnered a rating of "Very Good."

On May 21st, Battery D of the 18th CA conducted practice with two 6-inch disappearing carriage rifles on the heights north of Baker Beach. A witness to this firing remembered the formality of the table setting with punch bowls and polished coffee service for the invited guests. Then Battery F followed that evening with its turn at target practice. Though trained on Battery Saffold at Scott, this unit borrowed the 12-inch disappearing guns of Battery Mendell at Fort Barry for the shoot. Battery F attempted to fire in darkness, using seacoast searchlights to illuminate the target. But bad weather that

in the life of the battery. This put to the test months of gun drill and plotting drill. The range section waited in the plotting room or in distant observation pillboxes. Gun sections stood ready on the firing platform. Ammunition details rolled out projectiles and powder bags from magazine rooms deep underground. The battery commander might have tensed a bit at his command post, for his reputation was on the line. Perhaps on the slope behind the emplacement, the mess sergeant had set up a buffet table with coffee and refreshments for the officers and civilians invited to observe the firing. When the pyramid-shaped target, towed by a tug sailing right to left, appeared in the designated fire zone at sea, the battery went into action. "If you didn't do good," remembered an HDSF lieutenant, "you were pooh-poohed all over the post."

The 2nd Battalion of the 18th Coast Artillery also had guns registering with live fire in May; commencing with E's two 6-inch rapid fire guns on Baker Beach. When the towed target came into view, the guns usually fired at least four sensing rounds. After the range officer made final corrections, "you fired for the record," said Lieutenant Tom Scally of the 18th CA, "and this was for your reputation until the next time you fired." Battery E's target

Battery K, 6th CA fires 12-inch barbette seacoast gun of Battery Wallace, Fort Barry, April 28, 1941. (San Francisco Archives, S.F. Public Library)

Scene from Battery Commander's Station during target practice of 12-inch Battery Wallace in 1941. Battery CO Captain Samuel McReynolds in the pit was later captured at Corregidor. Shorter officer in middle distance is Lieutenant Colonel William LaFrenz, HDSF plans and training officer. (Presidio Army Museum)

night, and a broken tow line on the target caused postponement of the practice. Battery F resumed action on the night of May 27th. The 12-inch guns at Barry lit up the evening skies, which the *Coast Artillery Journal* claimed, "gave nearby San Francisco an unexpected thrill." Results for all 18th Coast Artillery batteries "were very creditable," reported the magazine, especially since many of the men were experiencing their first major caliber shoot. Praising the work of his batteries, battalion commander Colonel F.H. Holden wrote: "While we cannot call upon history to tell of our feats of arms, a record of loyal and conscientious work has been established which gives promise of dependability in any emergency." So ended the "raw recruit" phase at HDSF. From here on, future arrivals to the Harbor Defenses would have received their basic training elsewhere.

In the meantime, the AFL-CIO Machinist strike which began on May 12th, dragged into a second month. The shutdown affected work at eleven shipyards and repair plants. When the two thousand machinists struck, thousands of other workers walked out in sympathy. Local newspapers predicted two million work hours lost; enough time, they estimated, to construct two and one-half C-1 cargo passenger ships for the defense program. In Washington, President Roosevelt watched the labor-management impasse with mounting concern. Calling the Bay Area shipyard strike a threat to national security, Roosevelt declared a July 4th deadline for settling the dispute.

If the matter could not be resolved, the 6th Coast Artillery drew the assignment to remove the picket lines. One week before July 4th, several batteries of the regiment began training for strike duty. One platoon sat on the Scott parade ground, portraying recalcitrant strikers, while another platoon, armed with clubs, came upon them in wedge-formation. The units learned to dismantle a roadblock of trucks by placing 6x6 wooden beams hooked to a winch against the inside of the wheels and dragging the trucks sideways. Winning platoons in these strike-breaking games won gold-plated cups purchased in trophy shops. Since the strike-affected shipyards were along the waterfront, Lieutenant Colonel Felix Usis scouted the Embarcadero by motor boat. At the foot of a Bay Bridge tower, the boat propeller tangled in something under the water. Usis ordered the sergeant to gun the engine and the boat pulled away. He never figured out what was grabbing

Target practice with Battery D, 18th CA on 6-inch disappearing guns above Baker Beach.

the propeller in the green waters under the bridge. With the deadline almost at hand, the platoons that had performed best in training were picked to face the strikers. Lieutenant Harry Payne of Battery B, leading one of the chosen platoons, canceled his July 4th wedding plans as the deadline neared. On June 29th, the strike ended in a settlement between the machinists and shipyard management. Lieutenant Payne, who sent out cancellation notices, now had to notify guests that wedding plans were still on.

While troops practiced strike-breaking at the Scott parade ground, new men joined the Harbor Defenses on the Marin side. On June 2nd, the 3rd Battalion of the 6th Coast Artillery was activated at Fort Barry. Twenty days later, the battalion's enlisted personnel arrived from Camp Callan, a coast artillery basic training camp near San Diego. The men were assigned to Battery G which fired a trio of Barry 3-inch antiaircraft guns on fixed mounts, and to Batteries H and I which manned 6-inch rapid-fire armament at the fort.

Soldiers at Fort Barry, gazing across Rodeo Lagoon, saw construction of new Army barracks at Fort Cronkhite. Unpretentious and functional, the two-story wooden barracks were the intended home of the 56th Coast Artillery Regiment soon to arrive with their mobile batteries of 155mm guns reinforcing the "concrete artillery" at the Golden Gate. Before completion of barracks at Cronkhite, the officers and NCO cadres of the 56th moved

in ahead of the troops. The commander was Colonel Frank Drake, a West Point officer who had been ROTC instructor at the University of San Francisco since 1936. Most of the junior officers at the founding of the regiment were ROTC graduates. Upon arrival of enlisted troops on June 20th, the entire regiment moved into the new barracks. Again, the men were recruits from the Midwest, mainly Michigan and Illinois. All had trained together at Camp Callan and had brought with them the 155's they had trained on. These guns were holdovers from the First World War, still painted orange upon arrival at HDSF. At that point, the guns spent some time in a modification center being repainted olive-drab and having their rubber-rimmed steel wheels exchanged for pneumatic tires.

The Army barracks of the 56th Coast Artillery stood by the ocean, five hundred yards from the waves crashing heavily against the beach and cliffs of Rodeo Cove. At night, the coast artillerymen in their barracks heard the roiling surf and the melancholy sound of fog horns and clanging bell buoys out past the breakers. "We heard the foghorn an awful lot at night, especially with the great thick fogs we had," reminisced 56th CA veteran Dale Barnhart. "Through the Golden Gate or over the hills of Marin County, they roll without warning and spread between the bay and the bright daylight," as one 1939 author described the thick drifting fog. "One moment you may be over them. A minute later they will be wrapped around you." Dale Barnhart saw the fog time and again move in over Rodeo Lagoon. "We'd get out there in the morning in our thin fatigues and we'd do our calisthenics in that chill." When the men had nothing else to do, the officers created a special detail. "When they didn't know what to do with us," recalled Barnhart, "we planted tons of iceplant as ground cover around the barracks."

The 56th Coast Artillery de-

Fort Cronkhite wooden barracks soon after completion in 1941. (San Francisco Archives, S.F. Public Library)

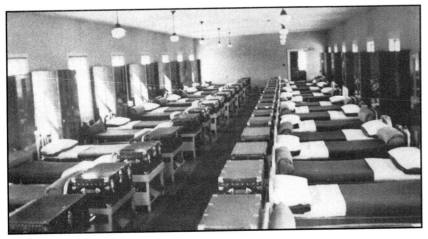

Barracks interior at Camp Spurr, Fort Barry. (Presidio Army Museum)

ployed three battalions, each with three gun batteries. Each battery fired four mobile M1918 155mm guns. The regiment had 36 of these seacoast artillery pieces. In case of war, the mission of the 56th at HDSF involved rapid movement to areas uncovered by the fixed defenses, like landing beaches to the north and south of the Golden Gate. The 155mm gun was a World War I artillery piece of French design. The coast artillery model fired a 95-pound projectile to a maximum of 17,716 yards, or roughly ten miles. It supplemented the 6-inch fixed guns in harbor defense by countering lightly armored or unarmored vessels, especially destroyers, submarines, and minesweeping craft.

The 56th CA batteries practiced moving the guns and emplacing them along the coast. Training occurred at Cronkhite, sometimes at night, with the goal of having the guns in place and ready by daylight. Trucks towed the 155's on the open road and caterpillar tractors pulled them through rough terrain. Range details established base-end stations on the hills beyond Battery Townsley. The crews loaded their tripods, communications gear, and M1910 Warner and Swasey Azimuth Instruments onto four-wheel drive reconnaissance cars and headed for the highest areas of the fort. "It

Training on 155mm mobile seacoast guns at Camp Callan near San Diego by future members of 56th Coast Artillery who brought these same guns with them to HDSF. (D. Barnhart)

was so steep," Dale Barnhart recalled, "you'd wonder if you were going to tip over up there." Stopping where they sometimes saw a tower of the Golden Gate Bridge peeking over a distant hill, the observation details mounted range scopes on tripods and surveyed the mobile base-end stations to establish their exact position on the battery plotting board. One of the sergeants who did the surveying was, in civilian life, a graduate civil engineer. Actual firing of the 155mm guns occurred only a few times.

The men of the 56th also trained on smaller weapons. Everyone fired the .50 caliber water-cooled machine gun on its antiaircraft tripod. Each battery had four of these weapons for close-in aerial defense. The semi-automatic Garand M1 rifle had just come into service, and the troops practiced marksmanship with these on the firing range. Wearing combat gear, gas masks, and carrying rifles, troops charged down the tear gas field at Cronkhite. As gas poured from generators and wafted across the field, dynamite charges in the ground exploded, adding to the realism.

Colonel Drake put Lieutenant Ralph G. DeMoisy of the 56th's Headquarters Battery in charge of the Officers' Mess. DeMoisy heard

that Colonel Drake operated a hotel during the 1920's. "When he went broke in his hotel," the rumor went, "he decided he was going to do it right at Fort Cronkhite." In the Officers' Mess, Colonel Drake wanted to charge officers extra money "and buy automatic potato peelers and everything else." Certain the regiment would vacate the barracks once hostilities began, Lieutenant DeMoisy resisted the idea of spending mess funds on extraneous kitchen equipment.

One day DeMoisy entered the Headquarters Battery office, "glowing and beaming." He had just been promoted to first lieutenant, and was showing off his silver bars to fellow officers and enlisted men. According to DeMoisy, Colonel Drake "lit right in the middle of me and made me stand at attention while he dressed me down." Drake had come from inspecting the kitchen of the Officers' Mess. "The cook had gotten into the vanilla extract and told Colonel Drake what he could do with his Officers' Mess," DeMoisy later found out. With the office staff looking on, the new first lieutenant stood at attention as Colonel Drake held him responsible for the cook's actions, and threatened him with court martial. "Humiliated---that took away from my joy at my promotion for the moment," remembered DeMoisy. From that incident, the regiment's executive officer concluded DeMoisy and Colonel Drake would never get along. A few months later, the lieutenant became "one of the people that was selected to

go to Chile," an unusual sidelight to the HDSF story.

On July 4, 1941, units of the 6th and 18th Coast Artillery marched in an Independence Day parade in Redwood City, about 20 miles south of San Francisco. The harbor defensemen sweltered as they paraded under the hot July sun. The march ended at the fairgrounds, where the troops were dismissed. Each soldier received one dollar's worth of scrip, which the local Chamber of Commerce said bars in town would honor as cash. The soldiers headed straight for the fairgrounds bar, expecting to buy ice-cold beer to slake their thirst. The bar refused to accept their scrip. Hot and tired, the coast artillerymen stood incredulously for a moment as the indignity of the situation soaked in. Then the bar erupted in a brawl. "They threw the joint up for grabs," said 18th CA veteran Charles Sullivan. Civilian and military police rushed in to restore order. Colonel F.H. Holden, commander of the 2nd Battalion, 18th Coast Artillery, came to hear for himself what had happened. First the police spoke, then the first sergeant explained the men's side. If the bar would not accept the scrip, Colonel Holden reportedly said after listening, "throw it up for grabs again."

"Before the war began, many civilians felt that soldiers were prone to be disorderly, carousers, and drunks," remembered HDSF officer John Schonher. "The harassment of off-duty troops in Marin county communities was commonplace. In military circles, it was believed this was supported to force the military to provide military police patrol in these diverse communities." Once during this prewar period, M.P.'s informed Schonher that three of his men sat in jail at the Hall of Justice in San Francisco, waiting to appear in court. The battery commander went downtown to represent his men before the woman judge as the arresting officer read the charges. The policeman claimed the soldiers "were raucous and noisy." The judge listened for a moment, put her palm over the microphone, and told Schonher the arresting officer "didn't know

Corporal Barnhart is about to set up azimuth instrument for 155mm battery at Cronkhite. Note 16-inch gun emplacement on heights at right. (D. Barnhart)

what he was talking about." After the judge dismissed the charges, the captain and his men left the courtroom for the friendlier atmosphere of the Army post.

The growing soldier population brought on by the draft prompted the Army to increase recreational services. Officers had the Harbor Defense Officers' Club at Fort Scott, with a social schedule including Saturday night dances three times a month, and a Sunday tea dance on the fourth weekend. The Officers' Club had two adjacent tennis courts and a nearby 18-hole golf course. The non-commissioned officers went to their own club, built in the style of a log cabin at Fort Scott. The enlisted men held dances at the post gymnasiums of Forts Scott and Baker. Fort Scott also boasted a 1038-seat air-conditioned theater for films and theatricals. Several bowling lanes were scattered among the posts. Sports constituted the main recreational activity provided by the Harbor Defenses. An Athletic Officer with additional military and civilian staff organized games "to insure full opportunity for every officer and enlisted man to enjoy some type of athletic activity." Favored sports included baseball, softball, basketball, volleyball, ping pong, bowling, and horseshoes. The Athletic Officer supervised inter-battery competitions which aroused "considerable interest among the members of the command with considerable rivalry between the batteries for the various championships," observed the 1941 HDSF yearbook. Occasionally the Athletic Officer booked a boxing or wrestling exhibition in the gymnasium "to please the patrons of the square circle."

Once national conscription began in earnest, civic-minded civilians began organizing the type of social services the Army could not provide. A year before the U.S. entry into war, eighteen private organizations, like the YMCA, the YW-CA, the Salvation Army, the National Jewish Welfare Board, and the National Catholic Community Service among others, pooled funds, experience, and facilities to form the USO---United Service Organization for the National Defense.

Fort Scott NCO Club in 1941.

The YMCA Presidio Branch offered "full USO services" in a four-story building on the post. These centers typically had libraries, recreation rooms, and tourist services for check-cashing and travel information. In addition, the Presidio branch organized church parties and Sunday Vespers. It also served as "the official Information Bureau for all posts within and related to the Presidio," being the contact point for locating enlisted personnel serving at the Harbor Defenses.

The Sunday *San Francisco Chronicle* on July 6th announced a week of all-out fund raising in the city to raise $35,000 for the USO. "One hundred young women are needed for volunteer USO work at Seals Stadium this afternoon." The San Francisco Seals were playing a Sunday double-header against the Hollywood All-Stars in Pacific Coast League baseball. Ten thousand fans bought raffle tickets to win the historic bat Joe DiMaggio used to extend his hitting streak to forty-five games. Between games of the double-header, the DiMaggio bat was ceremoniously escorted to home plate by a detail of sailors, the USO committee, the United Airlines stewardesses who brought the bat from New York, and ten NCO's and enlisted men from Battery A of the 6th Coast Artillery. The memorable bat was presented to the winner of the raffle drawing, and contest proceeds amounting to $1,675 went toward the USO fund drive. President Roosevelt dispatched a telegram hailing the patriotic spirit of the ceremony, proclaiming, "The response of San Franciscans thrill me." The support of the USO "has characterized

San Francisco and San Franciscans since the first day of the Argonauts." On that Sunday, the Seals won both ends of the double-header.

San Francisco Mayor Angelo J. Rossi kicked off the citywide USO fund drive the following day, issuing a proclamation stating, "The funds received by the USO will be used for the benefit of men who have left civilian life to learn how to defend our nation." Business groups devoted one week of "all out" campaigning to fill the city's USO quota of $35,000. The Chinese Chamber of Commerce and the Chinese Six Companies promised to "mass their efforts for a 100 percent contribution of the Chinese Community." Two hundred employees of downtown businesses armed with subscription lists made the rounds of prospective donors.

On Saturday evening, August 9th, show business personalities Eddie Cantor, Linda Darnell, Edward Arnold, and Ann Rutherford highlighted performances at the San Francisco Civic Auditorium for the official opening of Hospitality House, the recently completed downtown servicemen's center. The *Chronicle* reported top military commanders and ordinary "sailors, flyers, and harbor defensemen" from the bay region attended the show. After the Civic Auditorium show, the performers walked over to see the new center. As "concrete proof of San Francisco's regard for the Nation's servicemen," the Hospitality House offered a library, reading rooms, and waiting rooms, where servicemen could stop for rest and refreshments as they visited the city. The building, a streamlined Art-Deco structure across the street from the Main Library, was built by union labor with material supplied by building contractors on land provided by the city. The idea belonged to Colonel Charles Crockett of the Presidio's 30th Infantry Regiment, who coordinated the project. Dr. Howard McKinley, chairman of the Citizen's Hospitality Committee,

addressed the visitors. "This building will know no distinction between race, color, and creed," declared McKinley. "Within its walls will be welcome men of every national origin who are now Americans."

The official opening of Hospitality House the next morning featured a touring cavalcade of automobiles. Boy Scouts and members of fraternal orders drove each carload of GI's along San Francisco's famed 49-Mile Drive. The riders got along famously, reported the *Chronicle*. "Already many citizens have invited their service passengers to their homes for dinner." The 6th Coast Artillery Band led the way, occasionally striking up a military march as the sightseeing cavalcade cruised past the city's spectacular coastline and down Van Ness Avenue to the open doors of Hospitality House.

By the summer of 1941, the United States had done everything it could, short of war, to oppose Germany and Japan. U.S. naval forces garrisoned Iceland on July 7th and carried out antisubmarine patrols to protect British convoys. On July 21st, President Roosevelt asked Congress to extend draft terms of service from one year to thirty months. This measure passed by only one vote, evidence of divided American opinion on war preparations. On July 26th, the U.S. and Britain froze Japanese assets in their respective countries. Days later, Japan was barred from the oil fields of the Dutch East Indies, resulting in a seventy-five percent freeze in Japanese trade

Construction of Hospitality House at Civic Center. San Francisco City Hall looms in background. (San Francisco Archives, S.F. Public Library)

and a ninety percent reduction of Japan's oil supply. Desperate for petroleum, Japan now decided to invade Indochina, even if this meant risking war with the United States.

As part of American military preparations, President Roosevelt instituted a youth movement in the higher echelons of the Army. The president advanced younger men to field and general grade ranks so American officers would match the ages of their British and German counterparts. "Among Colonels nominated to temporary Brigadier Generals," the *Chronicle* reported on July 11th, "was Edward A. Stockton, commanding harbor defenses at San Francisco." The West Pointer served in World War I with the big railway guns and later in the Office of the Chief of Coast Artillery. As a colonel, Stockton had been in charge of HDSF since October 1940. At age fifty-five, Stockton became a Brigadier General on July 17, 1941.

"Coast artillery at Fort Scott will fire on the north short ranges from 9 a.m. Monday until finished, according to a warning issued to mariners." Further notices appeared in San Francisco newspapers during the summer of 1941 as gun batteries continued their target practices. July 14th marked the formal proof-firing of Fort Funston's 16-inch rifles manned by Battery C, 6th Coast Artillery. Since their emplacement in 1937, the two guns had fired a total of twelve rounds, most of them expended in the unofficial proof-firing the year before.

Mayor Rossi (left) and servicemen watch Anne Rutherford sign guest book at Hospitality House. Linda Darnell and Edward Arnold were also on hand for opening of downtown servicemen's center, August 9, 1941. (San Francisco Archives, S.F. Public Library)

Captain Arthur Kramer, who conducted the proof-firing at Fort Cronkhite's Battery Townsley the previous summer, was now the Battery C commander. Before firing, the Ordnance Department checked the 16-inch guns and their firing circuits. Then the battery fired five rounds from each gun. The huge rifles sounded with a lengthy "Booommm" accompanied by a bright muzzle flash and some smoke. The roar of these guns, Kramer reminisced, lasted "definitely longer than the relatively sharp crack of a 155mm gun." At some point in the firing, Captain Kramer stood five feet from the breech and "enjoyed watching the [40-inch] recoil of that 110-ton gun." Though the guns fired "smokeless" powder, some smoke was seen swirling about the muzzle flash. "It was quite thrilling to see," thought Kramer.

Some inspecting officers complained of seeing fouling deep inside the barrel of the 16-inch rifles. Captain Kramer called for a vol-

GI's relax in main lounge of Hospitality House, August 9, 1941. (San Francisco Archives, S.F. Public Library)

unteer to go into the barrel and clean it out. "A real skinny little fellow" in the battery said he would try. Because Kramer did not want his volunteer to suddenly develop claustrophobia inside the barrel, Kramer made sure the man knew the job was voluntary. Then they tied a rope around the volunteer's shoulders and ran the free end through the barrel from muzzle to breech. Another line was tied to his leg from the breech end. Armed with a trouble light and wire brush, the soldier was pushed into the gun until he came to rest one-third of the way up the barrel. Later when they pulled him out, the volunteer reported the foulings to be peels of copper from the rotating bands of fired projectiles. Try as he did with the steel brush, he could not scrape them loose.

During this period, Battery C's Maintenance Section contained some capable individuals. Mess Sergeant Robert C. Henneberg made food available to men returning from parades, formations, or night drills. When the troops came back, "the mess hall was open, coffee and doughnuts were out." Melvin O. Bachman, a former Chicago pastry cook, was a Battery C favorite for his banana cream pies. Lieutenant Colonel LaFrenz, HDSF Plans and Training Officer had "an intelligence network," Captain Kramer figured; LaFrenz turned up for morning coffee at Battery C whenever Bachman made banana cream pies. Meyer Schatz, who had run a second-hand furniture store in Chicago, was another distinguished recruit. He improved a weak supply room operation and rose rapidly to the rank of sergeant. The captain felt Schatz deserved the promotion, "because everything we needed, he got. He learned the ropes very quickly."

One of Battery C's gun chiefs was an-

(Inset) Brigadier General Edward A. Stockton, Jr., HDSF commander at start of World War II.

other story. He often disappeared on a three-day drunk at payday without first requesting a pass, though Captain Kramer reminded him one was available "anytime he would ask for it." The sergeant never availed himself of the captain's offer, preferring to stay away without permission. In exasperation, Kramer forced the section chief to sign an undated resignation, reduction, and request for transfer; this document went into the battery safe. If the sergeant turned up missing again without requesting a pass, Kramer promised to sign and date the order. The sergeant did not heed the warning. By December 1941, he was no longer listed on the battery roster.

The Harbor Defenses, brought up to strength since January, demonstrated its forceful presence on Tuesday July 29th as "the largest formation of Harbor Defense groups assembled in review since the World War" gathered at Fort Scott, the *San Francisco Chronicle* reported. An estimated six thousand men of the harbor defense command marched in farewell ceremonies for Major General Henry T. Burgin, as he left the 9th Coast Artillery District for the Coast Artillery command of the Hawaiian Department. Leading up to the 3 p.m. review at Crissy Field, the Golden Gate Bridge and nearby roads swarmed with military traffic, as "army trucks rolled between the six harbor defense posts carrying men to the parade ground." At Crissy Field, several hundred civilians gathered around the reviewing stand of General Burgin and other harbor defense officers. As the 6th Coast Artillery Band played, a composite group from the 6th, 18th, and 56th CA Regiments circled the field in regimental review formation. The troops paraded in Class A uniforms, the *Chronicle* reported, "wearing trench helmets and carrying bayonet tipped rifles." As they marched past General Burgin, unit guidon bearers dipped red and white guidons in salute. After Burgin's departure, Major General

Battery C, 6th Coast Artillery drills on Fort Funston 16-inch gun in 1941. Hydraulic rammer pushes projectile into breech. (K. Cooper, Jr.)

Walter K. Wilson took command of the 9th Coast Artillery District.

Each year, the Junior Chamber of Commerce sponsored Harbor Day, which commemorated the commercial and recreational activities of San Francisco Bay. On Saturday, August 4th, the Jaycees held a water carnival, parade of boats, and other events at Aquatic Park in the sheltering man-made cove between the curving arm of Muni Pier and the stone-stepped shoreline of the casino. An official luncheon came later at the St. Francis Yacht Club. The young woman crowned Miss Harbor Day of 1941 sat at the dais of course, but luncheon guests "dwelt on Bay Area shipbuilding, harbor defenses, and other aspects of the national emergency," reported the *San Francisco Chronicle*. Bay Area military officials at Harbor Day represented the 4th Army, the 12th Naval District, and the Pacific division of the U.S. Marine Corps. A local FBI agent spoke about sabotage prevention at bay defense plants. Then rose an officer from 4th Army who spoke of the harbor with the stirring words favored by Bay Area civic boosters in prewar years. "Possibly from its waters may sail at some time in the future those forces which may have to be dispatched for the defense of vital areas of the Western Hemisphere," Lieutenant Colonel D.A. Stroh foresaw. "The nerve center of this vast area is centered at the Presidio, over looking your Golden Gate and that magnificent Harbor which is being publicized today."

The U.S. Navy underlined the strategic importance of the harbor on August 7th, when they announced a zone of operations "at the entrance to San Francisco Bay." The Navy marked a zone across the inner waters of the Golden Gate from the Marina to Sausalito Point and from there to Angel Island. "Although no confirmation has been received," surmised the *San Francisco Chronicle*, "it is believed the submarine nets are being placed in the operations area." Though the Navy kept silent about their plans, the submarine net project had begun in July. In principle, the net was not intended to trap enemy submarines, but to discourage them from entering the bay.

The U.S. Navy studied the major harbor entrances of the world and concluded the mouth of the Yellow River in China and the entrance to San Francisco Bay had the fastest and strongest currents of all. Two visiting British naval officers, accustomed to the calmer anchorages of the Royal Navy, thought a net could not hold in the six-knot current of the Golden Gate. The Navy again consulted Charles Rice, a local salvage expert who participated in pier construction of the Golden Gate Bridge. Rice recommended using 10-ton concrete slugs instead of the standard 6,000-pound anchors to weight the nets. The Navy eventually produced concrete slugs by the thousands at the Tiburon Net Depot.

The first mooring buoy of the net project was in place by July 1, 1941. The transport *Henderson* promptly ran over it despite public warnings issued by the Navy about the operations area at the harbor entrance. For all their declarations, the Navy could not have done much to prevent anyone from entering the zone. At the time, the U.S. was not at war, and no federal agency had full control of passage through the Golden Gate. Work continued on the submarine net at San Francisco through the summer of 1941. But not until September 15th, did Washington give belated authorization for its installation. Despite lack of higher approval, Navy Captain Stanley M. Haight of the Tiburon Net Depot pressed on with the net project until December 7th, when the installation would be nearly complete.

The resulting submarine net formed a continuous barrier across the main channel of the harbor entrance from the St. Francis Yacht Club at the Marina to Point Sausalito, a distance of about three miles. The rough tides forced the Navy to position the net far enough from the narrows of the Gate, yet close enough to block the entrance. On the surface, the installation presented only a line of rusty steel buoys strung along the top of the net. Underwater, the net was a formidable curtain of tough steel wire connected with shackles and clamps. The height of the net varied, from thirty feet near the shores to 150 feet in the main channel. 10-ton concrete anchors held the net against the rough tides. One quarter-mile off the San Francisco side was the net gate, a one-thousand yard long movable section which opened, permitting friendly vessels to enter the harbor. Submarine net tenders moored at either end of the opening were secured to the sea floor by concrete anchor and chain. These 146-foot Navy vessels sported powerful winches on their prows which pulled the movable gate section to one side. Two ships were stationed at each side of the opening; one to open the gate and one to pull it shut.

The harbor defense troops of San Francisco had already appeared publicly at Army Day and several review ceremonies and re-

ceived some pictorial attention in the local press. But on Saturday August 16th, city residents had their first glimpse of other Army units that formed in California since January. San Francisco newspapers reported movement of "great olive-drab troop carriers and prime movers [as they] roared up the Funston approach." The new 7th Infantry Division, composed of draftees, and the 40th Infantry Division, activated from the California National Guard, streamed through the city, en route from Fort Ord and Camp San Luis Obispo to field maneuvers at Fort Lewis, Washington. For three days, military convoys rumbled across the Golden Gate as M.P.'s directed them onto special lanes of the bridge. Calvin Chin, an ambulance driver in a medical company of the 7th Infantry Division, recalled the convoy line coming to a stop by a peach orchard near Santa Clara. Before the troops could start picking the ripe fruit, a farmer emerged and gave the men all the baskets of peaches they could carry. For days after, Chin drove up the coast with the convoy, as he munched on the horde of juicy, summer peaches by his side. After conclusion of maneuvers in the Northwest, the same divisions headed back to their California bases, crossing the Golden Gate Bridge during the Labor Day weekend. The Harbor Defenses of San Francisco would soon also carry on large-scale maneuvers, but in its own sphere of operations.

Return of California-based infantry divisions from maneuvers at Fort Lewis, Washington, Labor Day weekend, August 31, 1941. (Presidio Army Museum)

Chapter 4:
"An Enemy Will Attack the Golden Gate Bridge"

The Harbor Defenses of San Francisco were fully manned by the late summer of 1941. Troops dug in and constructed field fortifications around their concrete emplacements. On Baker Beach, the commander of Battery E, 18th Coast Artillery wanted shelters dug in the slopes behind the 6-inch guns so the gun crews on alert could live close by. But building material was hard to get. At the Presidio's National Military Cemetery, a routine pruning of the eucalyptus trees on the cemetery perimeter yielded a large quantity of felled logs. Battery E hauled the scrap to Baker Beach. The men put the eucalyptus logs into the construction of underground quarters and a network of log-lined trenches connecting various parts of the battery.

With the assistance of HDSF artillery engineers, the men garnished their fortifications with camouflage. Army field manuals suggested the disruptive paint scheme. No attempt was made to match colors to local terrain, but the irregular patches of olive, maroon, and yellow ochre paint applied to emplacement walls gave the necessary effect. Nets hung like tents above entire emplacements. To the nets, the men attached strips of colored burlap and salvaged raincoats painted with infrared oil paints. Sometimes, the camouflage netting was layered three-deep so nothing could be visible through the density. In addition, artificial bushes and movable panels broke the outline of the concrete blast aprons in front of the guns.

Captain Richard Moorman, battery commander of the Funston 12-inch mortars, wanted to disguise his emplacement as a tourist camp with a tourist cabin covering each mortar. The canvas and scrap lumber cabins would be mounted on wheels so they could be quickly rolled back when the mortars had a fire mission. The men built one cabin as a test, and positioned it over one of the battery's four 12-

The first sergeant shows battalion staff officer through the eucalyptus log-lined trenches at 6-inch Battery Chamberlin on Baker Beach. Through netting in right background is the battery commander's station. (Presidio Army Museum)

(Left) A view of the camouflaged Baker Beach rapid-fire battery from the air. (K. Cooper, Jr.)
(Below left) Candid shot of Baker Beach emplacement under the nets. Note basketball backboard and small dog.
(Bottom right) Gun drill on Baker Beach as crew of Battery E, 18th CA moves aside netting in front of 6-inch gun. (San Francisco Archives, S.F. Public Library)

calculated stress points and positioned beams for maximum support. Lieutenant Payne scrounged timber from the fire-gutted Tait's-at-the-Beach roadhouse inn near Fleishhaker Zoo. Tait's, a hangout for the city's gourmets and leisure crowd, had its business reversals over the years, then burned down in December 1940.

The new antiaircraft emplacement bunkers were ingenious. The range section and the three gun pits had dugouts concealed under three feet of earth. Heavy timbers lined the dugout interiors, which contained double-deck bunks and eight-foot ceilings. One end of each wooden dugout had an opening facing the ocean for cross ventilation. The command post was built on two levels underground. Rough-hewn wood lined the interior, warmed by two old-fashioned potbellied heating stoves on each floor. As Captain Moorman figured it, "all the men had to do was carry their beds and shelter halves down the road to the dugouts from the barracks. They were then in position and could be called out and on the guns in thirty to sixty seconds."

During construction of bunkers, Cap-

inch mortars before the 9th Coast Artillery District's commanding general came to inspect. When the general saw the emplacement, he remarked to Captain Moorman that he had never before seen a three-gun mortar battery. Then the men rolled aside the fake cabin to reveal a fourth mortar. The general said, "Tear it down and camouflage the battery with fishnet!"

At the Funston antiaircraft emplacements, Captain Moorman gained inspiration for another project after seeing "a very low underground command post" erected by one of his lieutenants during a maneuver. Moorman expanded on the concept and assigned his engineering officer, Lieutenant Harry Payne and Payne's platoon to build underground living quarters. Armed with his knowledge of physics and some field manuals Captain Moorman had given him, Payne designed the structures. He meticulously

(Right) Fixed 3-inch antiaircraft gun in camouflaged gun pit at Fort Funston.
(Below) Captain Richard R. Moorman (taller man) and lieutenant in the log-lined dugouts of Battery B, 6th Coast Artillery at Funston.

tain Moorman told Lieutenant Payne to furnish them with running water from the Funston hydrant. Once more, Payne went to Tait's-at-the-Beach---this time to scrounge water pipe. The platoon dug ditches and installed the pipeline with special wrenches obtained by Payne's father. Battery B had a number of recruits from rural backgrounds. The men did not take easily to plumbing work, and Lieutenant Payne had to stand in the ditch, working with them.

Meanwhile, Captain Moorman told his battalion commander about the underground construction at Fort Funston. To verify the safety of the bunkers, the battalion CO sent copies of Lieutenant Payne's dugout designs to the local Corps of Engineers. General Stockton and several HDSF staff officers came to Funston for a personal look. Lieutenant Payne was standing in a ditch, supervising his men in pipe work when he heard the sergeant call out, "Ten-shun!" Payne scrambled out of the ditch. Except for the gold bar on each shoulder, the second lieutenant, wearing mud-splattered overalls, was indistinguishable from the enlisted men in the ditch. General Stockton tapped the bar on Payne's shoulder with his command stick, saying, "Officers supervise. They don't do the work." To which Payne protested that his men were "farmers" and didn't know pipe work. "You should teach 'em," replied General Stockton. When Payne explained that Captain Moorman had imposed a deadline for the pipes and there was no time for teaching the men, the general growled, "You better take time." Stockton's staff stood silently watching this exchange between the general and a mud-splattered lieutenant. They were impressed with the design and construction of the wooden dugouts. One of the staff officers, Major

George D. Burr, the HDSF artillery engineer, stepped up to Payne. "You're a very conservative engineer," Burr said, commenting on the underground barracks. "They're never going to fall down."

Soon after, Major Burr transferred Lieutenant Payne to HDSF Headquarters as an assistant artillery engineer. Burr told Payne to report for work in "boots and old uniform." At Hill 129 on the boundary of Forts Baker and Barry, on a site eight hundred feet above sea level, Army engineers started laying the foundation for a massive 16-inch gun emplacement. Ten concrete mixers mixed and poured in tandem twenty-four hours a day. Burr showed Payne how to measure the density of the concrete with a slump cone, which measured the amount of water that rose above the crust of mixed concrete. The civilian contractors on Hill 129 would have liked more water in the concrete for easier laying and smoother appearance. But military regulations demanded only the minimum of water for the pour; excess liquid weakened the concrete.

By July 1941, of the nine 16-inch emplacements already built or under construction in the United States, two of them already guarded the Golden Gate. The battery on Hill 129 was to be the third. These guns reflected the Bay Area's importance to national defense. But tank and field artillery manufacture held priority over seacoast artillery production, and the 16-inch gun program lagged behind optimistic quotas. By late summer 1941, American air and sea power had improved to the extent that further 16-inch batteries seemed superfluous, so the War Department limited work to those batteries slated for completion in three years. The battery on Hill 129 was completed but never armed.

Artillery engineers undertook numerous smaller but equally vital construction jobs. The extreme range of the 16-inch guns required widely scattered stations for accurate observation over the vast fields of fire. To obtain the best view over a given water area, engineers erected fire control posts on remote heights overlooking the ocean, like the two stations, one above the other, on Devils Slide, a rocky and precarious spine of hill seven miles south of San Francisco. Civilian contractors first built a long concrete stairway going to the top of the incline. Then jackhammers chiseled out a ramp running beside the steps. A wheeled chair lift climbed the ramp on an endless cable. The lift took hardware and construction lumber to the crest of the hill. Workmen dug a hole for the stations, and built up wooden forms for pouring the concrete. Down the coast highway came mixer trucks with their loads of ready-mixed concrete. The lift hauled wet concrete to the hilltop where it was poured into the wooden forms. Trucks brought the stations' protective steel domes from the foundry to Devils Slide, where they were bolted and welded to the concrete foundations. The artillery engineers installed bunks, telephones, and observation scopes and surveyed the station "down to a yard" for accuracy in range finding.

The Fort Baker Station Hospital was another big project in the works during 1941. Construction crews labored overtime for the October 1st completion of the twenty-four building complex. The Fort Mason Construction Quartermaster supervised the job. At a cost of $412,000, the 229-bed facility was intended specifically for the needs of the officers and men of the Harbor Defenses, easing the burden on Letterman General Hospital at the Presidio.

Meanwhile, across the Pacific, the Japanese felt the effects of the Allied oil embargo. In light of Japan's declining oil reserves, Japanese military leaders demanded a war decision by the Japanese government. On September 6th, an Imperial Conference resolved to make a final decision about war if no political agreement with the United States was struck by mid-October.

At the Golden Gate, coast artillery target practice continued. "Subcaliber and record service target practice now under way" at Forts Barry and Cronkhite through September 13th, came the warning from the Harbor Defenses. "Danger areas will be north and south short ranges except on September 5, when they will be the north long range and south short range." At Cronkhite, Battery E of the 6th Coast Artillery participated in the September target shoot with their 16-inch rifles.

When Lieutenant Preston B. Cannady, a Thomason Act officer, joined the battery during the summer of 1940, E manned three separate installations; the 3-inch antiaircraft emplacements on Wolf Ridge, the 6-inch rapid fire guns at Fort Barry, and the 16-inch rifles of Fort Cronkhite. Battery personnel trained on all the armament in order to serve as cadres for new units if war came. "But before that happened," recalled Cannady, "we got in a bunch of recruits," who took over the Wolf Ridge AA guns and the rapid-fire emplacement, leaving Battery E with the 16-inch rifles.

When a new unit began training on the 3-inch antiaircraft guns, sometimes Battery E men like Corporal Willis E. Spitzer helped train the green gun crews. Spitzer was serving as breechblock operator, when an inexperienced ammunition handler dropped a live round. The thirteen-pound shell (with fuse cut, set to explode in twenty, thirty or forty seconds) landed on the floor of the gun pit. The crew scattered in all directions, leaving Corporal Spitzer at the breechblock. "I reached down and I never moved so fast in my life," he later recalled. "I grabbed the shell, put it in, slammed the breech, pulled the trigger and it went out a thousand feet or less and exploded."

A former North Dakota National Guardsman, Willis Spitzer told Army recruiters

Fixed 3-inch AA gun at Barry Ridge, looking inland. (Presidio Army Museum)

he wished to serve on the biggest guns possible. Eventually he arrived at Battery E, 6th Coast Artillery with the 16-inch rifles, the largest guns in the Army. The crews drilled thoroughly on the big artillery pieces. "Every person had to do their job at the right time at the right moment," Spitzer said of the heavy training course. "That's the only way they could operate the 16-inch guns and do it as fast as they did." Training stressed safety in handling the ammunition around the powerful machinery of the guns. Job assignments changed from time to time, with individuals switching from the gun crew to the ammunition detail in the magazine deep underground; or they went down the hill to the plotting room, or out with an observation detail to a distant base-end station.

The firing of the 16-inch gun commenced when the camouflage netting and supporting cables at the mouth of the casemate were carefully rolled up and kept to one side. In the shell room, the ammunition detail clamped heavy tongs around a 16-inch projectile. The tongs were suspended by chain to a differential hoist hanging from trolleys to the overhead rails on the ceiling. The hoist rode along the rails leading out to the gun as the men pushed the shell along by hand. In the powder room, men who wore belts without metal buckles to prevent sparks, took 110-pound powder bags from their moisture-proofed

cans and loaded them onto wheeled shot trucks. The powder was brought out to the breech end of the big guns and deposited beside the 16-inch projectile already on the loading tray.

The gun barrel rested in a fully depressed loading position, opened breech facing the loading tray. The Waterbury speed gear, a large hydraulic ramming machine, similar to the type used in naval gun turrets, pushed the heavy shell into the breech, followed by the powder bags. Under air pressure, the breechblock swung shut and the gun elevated and traversed to the proper coordinates. The barrel raised and lowered effortlessly, since the gun was breech-heavy after loading and muzzle-heavy after firing. The crew moved a safe distance away, and the

News photographers got close to breech of Cronkhite 16-inch gun during October 1941 defense pageant in Bay Area. Note overhead rails for moving projectiles to loading table. (San Francisco Archives, S.F. Public Library)

gun fired. "The 16-inch gun was like thunder. It was a big rumble," according to Spitzer. Flame erupted from the muzzle accompanied by a whirling halo of smoke. The gun then recoiled and eased its tons of machinery back to firing position. When the breech reopened, air jets cleared the chamber of any debris. Though powder bags were made of a special silk that burned completely and left no residue after firing, no chances were taken, for the slightest ember left in the breech could set off the next round of powder. The compressed air evacuating the firing chamber was powerful enough, said one officer, "to blow a twenty-five pound youngster out the front of the tube."

The fired projectile shot up thirty to forty thousand feet before descending. In the higher atmosphere, buffeting winds affected the flight of the 2100-pound shell. Weather balloons went aloft five thousand feet and higher to record the direction and strength of the wind and the density of the air. The measurements went to the battery's plotting room, which also received current data on the level of tides and height of waves on the sea. Calculating devices combined the meteorological data and plotting board coordinates to arrive at the most accurate numbers to send the gunners.

Out at sea on the boat towing the target, observers from the battery noted the enormous splashes when the plunging shells struck the water. For one target shoot, HDSF hired a civilian tugboat with an Italian

skipper. During the firing, Willis Spitzer lay on the stern of the tug, watching his distant 16-inch battery through binoculars. When the telltale puff of smoke appeared on the Cronkhite hillside, Spitzer trained his binoculars in the vicinity of the pyramidal target towed four hundred feet behind the tug. The incoming round hit the water and sent a geyser up two hundred feet that could "scare the heck out of anybody." The 2100-pounds of steel cut the tow line between target and boat. The shot landed too close for the tugboat captain. Speaking excitedly in Italian, the skipper "turned that little tugboat around and that was it," Spitzer recalled. "He wasn't going to tow anymore targets."

Battery E held two target practices before the war; once in 1940, and again the following year, probably in September. Preston Cannady, the battery range officer, remembered the distinctive success of one of these record target shoots. Practice dictated two rounds from each 16-incher as ranging shots, then the guns fired five rounds apiece for the record. Coast artillerymen believed that gun crews needed a "warm-up" period to increase their accuracy as they fired more rounds. But the warm-up was hardly needed this time. Round one hit about a thousand yards over the target and the second ranging shot was short by a like distance. The range

Battery E, 6th CA fires 16-inch gun in Fall 1941 target practice. Small 3-inch gun used by unit in excaliber firing is visible beyond barrel of 16-inch rifle. The Army asked newspapers to paint out the background before publishing photo. (San Francisco Archives, S. F. Public Library)

Gun drill with 6-inch rapid-fire guns. (San Francisco Archives, S.F. Public Library)

officer adjusted fire and the third round destroyed the target. This service target practice won for the battery enlisted men the privilege of wearing the red "E" for gunnery excellence.

The 6-inch emplacement relinquished the year before by Battery E had been manned since June 1941 by Battery I, 6th Coast Artillery. The enlisted personnel came from the coast artillery training center at Camp Callan near San Diego. Among their number were college graduates, some with post-graduate degrees. Lieutenant Daniel Cook transferred from the Fort Baker mine battery to join the 6-inch gun outfit as range officer. His range section contained many motivated soldiers who showed interest in the techniques of fire control. In their free time, men practiced tracking targets on the plotting board. The weekend before their target practice, the enthusiastic range detail voluntarily went to the plotting room and adjusted calculating devices and tightened azimuth arm pivots on the plotting table for maximum accuracy.

The target of Battery I's 6-inch guns appeared at Potato Patch Shoal in the North Channel, five thousand yards west of Fort Barry. One gun fired a ranging shot. But instead of being a gauge to adjust on, this shot landed squarely, demolishing the target. Back to Sausalito went the tug to pick up another target for the artillery practice. Battery I registered a high score that day.

For their good work, the battery commander wanted to reward his troops with a beer party. Lieutenant Colonel John H. Fonvielle, the fort commander of Baker, allowed the festivities to be held at Kirby Beach, a quiet and secluded shoreline one thousand yards north of Lime Point. "But no more than three or four beers each, you understand," Colonel Fonvielle cautioned Lieutenant Daniel Cook. "You can sing all you want to out there, and you can sing all you want to coming in, but when you cross underneath that Golden Gate

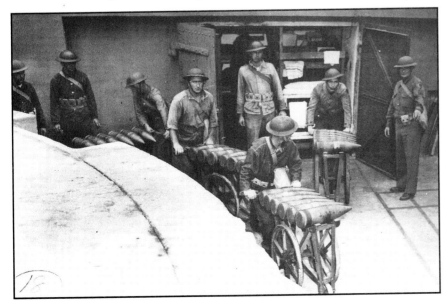

Sergeant directs ammunition crew pushing shot-trucks loaded with 6-inch shells in display posed for news camera. In practice, the 6-inch shells were carried by hand from the magazine. (San Francisco Archives, S.F. Public Library)

Bridge," warned the fort commander, "I don't want you waking up anybody at Fort Baker."

After the evening's celebration on Kirby Beach, the men policed the grounds and tossed empty beer bottles back in the trucks. Singing "For He's a Jolly Good Fellow," revelers hoisted Lieutenant Cook, their jubilant range officer, onto their shoulders and tossed him in also. The troops still sang as the trucks made their way in the night toward Fort Baker. As soon as they crossed under the Golden Gate Bridge, Lieutenant Cook signaled for the merriment to stop and the trucks rolled noiselessly past Fort Baker on their way to the Barry tunnel and the barracks beyond.

Battery I lived in old multistory barracks built on the landward slope of a Fort Barry hillside. Like Cronkhite across Rodeo Lagoon, cold fogs often kept Fort Barry covered in mist. Some of the men who had recently transferred to San Francisco from the tropical Philippines found the abrupt change in climate chilling. Even in the barracks, they "were so cold, they were shivering," one officer observed.

To Battery I came a recruit who worked on a Southern California lion farm which furnished animals to the motion picture business. The lion trainer, with his show business connections, said he could arrange for a movie celebrity to formally present the battery with a lion cub mascot. Battery commander George Thurston and his lieutenants felt the idea would be good for battery morale and public relations. With a three-day pass, the lion trainer went south to pick up the cub. It is believed a young Judy Garland later came to the bay on a visit, posed on the barrel of a 6-inch gun, and officially presented the infant lion to the battery. This event probably caused the mascot to be named "Judy."

Judy the lion cub resided in the barracks basement but had the run of the building. Following military protocol, barracks visitors first met the battery clerk, then the first sergeant, and finally the captain. At Battery I, visitors were also taken to the basement to meet the cub. Sometimes, Judy wandered about the other floors of the barracks and introduced itself to surprised strangers. Tom Scally, an officer with another unit, once came "roaring by" the Battery I quarters and startled the mascot. "The cub got all shook up," Scally remembered, "and leapt at me from about six or eight feet away, wanting to be petted." When General Stockton made a surprise inspection of the battery messhall, the mess officer hurriedly ran down to meet him, unaware the lion was playfully following along. Judy slipped into the messhall and walked up to the harbor defense commander. For an instant, General Stockton was unnerved. "What's that?" he demanded, pointing to Judy. "Get that thing out of here!" The mascot was growing, no longer a tiny lion cub.

By the autumn of 1941, the Golden Gate harbor defenses, in training since the first of the year, stood ready for action. "Today we have crossed the threshold of the greatest military activation in modern times," wrote General Stockton to the command. "Today as never before the Harbor Defenses of San Francisco are important to our country . . . we can depend

The lion mascot of Battery I, 6th CA leaps playfully at the animal trainer. As each cub grew too large, it was replaced by a younger one. (Presidio Army Museum)

that this area so glorious in history, so vital to the present, will remain as a strategic military center." The strength of U.S. harbor defenses had increased in two years. In 1939, the entire Coast Artillery Corps numbered only 4,200 officers and men. All fixed defenses remained on caretaker status until 1940, when induction of National Guard units permitted partial manning of some batteries. By 1941, thanks to the draft and the recruitment effort, the Coast Artillery Corps increased to 45,000 men, which brought all continental harbor defenses up to strength. The San Francisco defenses reflected this growth. In 1938, HDSF had only four batteries active, all assigned to mines and antiaircraft guns. By mid-1941, the 6th Coast Artillery and the 2nd Battalion of the 18th Coast Artillery manned all seacoast batteries, mine defenses, and antiaircraft emplacements. The 56th CA Regiment augmented the "concrete artillery" with mobile 155mm guns. Much had been accomplished to get the troops and defenses into shape. But as one HDSF regimental commander cautioned, "battle efficiency is the only true test of the value of any military organization."

The Golden Gate defenders' test of battle efficiency came towards the end of October 1941, when the Harbor Defenses conducted week-long war games in San Francisco and the surrounding waters. This pitted the full weight of HDSF against a fictitious "Black" invasion force of ships, planes, and paratroopers. The war game scenario called for Black air and naval raids on San Francisco to lure the U.S. Fleet away from the Atlantic Ocean to take pressure off Black's "European ally." War game organizers envisioned Japan as the Black power, with Germany as the European ally. This exercise meant to test all military service arms in the Bay Area. The "Blue" defenders included the Harbor Defenses, the 7th Medical Battalion, Company A of the 113th Engineers, the 1st Battalion of the 30th Infantry Regiment, the 1st Platoon, Company A of the 147th Field Artillery Regiment, a medium bombardment squadron from the 4th Bombardment Command at Hamilton Field, and the 115th Observation Squadron from the California Air National Guard. The Blue defenders' naval patrol force comprised two Eagle boats, four patrol boats, five minesweepers, one net and boom defense boat, and several Navy bombers and observation planes. Brigadier General Stockton commanded the Blue forces, and he intended to find out if the Harbor Defenses could fulfill its seacoast defense mission while protecting itself against attack from the rear.

The Black attacking force consisted of a submarine, three destroyers, and two Coast Guard aircraft under Commander J.E. Huff of the Navy. The destroyers would play the role of two enemy cruisers and an aircraft carrier. The war game scenario allotted defending seacoast batteries "theoretical shots" based on actual ammunition supplies. Navigation buoys in the harbor entrance would go out of action intermittently as they might in a real emergency. Soldiers of the 56th Coast Artillery organized themselves as enemy paratroops, ready to make a simulated airborne landing on the city. Defending Blue infantry carried blanks in their rifles to create realistic battle sounds. The Presidio closed the 25th Avenue gate to civilians for the duration of the exercises. From other Pacific coast military organizations came official observers to the San Francisco war games, including officers from the Canadian Coast Artillery.

MONDAY, OCTOBER 20: "The 'alert' has been sounded in the ring of steel and concrete fortifications that form the Harbor Defenses of San Francisco," proclaimed the San Francisco Chronicle. Sometime after midnight, the war games began. "Artillery batteries were manned, and anti-aircraft stations were on alert." To recreate the suspense and uncertainty of an impending attack, officers controlling the war games released information in such a way to confuse the Blue defenders. First, they reported contact with the Black navy five hundred miles off Hawaii. Then came an announcement that contact was lost but the Black fleet could arrive off San Francisco at dawn. Throughout the night, "searchlights stabbed the darkness over the bay," and Coast Guard lookouts along the shoreline kept watch for the Black fleet.

At 5:27 a.m. Monday morning, observation posts reported seeing an enemy submarine seven miles off the Golden Gate. The vessel could also be heard underwater by

In a scene reminiscent of World War I, gas-masked harbor defensemen in combat gear pose threateningly with pistols and bayonet-tipped rifles at entrance to underground dugout.

officers kept in contact by telephone to air and boat patrols.

Morning rush hour commuters saw soldiers patrolling the Golden Gate Bridge. The Highway Patrol dispatched officers after receiving "an excited report that a woman was on the span, about to leap off," newspaper columnist Herb Caen revealed the next day. "It was only a soldier in a bulky overcoat, standing guard for passing convoys!" Evening motorists crossing the bridge witnessed similar scenes. The Army controlled all roads leading to the span. With both sides of the Waldo Tunnel guarded by troops, the *Chronicle* reported that Marin commuters got "a feeling of what war might bring." At the Presidio and Fort Scott, guards had orders to be on alert for enemy saboteurs.

WEDNESDAY, OCTOBER 22: Sometime after midnight, the Black fleet emerged from the darkness within sight of the Golden Gate. The naval attack challenging the shore

hydroacoustic devices. Over the same water area, a Black seaplane was spotted. Coast Guard boats and Hamilton Field aircraft went out to search, but found no sign of the enemy. The *Chronicle* wrote of harbor defense gun crews on twenty-four hour duty beside their armament and of mobile units posted throughout the Bay Area to guard against surprise airborne attacks. But on Monday, the main force of the Black raiding fleet did not appear.

TUESDAY, OCTOBER 21: A Point Bonita observation post sighted the Black submarine and seaplane. Other enemy ships were said to be approaching the Golden Gate from various distances. Newspaper accounts hinted at the extensive harbor defenses of San Francisco, where gun crews slept in "eucalyptus log dugouts that honeycomb the coast hills from Fort Funston to Fort Cronkhite" in a "labyrinth of fortifications set in the gray-green hills flanking the Golden Gate." Though the press did not disclose the location of the harbor defense command post, they alluded to "a heavy concrete pillbox," where Army and Navy

Gunners of Battery E, 18th CA living in their Baker Beach emplacement. (San Francisco Archives, S.F. Public Library)

batteries of General Stockton's Blue defenders had arrived in the form of three destroyers portraying two cruisers and an aircraft carrier. Creative newspaper reporters described a "battle of unprecedented fury" lasting through the night, with warships and harbor defenses trading "paper shots."

At 2 a.m., a formation of Navy planes roared over San Francisco and the war game umpires announced that paratroopers of the Black force had dropped on the city. This was the signal for soldiers of the 56th Coast Artillery to go into action as landed enemy airborne raiders. In three groups of forty to sixty men, troops from the 56th invaded Forts Barry, Cronkhite, and Funston. They overwhelmed machine gun nests and cut some communication lines before defending Blues rounded them up.

At the same hour, a special detachment of the 56th, playing fifth columnist saboteurs in civilian garb, drove across the bridge and into Fort Scott. They carried paper sacks filled with flour, and intended to wreak havoc on the rear lines of communications. During the war games, machine gun nests guarded manholes leading to underground fire control telephone lines. These terminals became the special target of the saboteurs; in their civilian cars and clothes, the fifth columnists bypassed unsuspecting guards and plastered manholes with white flour, knocking the terminals out of the games.

The 56th's flying squad of saboteurs then sped south to Fort Miley. At 2:30 a.m., they crashed guard posts along streets leading into the fort. The raiders penetrated a dugout, capturing some sleeping Blue defenders and their ammunition. After cutting additional communication lines, the fifth columnists headed down toward Ocean Beach to continue their rampage. At the junction of Fulton Street and the Great Highway, the saboteurs disabled the Coast Guard life-saving station, then approached the rear of a 12-inch battery at Lands End before the war games umpires declared the attackers "wiped out."

While harried Blue defenders chased down enemy raiders, Black paratroops five hundred strong "landed" on the Presidio golf links. A two-hour battle ensued "across putting greens and bunkers," with elements of the 30th Infantry Regiment and 147th Field Artillery attempting to repel the invaders, reported the *Chronicle*. Sleeping residents in the adjacent Richmond District awoke to the firing of rifle blanks. Some of the attackers infiltrated past Blue lines and encircled a 75mm field gun position on the slopes above the U.S. Marine Hospital on the southern edge of the Presidio, at Lake Street and 14th Avenue. Another group of invaders attempted to capture Blue headquarters by "working their way through the grove of eucalyptus trees toward the command post at Fort Scott." The Black force never reached the underground harbor defense command post. Umpires ruled the attackers destroyed by 7 a.m. Wednesday morning.

By the early light of day, the ship-to-shore artillery duel between Black naval units and HDSF batteries also came to an end as the attackers retreated. During the engagement, a

Fort Miley at Lands End. The "saboteurs" of the 56th Coast Artillery encircled the seacoast battery and threatened other HDSF installations below the Veterans' Hospital during October 1941 war games. (K. Cooper, Jr.)

A pursuit group of Curtiss P-40's at Hamilton Field in Marin County, January 2, 1941. (San Francisco Archives, S.F. Public Library)

Chronicle, "stealing through heavy Pacific fogs toward San Francisco bent on destroying vital artillery emplacements."

Speaking with reporters, Vice Admiral H.W. Osterhaus of the 12th Naval District and General Stockton commanding HDSF agreed the maneuvers had "more than justified themselves" in finding and fixing mistakes, probably referring to the difficulties experienced the night before in repelling the mock airborne attacks and sabotage raids on the harbor defense posts. The Navy announced plans to conduct a seaplane mineplanting exercise the next day. "This is one of the most important phases of the entire maneuver," a naval officer told reporters. "It probably is the first time the navy has ever attempted this task during peacetime maneuvers." Seaplanes previously attached to the Blue defenders now switched to the Black side for minelaying "as soon as weather permits."

FRIDAY, OCTOBER 24: The fog lifted early enough to permit the aerial minelaying exercise to take place in the morning. Three Black navy bombers flew at low level over the harbor entrance and dropped one hundred-pound water-filled canisters. HDSF observation stations noted the splashes of the canisters and marked their locations. Naval minesweepers went to the targeted area of the channel where they began sweeping operations. Interested officers of the Army and Navy keenly observed all phases of the mine exercise.

At noon Friday, "with a stroke of his pen," General Stockton declared the exercises over. "The General's literary victory heralded conclusion of extensive war games," the Chronicle reported, which proved that combined land, sea, and air defenses "operating as

Black submarine was declared sunk. The three destroyers representing capital ships of the Black navy survived the shore batteries only to be caught and "sunk" off the Farallones by B-18 Army bombers of the 41st Bombardment Squadron from Hamilton Field. Though bombardiers aimed their "new, secret bombsights" on the destroyers, the Army planes carefully dropped the bombs a safe distance away.

THURSDAY, OCTOBER 23: No battle at the Golden Gate would have been complete without the appearance of fog. A day after the heaviest war game action yet seen, the changing climate of the Golden Gate put a halt to further activity. At Hamilton Field north of San Rafael, the Blue squadrons were grounded, "helpless against the gray pall," said the Chronicle. "One of San Francisco's famed fogs protected the city throughout daylight hours from enemy bombing attack." The same fog "likewise silenced the big 14 and 16-inch guns of 'Blue' harbor defenses," stated a reporter who was mistaken about 14-inch guns which did not exist at HDSF.

At 11:20 a.m., Blue destroyers sighted a surfaced Black submarine off the Farallones. "Paper shots" were fired at the submerging enemy, but war game umpires ruled them all misses. Later, underwater ranging devices detected the noise of naval motors somewhere south of the Farallones. But no submarines were sighted and the engine sounds ended at dusk. Naval officials surmised the Black force was gearing for another push, reported the

a single unit form the mightiest offense or defense." Later in the afternoon, Admiral John W. Greenslade of the 12th Naval District and Vice Admiral H.W. Osterhaus commanding the naval patrol, met with General Stockton, General Walter K. Wilson of the 9th CA District, and representative officers from the harbor defense sub-posts to review the maneuvers "which incorporated all the blitz tactics of European warfare." General Wilson later told reporters the maneuvers revealed "certain kinks in the system which we will straighten out. We have established a foundation for co-ordination with the Navy and Air Corps." The simulated airborne attack using 56th Coast Artillery troops impressed Wilson. The landings on the Presidio golf links demonstrated to harbor defensemen the "necessity for infantry support of harbor fortifications." In the the war games' aftermath, HDSF planning officers analyzed battle results to determine if the command could defend its own rear while repelling a naval attack. "It was determined that we could not," revealed Jack Lehmkuhl, General Stockton's aide. As a result, the harbor defense battle plan was redrawn; immediately at start of hostilities, an infantry unit was to establish a perimeter defense behind the Harbor Defenses.

Shortly after the San Francisco maneuvers, Army continental defenses reorganized to meet possible attack on U.S. shores. The War Department directed HDSF and other harbor defenses on the Pacific Coast to pass from control of the 9th Coast Artillery District to control of Western Defense Command, one of four regional commands dividing the country into defense zones. With headquarters at the Presidio, Western Defense Command controlled certain air and ground forces in addition to harbor defenses on the Pacific shore. If enemy attack threatened the Western states in time of war, Western Defense Command could be declared a theatre of operations. The defenses along the coastline were part of Western Defense Command and received their own designation; the Pacific Coastal Defense Sector, with HDSF as part of the Northern California sub-sector. In the Bay Area, HDSF personnel in uniform could be recognized by the circular shoulder patch featuring a red artillery shell on a yellow nine-pointed star, an insignia originally created in 1941 for the 9th Coast Artillery District, but now worn by all Pacific coast harbor defense units.

The coastline under HDSF control stretched for fifty miles, from Point Reyes on the north to Pillar Point on the south. Army textbooks defined a harbor defense as "a unit provided for the defense of a harbor or other water area." The San Francisco defenses had a specific mission: to protect harbor facilities and shipping from enemy gunfire, ensure freedom of movement for friendly ships at the harbor entrance, deny enemy ships access to the harbor, and support the land defenses against enemy beach assaults. In wartime, the Harbor Defenses would be authorized to control all friendly shipping within a thirty mile radius of Point Lobos. Groupments of seacoast artillery and submarine mine batteries provided the firepower for HDSF to fulfill its mission. Antiaircraft guns defended the seacoast batteries from aerial attack, and all units organized land defenses for their own protection.

The Harbor Defenses grouped individual gun batteries to direct their fire at enemy ships in an efficient, controlled manner. Batteries with similar fields of fire belonged to "groupments." Thus HDSF organized the Mine Groupment, comprising the mine batteries with their minefields and the 6-inch rapid fire batteries to protect them. Funston Groupment had 12-inch mortars and 155mm guns which covered the southern waters. The AA Groupment coordinated all antiaircraft guns, automatic weapons, and searchlights. The Separate Groupment contained all the 12-inch and 16-inch major caliber batteries; the fields of fire of the large guns spanned the length and width of the HDSF defensive area. Each groupment was in turn divided into "groups," batteries of similar armament firing on the same target. Thus the two 16-inch batteries worked together under a group commander, who directed their fire as a unit. At Funston Groupment, because their armament was not similar, the mortar battery made up one group and the 155mm battery another.

The groupments, groups, and batteries took orders from the harbor defense command post, or H-Station. In wartime, the harbor defense commander or designated officers from his staff would man the H-Station twenty-four hours a day, ready to lead the defenses should the enemy appear. The H-Station was established just west of the Fort Scott parade ground, in the deep gun pit of an abandoned emplacement. The wooden structure was used originally in 1911 as a fire control station. By January 1941, HDSF had adapted it for use as the harbor defense command post. The lower level in the gun pit, 37 feet by 87 feet, housed radio and coding equipment enabling the Army and Navy staff in the command post to direct the defense of the harbor entrance. Concrete columns raised the second level of the H-Station eighteen feet off the emplacement floor. This upper level consisted of two side-by-side observation rooms, one each for the Army and Navy. Nicknamed the "bridge," much of the potential battle area could be observed from the cupolas. The San Francisco Chronicle referred to the harbor defense nerve center as "a heavy concrete pillbox." Though the structure was built in a deep concrete emplacement, like many of the older observation posts at HDSF, the roof was only composed of wood and graveled tarpaper. HDSF considered the station a temporary one, and lobbied the War Department for a casemated command center.

By November 5, 1941, diplomatic negotiations between Japan and the United States had reached an impasse. The American government rejected the latest Japanese peace terms because Japan would not repudiate the Axis Tripartite Pact nor would the Japanese renounce occupation of China. As negotiations came to a halt, the Japanese government secretly set a deadline for themselves; by the end of November, if talks with the United States did not bring results, Japan would begin military action.

The War Department wanted data on the effectiveness of overhead concrete protection against aerial bombs. To simulate the terminal velocity of bombs, the War Department planned to fire projectiles with reduced powder charges from a 16-inch seacoast gun against concrete blocks. Battery Townsley at Fort Cronkhite was chosen for the test since its Gun No. 1 was the only 16-inch gun in the continental U.S. that could be traversed to fire onto a portion of adjacent land. In November, Army engineers constructed four large concrete blocks 620 feet distant on the right flank of the battery. Each steel-reinforced concrete target measured twenty-seven feet tall by forty-two feet across. Two blocks were twenty-three feet thick, while the other two were thinner by half, but contained more steel reinforcement. Gun No. 1 was to fire point blank into the blocks and show whether thick concrete or whether more steel reinforcement in thinner concrete was stronger. Some officers of the 16-inch battery believed the tests also intended to simulate the effect of bomb hits on the Panama Canal. The trials were slated to begin after the weekend of December 6-7th.

In what might have been their final public peacetime ceremony, HDSF units participated in the San Francisco Armistice Day parade held on the evening of November 11th. Behind the limousine carrying Mayor Angelo J. Rossi and American Legion officials came the 6th Coast Artillery Band and a battalion from the regiment. The rest of the marchers came predominately from the city's ROTC units. The procession started at aptly named Battery Street and marched down Market Street to City Hall.

On Sunday, November 16th, the harbor defense command dedicated the new Fort Barry Army chapel. Major General Walter K. Wilson of the 9th Coast Artillery District, along with General Stockton, Colonel Drake, and Lieutenant Colonel Fonvielle of HDSF, led military and civilian dignitaries in ceremonies marking the chapel's completion. In 1941, the Army built chapels at Forts Scott, Baker, and Barry. Each had a steeple and an electric organ. Four hundred worshipers at a time could be accommodated, with services offered in three religious denominations; Protestant, Catholic, and Jewish. The conscript troops presented a challenging task to the Army chaplains of the Harbor Defenses. "Men who are taken from the normal relationship of their respective communities and placed in strange localities with new men and women present tremendous social problems," wrote one HDSF padre in the 1941 harbor defense yearbook. The post chaplains sponsored dances, athletic events, stage shows, and other theatrical activities "in an effort to provide wholesome entertainment as

The 1941 Fort Scott Chapel. (San Francisco Archives, S.F. Public Library)

well as to introduce the men to reputable girl companions." The HDSF chaplains also cooperated with the USO and other servicemen's clubs.

The Thanksgiving Day menu for Battery C, 6th Coast Artillery indicated the sort of meals served on traditional holidays. A special mess allowance was authorized throughout the Harbor Defenses and every battery featured the same holiday fare. Menus resembled greeting cards, personalized with the name of the individual battery. Opening the card revealed the battery personnel roster along with the menu offerings: Appetizers included Puree of Oyster, Blackstone Salad, Smoked Herring, and stuffed olives. For Thanksgiving, the main course was "Roast Tom Turkey, Savory Dressing," followed by snowflake potatoes, candied yams, French peas, and asparagus tips. Then came dessert offerings of mince pie, pumpkin pie, and various cakes. The men finished off the meal with mixed candies and nuts, coffee, cigars and cigarettes, bottled beer, fruit punch, apples, and oranges.

Several batteries changed tactical assignments in November. Reorganization moved most of the 2nd Battalion, 18th Coast Artillery to Fort Funston, where Battery D now manned 155mm guns and Battery E took the 12-inch mortars. Battery F relocated to the 12-inch rifles overlooking Lands End at Fort Miley. In return, the 6-inch guns on Baker Beach and those on the adjacent heights went to Batteries B and D of the 6th Coast Artillery. Though assignments officially changed on November 28th, some units took several weeks to complete the transition.

By the last week of November, the American government had presented final terms to the Japanese. Washington demanded Japan leave China and Indochina, and recognize the Chinese Nationalist government. In return, the U.S. promised to negotiate new trade and raw materials agreements with Japan. The Japanese found this offer

unacceptable, but the Americans would offer no better deal. On November 26th, the Japanese government secretly ordered its carrier fleet to start moving east across the Pacific. Five days later, the fleet received the signal to begin hostilities as planned.

"An Enemy will Attack the Golden Gate Bridge," stated a small headline in the *San Francisco Chronicle* of November 28, 1941. Two infantry brigades from Camp Haan at Riverside, California were to take part in maneuvers testing their ability to join air force units in defending San Francisco and Los Angeles, the *Chronicle* reported. The writer was either misinformed or forced by military censorship to be misleading, since the units involved were not infantry, but two antiaircraft artillery brigades. In all other details, the newspaper was correct. The 101st Antiaircraft Artillery Brigade planned to arrive in the Bay Area the following Tuesday in maneuvers to "protect the Bridge," while the 37th AA Brigade guarded oil fields and airplane factories in Southern California. The exercise would test coordination of the antiaircraft artillery units with the 4th Interceptor Command and the new Civilian Aircraft Warning Service.

At Camp Haan, the 101st AA Brigade, composed of the 216th and 217th Coast Artillery (Antiaircraft) Regiments, had been in training since the winter of 1940. These federalized Minnesota National Guard units converted from infantry to antiaircraft artillery when the war in Europe demonstrated the importance of air defense. The officers and men came mostly from little towns around St. Paul, Minnesota. During the Depression, they eagerly joined the Guard, since "being paid for drill once a week was pretty attractive," remembered one officer. In California, the two regiments maneuvered near Palm Springs and fired their armament in the Mojave Desert. Each regiment had two battalions. One battalion included a searchlight battery and three 3-inch AA gun batteries. The other battalion had a machine gun battery and three 37mm automatic weapons batteries. But the regiments had only enough equipment to arm one battery of each type, which meant all units took turns training on the armament. "We were better trained than we were equipped," recalled a battery commander.

On the last weekend of November, 101st AA Brigade convoys began leaving Camp Haan for the Bay Area. The regiment was short of officers at the time, some being away at AA school or on other assignments. Harry Freeman, then a first lieutenant, was in charge of one battalion convoy. The line of vehicles drove over the Cajon Pass and through the Central Valley. En route, Lieutenant Freeman received orders to dispatch three trucks to a Bakersfield arms depot to pick up ammunition for the 3-inch guns and automatic weapons. "The rank and file really wasn't too conscious of the immediacy of war," but Freeman took this as an indication the "powers that be" knew more than could be disclosed.

"San Francisco's Protectors," as the *Chronicle* called the 101st AA Brigade, arrived in the Bay Area on December 3rd "to take defense positions against invasive air attack." The 4th Air Force would portray the enemy with mock air attacks on airports, factories, and harbors. The air defense exercises would take place from December 6th to 11th. The 217th Coast Artillery was stationed in the Oakland-Berkeley area. The 216th took up positions in San Francisco. Regimental headquarters and some of the batteries bivouacked at Aquatic Park. Still suffering from an equipment shortage, most of the batteries took up positions without their assigned armament. In the 216th's automatic weapons battalion, only Battery E, which defended the Hunters Point shipyard, had its complement of 37mm AA weapons. Battery F, guarding the Golden Gate Bridge, had no weapons except for three .30 caliber machine guns. Lieutenant Harry Freeman, the battery commander, saw the irony of this "most romantic assignment," as he sited his modest weapons next to the Toll Plaza in "the defense of the beautiful little bridge." The 101st Antiaircraft Artillery Brigade had come to the Bay Area as a rehearsal for their assigned deployment in event of war. Their timing could not have been more coincidental.

The Harbor Defenses went on alert Friday morning, December 5th. Before this, the command maintained a state of readiness by rotating alert duties among its gun batteries. But this time, the men sensed an air of urgency when they were each issued forty rounds of small-arms ammunition. "That was the first time we ever had so much live ammunition," Charles Sullivan of the 18th Coast Artillery recalled. On Saturday morning, the heightened alert was canceled, and the usual number of men left for the city on weekend pass. Some planned to attend church services the next day in San Francisco.

Chapter 5:

High Tide of Danger

On the morning of December 7, 1941, the Japanese attacked Pearl Harbor, and Brigadier General Edward A. Stockton of the Harbor Defenses of San Francisco needed to gather his forces. Stockton, with the help of Colonel Carl S. Doney, the HDSF executive officer, and Captain Jack R. Lehmkuhl, the general's aide, had phrased a tersely worded statement. Requesting "circulation of this message throughout the Nation," Stockton released the following words to newspapers and radio stations: "All Coast Artillery officers and soldiers of the Harbor Defenses of San Francisco are ordered to report to their stations immediately. All leaves and furloughs are canceled."

On holiday in Washington D.C., First Lieutenant Ralph DeMoisy and his wife came down from the Washington Monument and learned of the Pearl Harbor attack from their taxi driver. DeMoisy later heard General Stockton's message broadcast on the radio. "This was very specific and surprising to me," DeMoisy recalled, "because I was so very far away." Officers and men of HDSF on their way home on leave and furlough, stopped in train and bus terminals, and reversed their destinations. Captain Lehmkuhl, assistant adjutant of the Harbor Defenses, was "swamped with telegrams and phone calls" from those headed back to San Francisco.

A change in weekend plans was no less sudden for off-duty harbor defense personnel who had not left town. Lieutenant Preston Cannady, returning from church in the city, heard General Stockton's radio announcement en route. Back at his Sausalito quarters, Cannady received a call-to-arms by telephone from First Lieutenant Ivan M. Teuscher, the battery executive. Cannady then contacted those on his own emergency list before going to Fort Cronkhite. Men poured out of the Cronkhite barracks and into the 16-inch gun emplacement on the hill, ready to live in the tunnels for the foreseeable future. From the safety of their casemate, the men saw desolate Rodeo Beach below. Some feared an enemy landing, especially since Battery E could not man the 16-inch guns and guard the nearby beach at the same time. "They could have landed on the beach down there," one of the artillerymen observed, "we were wide open."

All through the Harbor Defenses, batteries responded to the emergency call, putting their assigned armament on "A" Alert, ready to open fire at a moment's notice. Battery I hurried from their barracks at Fort Barry to the 6-inch rapid-fire guns, bringing their lion cub mascot with them. In the ammunition chambers at the emplacement, most of the 6-inch projectiles still wore protective coats of yellow paint from World War I. The men set to work scraping off the old paint so the shells could be fired. The men of Battery F, 18th Coast Artillery were firing their 1903 Springfield rifles at the Funston range when they heard about Pearl Harbor. They went back to Fort Miley and the 12-inch guns of Battery Chester. These forty year old seacoast guns and the equally ancient 12-inchers of Battery Mendell at Fort Barry, together with the modern 12 and 16-inch rifles of Wallace, Townsley and Davis, composed the "harbor defense commander's reserve." If the Japanese navy attacked San Francisco, as many believed possible that day, these big guns were counted upon to slug it out at long range with the enemy battleships.

Captain Arthur Kramer, commanding the Funston 16-inch guns, had become the father of a baby girl the day before. On Sunday morning, at the University of California Hospital on Parnassus Avenue and Arguello Boulevard, the telephone call from the Harbor Defenses reached Kramer in his wife's hospital room. The captain quickly bid his wife good-bye and dashed back to their Fort Scott apartment to change into uniform before heading out to his Funston battery, where his men had moved into the tunnels and set up their folding cots. The officers' quarters were established next to the power room, midway between the 16-inch guns.

The Harbor Defenses had no minefields in place at the Golden Gate on December 7th. Until hostilities commenced, HDSF had no jurisdiction to lay minefields at the bay en-

trance. By 11:00 a.m. that Sunday, General Stockton ordered Captain Frank Liwski of the Fort Scott mine battery to begin minelaying. Meanwhile, the commander of the mine battalion, Lieutenant Colonel Felix Usis, had just arrived home in Berkeley after four months at the Command and General Staff School at Fort Leavenworth, Kansas. With no time to rest, he left for Fort Scott. Usis drove onto the Bay Bridge, heading to San Francisco. The bridge traffic streaming east, "all leaving San Francisco, was incredible," Usis thought. The heavy flow of eastbound cars sometimes spilled over to the wrong side of the divided roadway on the upper deck.

Some gun batteries had no guns to man on December 7th. The 155mm armament of the 18th Coast Artillery's Battery D awaited construction of concrete Panama mounts at the southern end Fort Funston; so the men grabbed their rifles and went on guard duty at Forts Scott, Miley, and Funston. Battery F of the 216th CA antiaircraft regiment, though not a part of the Harbor Defenses, was supposed to defend the Golden Gate Bridge from aerial attack with 37mm automatic weapons. But these had not yet arrived. "All we did was form up and make sure everybody was there and stand by," recalled Harry Freeman, the battery commander. Down at Fort Point, wooden machine guns stood conspicuously on the upper tier to deceive enemy reconnaissance. The official history of Western Defense Command stated that "All stations and installations of the H.D.S.F. were manned by 1200, 7 December 1941."

Back at the Fort Cronkhite 16-inch battery, Sergeant Willis Spitzer waited with a truck-load of men. Captain John Schonher peeked in the back of the truck and said to Spitzer, "You only have six men in there." The sergeant counted them off; three men for the base-end station at Fort Miley

Battery E, 6th CA commander John Schonher in front of Fort Cronkhite 16-inch gun. (Presidio Army Museum)

and three for the station at Hill 640 above Stinson Beach. Spitzer admitted he would still need another three men for Milagra Knob, fourteen miles south of San Francisco. "You'll need more than that," Captain Schonher responded. "We have four more stations." Before the war, Battery E did not practice with all assigned observation stations. The battery had about eight metal-domed stations scattered between Half Moon Bay and Drakes Bay, but Spitzer was familiar with only some of them. And now he had to post observation details to each station as quickly as possible. After finding enough men to staff all the stations, Spitzer set out with the men on a marathon truck ride across the length of HDSF territory.

By 4:00 p.m., special guards began checking vehicle traffic on the two bridges linking San Francisco with Marin and the East Bay. "Japanese driving cars over the Bay Bridge were stopped and searched for explosives," claimed the *San Francisco Chronicle*. The Fort Scott provost marshal stationed military police at the Toll Plaza and on all roadways leading to the Golden Gate Bridge. M.P.'s and Highway Patrolmen scrutinized all cars but stopped no motorists.

At Fort Miley Veterans Administration Hospital, the three hundred patients, some of them Spanish-American War veterans, were either discharged or moved by ambulance "to less vulnerable positions," said the *Chronicle*. The eight-year old hospital was "surrounded by military emplacements protecting the Golden Gate." Searchlight stations, a group of command posts, and the 12-inch guns of Battery Chester stood several hundred feet west of the veterans' facility. Commenting to reporters on the reason for the hasty move, the hospital manager said, "We're just sitting here in the midst of the bullseye."

While some citizens stayed away from areas thought to be potential targets for enemy guns or bombs, others flocked to the shoreline to watch the western horizon for the arrival of the Japanese fleet. Columnist Herb Caen saw cars jamming the Great Highway and people standing on Ocean Beach, looking out to sea

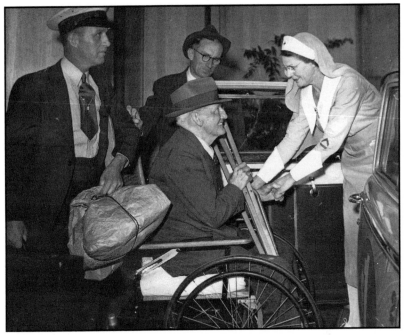

Nurse and taxi driver aid Spanish-American War veteran into taxi after Veterans Administration Hospital at Fort Miley was closed due to its proximity to harbor defense installations. Man with glasses is a World War I veteran. (San Francisco Archives, S.F. Public Library)

"in bewildered silence and shaking their heads in frustration--and unspoken fear for their futures." In downtown bars along the cable car tracks of Powell Street, and in taverns of the nearby Tenderloin, business was brisk and intense, with drinkers vowing to enlist the next day. "Older men were buying drinks for G.I.'s they'd ignored (or complained about) for months," Caen observed. On the streets, military sound trucks cruised the downtown district and blared announcements over loudspeakers telling all servicemen to report to their outfits. Some Chinese-American GI's on weekend pass in Chinatown heard about Pearl Harbor on their car radios that morning, but did not head back to Fort Ord until darkness came. During the day, they "hung around Chinatown" as usual. "There was no sense of urgency," one of them remembered. "The war started already."

Sergeant Spitzer drove the Army truck along the coastline, making stops at Miley, Funston, and Milagra Knob to drop off three-men crews at each observation station. One station on the south shore remained to be found. By driving around and asking local residents if they had noticed any military construction in recent months, the sergeant tracked down Battery E's most southerly outpost, which perched on the steep and narrow blade of Devils Slide. Patches of camouflage paint covered the smooth metal dome of the new station. The crew opened the counterbalanced hatch cover and entered through the dome top. Once inside, the men closed and padlocked the hatch cover for security. Range-finding telescopes stood on concrete mounts at the vision slit. A heavy metal visor could be swung down to seal the slit. Telephones connected the station to the battery. Two wire-framed bunks hung from the far wall, but the station lacked other living accommodations. There was no stove, no food, and no water. The men would have to live on what they had brought in their canteens and field packs. Spitzer left the crew to fend for themselves, promising to return as soon as possible.

By late afternoon, the truck from Battery E returned to the Marin side. Sergeant Spitzer posted a crew at the station on Hill 640 above Stinson Beach. Then with help from a farmer, the sergeant found the Bolinas Bay station at the top of a steep hill. Even in low gear, the four-wheel drive Army truck could not ascend the incline, so the men climbed to the station on hands and knees. Night had fallen by the time Spitzer drove toward the most northerly observation post on a rugged promontory at Drakes Bay known as Wildcat. Along the way, Spitzer found a farmer who knew of the station, but the local citizen had a warning for the soldiers. The Army path leading to Wildcat was too deeply rutted by rain to support their truck. Spitzer and the observation crew continued on foot, walking two miles through a forest to reach the station.

The Wildcat station supplied range data to the Cronkhite 16-inch guns, but also had a direct line to the Fort Scott H-Station. From Wildcat, the observers saw the desolate, curving beach that extended in a slow arc to

Imitating an advertisement of the time, observation crew on steel dome of Wildcat base-end station compares cigarettes . Entrance hatch and counterweight visible behind them. (W. Spitzer)

the tip of Point Reyes. Any suspicious activity on the waters or on the flat shoreline of Drakes Bay was reported by the station crew to the harbor defense command post. Drakes Bay, isolated, undefended, but so near the Golden Gate, might become a landing spot for Japanese submarines, the high command felt. Consequently, before midnight on December 7th, Battery B of the 56th Coast Artillery towed their 155mm guns north to Drakes Bay. By dawn the next day, the four-gun battery was on the beach, ready for action at the water's edge. Japanese farmers owned the land where the 155's were emplaced. Another battery of the 56th later went to Granada near Half Moon Bay. Other 155mm batteries of the regiment remained in position on the Marin sub-posts as attached support for the HDSF Mine Groupment.

Newspapers reported incidents of enemy submarine activity on the high seas. Five minutes after the Pearl Harbor attack began, the Japanese submarine I-26 had sunk the lumber freighter *Cynthia Olson* one thousand miles northeast of Hawaii. The troopships *Etolin, Bliss, President Johnson,* and *President Garfield* with sixty-four hundred men sailing for Hawaii, retreated to the safety of San Francisco harbor within two days of the Pearl Harbor attack. Following December 7th, the Navy had only a handful of destroyers and Catalina flying boats to patrol the coast from Alaska to Southern California. TF-1, a task force composed of the battleships *Idaho, New Mexico,* and *Mississippi* would not arrive on the West Coast until late January. The 4th Air Force defending California possessed 113 fighters and thirty-four bombers. This shortage of coastal air and naval patrol left the American defenders unsure about Japanese intentions. Captain Schonher, commanding the 16-inch battery at Fort Cronkhite, doubted a Japanese naval force was anywhere near the coast. But he had to admit "there was a paranoia because of the sneak attack." At this stage of the war, the big seacoast guns he commanded represented the first and last line of defense if the enemy appeared off the Golden Gate. "As long as we had no navy and aircraft to patrol the seas," Schonher knew, "we didn't have too much cover."

On the afternoon of December 7th, Western Defense Command had received an erroneous report indicating a Japanese fleet thirty miles from the Presidio. The next day, more messages poured in, signaling assorted threats; aircraft carriers off the coast, submarines spotted off San Francisco, and enemy bombers and destroyers heading for San Diego. Western Defense Command investigated these sightings, but could verify none of them, later concluding "the information appeared to be very positive at the time." That evening, the 4th Interceptor Command, charged with the aerial defense of the Bay Area, detected something on their radar screens one hundred miles west of San Francisco.

At 6:00 p.m. on December 8th, air raid sirens wailed over the city. Fire engines and police cars raced through the crowded downtown streets during Monday evening rush hour. Vehicle sirens warned startled residents and shop keepers to turn off lights and pull down blackout curtains. Meanwhile, the hydroacoustic listening post near Sutro Baths picked up sounds of a submerged submarine approaching the Golden Gate. They notified Captain Jack Lehmkuhl on duty at the H-Station. "Whose submarine was

it?" Captain Lehmkuhl wanted to know, as he phoned various command posts in an attempt to find out more before taking action. Then, someone at the Presidio mistakenly pulled the master power switch in response to the general blackout. This shut off electricity throughout the Harbor Defenses and cut telephone contact between the H-Station and the 16-inch batteries. The hydroacoustic station tracking the unidentified submarine also went out of action. When the Presidio master switch was turned back on, the underwater intruder had disappeared. By now, the submarine could have passed the Golden Gate Bridge, heading for the Navy's submarine net. Captain Lehmkuhl at the H-Station imagined the submarine "laying in the mud alongside the net gate and then following some ships in." He thought of alerting some HDSF guns to train their sights along the net, but he realized the only ones able to point into the bay were deactivated 3-inchers at Fort Baker. The submarine, whether a faulty contact or a real intruder, did not materialize.

During the blackout, the Golden Gate Bridge stood in the harbor entrance with roadway lights glowing and tower beacons rotating and signaling their presence for miles around. The illumination made the famous landmark an aiming point for the enemy. "There were more jurisdictions mixed up with that thing," grumbled Captain Lehmkuhl, as he placed phone calls to municipal authorities from Santa Rosa to Hayward. That night, Lehmkuhl made arrangements with bridge

December 8, 1941, night of first air raid alert in San Francisco. From Twin Peaks, the downtown business district shows poor blackout discipline. (San Francisco Archives, S.F. Public Library)

officials for handling future blackouts. As soon as enemy planes were detected, HDSF agreed to notify bridge authorities. This gave enough time to clear traffic from the span without causing a pile-up of cars. When the planes got closer, the bridge lights would be turned off.

In the city, civilians reacted in confusion to their first wartime blackout. Many ignored the sirens. Neon lights glowed from the business district and Christmas shoppers went into lighted stores. Residents on Twin Peaks saw downtown San Francisco sparkling "like New Orleans at Mardi Gras time." Not until late that night, did the majority of street lights and radio stations finally shut down. Out on the bay, the Federal penitentiary of Alcatraz observed no blackout. Its lighthouse flashed and floodlights played off the stark exterior walls of the cell house. General John L. DeWitt of Western Defense Command angrily ordered the lights shut, but the Alcatraz warden refused, citing the primacy of prison security. Yet, no aerial raiders had appeared over the Bay Area and residents wondered what all the commotion was about.

By 3:00 a.m., the night's excitement had subsided at the H-Station when Captain Lehmkuhl took a telephone call. The lieutenant colonel on the other end of the line told Lehmkuhl a perimeter defense of the HDSF rear had been established. This defense measure was adopted after the October war games when HDSF found it could not defend against both naval and airborne attack at the same time. The lieutenant colonel informed Lehmkuhl that machine gun positions were being set up on the four corners of the H-Station to defend it. At dawn the next morning, Lehmkuhl went up to the observation deck of the command post. He had not slept in forty-eight hours, being occupied with the tactical business of the station and carrying out his duties as assistant harbor defense adjutant. Captain Lehmkuhl looked out the vision slit of the "bridge" and saw two of the promised machine gun nests. But to his amazement, Japanese soldiers manned each gun. Lehmkuhl reported this to General Stockton on the direct line. Stockton assured his aide the situation was normal. Japanese-Americans made up a part of the California National Guard infantry unit assigned to perimeter defense of HDSF.

Chided in the press for calling a false alert, the 4th Interceptor Command defended their aerial detection system; however, the reason for calling the blackout was not revealed. To General DeWitt of Western Defense Command, the false alert showed how ineptly San Francisco handled its first blackout. In a heated meeting with civilian officials at City Hall, DeWitt scolded them. "It might have been better if some bombs had been dropped to awaken the city," he told the gathered reporters. From then on, San Francisco took the blackouts seriously. That night, businesses voluntarily turned off neon signs and major stores closed before five o'clock. When the next alert sounded in the darkness early Wednesday morning, newspapers reported the blackout "nearly 100 per cent effective."

Battery E, like all units in the Harbor Defenses, observed "A" Alert during the first days of the war; the ammunition magazine doors were open and the 16-inch guns were ready for action. Men slept on double bunks in the emplacement corridors. Battery cooks prepared food in the mess hall and sent it

December 9, 1941: Downtown does much better on second night of alert. AA searchlights illuminate from Twin Peaks in distance. (San Francico Archives, S.F. Public Library)

.30 caliber machine gun on AA mounting sited above plotting room of Battery Townsley at Fort Cronkhite. (San Francisco Maritime NHP)

up to the tunnel. To cover Rodeo Beach, the battery mounted a machine gun on the high ridge above the plotting room casemate. When an infantry battalion arrived to reinforce the northern part of the Harbor Defenses, some of the troops established themselves in machine gun nests and foxholes atop the 16-inch gun emplacement. Then the rains came. "It was windy, cold, and damp," so Battery E commander John Schonher invited the soldiers to bring in their gear and stay in the cavernous area behind the 16-inch guns. The captain's offer "was heaven" to the infantry who gratefully moved into the tunnel. Later that evening, the sergeant in charge of the powder magazine got a good look at some of the invited troops. He went immediately to Schonher. "Captain," the sergeant reported, "you know there are several Japanese in this company." "Well, it's all right," Schonher answered, "but I better report it to the harbor defense commander." At the H-Station, a duty officer handled Schonher's inquiry by replying, "I'll get back to you." A few minutes later, General Stockton came on the line, saying to Schonher: "These are soldiers of the U.S. Army. They're treated like anybody else."

In the days following December 7th, a variety of Army units moved into the Bay Area, not only to support the Harbor Defenses, but to guard vital installations. An infantry battalion defended the Fort Mason Port of Embarkation by posting troops from Aquatic Park to the Presidio. These troops set up field guns on Marina Green, where expensive homes, now deemed vulnerable by their owners because they faced the water, displayed "For Sale" signs in their front windows. The 211th Coast Artillery Regiment (Antiaircraft) of the Massachusetts National Guard came to Vallejo on December 14th, to provide air protection for Mare Island shipyard. The 17th and 53rd Infantry Regiments had moved up from Fort Ord by December 9th. They stayed north of the Bay Area in Santa Rosa and Sacramento, ready to move on enemy landing spots. At expected landing beaches at Drakes Bay, Tennessee Cove, and Fort Funston, Army engineers strung miles of serpentine wire. Shortly after, when Assistant Secretary of War John D. McCloy inspected the defenses he suggested also installing a line of barbed wire entanglements for the land approaches. "It was quite a project" for the Harbor Defenses, John Schonher recalled, "but we had the manpower to do it."

On Wednesday December 10th, San Franciscans saw their first signs of the shooting war when a Pan American Airways Clipper landed on the bay and taxied up to the terminal at Treasure Island. The huge civilian flying boat had departed Wake Island on December 7th, just after a strafing by Japanese planes. Newspapermen taking a close look at the escaped Clipper, counted sixteen bullet holes on its metal skin. The liner's captain told reporters he dodged enemy planes by diving into a drainage culvert.

Nearly a week after the first blackout alert, the HDSF command net still buzzed occasionally with reports of enemy sightings. One night at two o'clock, Second Lieutenant Tom Scally, on duty at the 6-inch disappearing guns above Baker Beach, received a call from the battalion CP to bring up ten rounds of ammunition and stand by for firing instructions. Scally hesitated, saying he wanted to first contact the absent battery commander.

After all, Scally thought to himself, "you do not give a second lieutenant carte blanche." "We're in a war now. You're in command and you're gonna do it," ordered the major on the phone. With those words, Scally alerted the battery. Supposedly a Matson liner loaded with evacuees from Honolulu was steaming for San Francisco with a Japanese submarine in pursuit. If the liner sped through the Golden Gate with the enemy sub close behind, the seacoast guns were to fire around the ship "to scare the hell out of the submarine." Battery B stood by, ready for action, but the order never came. Sometime later, a passenger ship did enter the harbor without incident.

Captain John Schonher, a more senior officer, could take a warning from battalion more calmly. He awakened in his Wolf Ridge command post after midnight when word came over the intelligence line of enemy ships four hundred miles off the California coast. Schonher acknowledged the message and relayed it to the group commander of long-range guns on the Marin side, Lieutenant Colonel Fonvielle, who slept in the adjacent bunk. "We were skeptical of the report's accuracy," Schonher recalled, "and since we were on alert and ready, and the threat was not immediate, we went back to sleep." After the Pearl Harbor attack disrupted the Navy, Schonher thought, the Americans had no way of locating an enemy fleet four hundred miles out at sea. Schonher's 16-inch battery at Cronkhite was ready for action "had they come closer." Dissemination of this unverified sighting annoyed Major General Joseph W. Stilwell, then senior tactical commander of Western Defense Command. He complained the report was not properly investigated, and faulted 4th Army, charged with defense of the Northern California area. "They had it from a 'usually reliable source,'" Stilwell wrote, "but they should never have put it out without check."

"As was to be expected, for the first week after the outbreak of war," reported the *Coast Artillery Journal*, "a constant flow of messages filtered through to Harbor Defense Headquarters, indicating activities far beyond that which actually later proved to be the

Command post on Wolf Ridge where Captain Schonher and Lieutenant Colonel Fonvielle received erroneous report of enemy fleet 400 miles off the coast. Photo taken July 24, 1940. (National Archives, Pacific Sierra Region)

case." Given the speed and ferocity of the Japanese attack in Hawaii and the Far East, 4th Army and Western Defense Command feared some form of enemy action off California. Spurred on by false alerts of the first week, the War Department rapidly reinforced Western Defense Command and proclaimed it a theatre of operations on December 11th. Fourteen antiaircraft artillery regiments were among the 250,000 troops sent to bolster the West Coast defenses.

"Official 'Keep Out' signs were nailed to San Francisco Bay yesterday by orders of President Roosevelt," stated the *Chronicle* on December 13th. The rules covered "virtually all" of the bay, "plus a large area off the Golden Gate." No private vessels sailed designated waters without permission from 12th Naval District. The Navy restricted all sailing to daylight hours and required advance notice of any departures from the harbor. Ships entering the bay first had to contact, by radio or visual signal, the harbor entrance control post. "Any ship entering the bay will do so at its own risk," the newspaper warned. "All areas presumably are mined." On December 16th, President Roosevelt signed an executive order establishing Defensive Sea Areas off U.S. ports. This officially instituted the regulations mentioned in the *Chronicle* and gave authority to the harbor entrance control post, or HECP, to govern maritime traffic inside and outside San Francisco Bay.

The HECP operated in conjunction with the H-Station. From the observation cupolas atop the two-story harbor defense command post, Army and Navy duty officers controlled vessels passing through the Golden Gate. As commander of the Harbor Defenses, General Stockton handled the Army side of the HECP, sharing authority with his Navy counterpart, who commanded the harbor entrance patrol boats and the submarine net gate. Ordinarily, Army and Navy duty officers ran the post on behalf of the senior commanders. Besides controlling maritime traffic, the HECP was entrusted to "take prompt and decisive action to operate the elements of the harbor defense and to deny enemy action within the defensive coastal area," as stated in HDSF's Standing Operating Procedure. Minefields were under direct control of the HECP, and no mines could be activated unless authorized by the control post. Since December 7th, Captain Jack Lehmkuhl, Stockton's aide, served seventy-two hours of continuous duty at the command post without sleep. When the situation calmed down, staff officers took twenty-four hour duty at the station every third day. Even in the HECP, Lehmkuhl noticed, "the Navy could never function without coffee." Upon taking up station, the Navy men promptly set up

a big coffee maker. While Army duty officers remained awake during a twenty-four hour watch, their Navy counterparts could retire to bunks. One morning at 3:00 a.m. Lehmkuhl buzzed the senior navy officer who was sound asleep. After making sure his friend was awake, Lehmkuhl said over the intercom, "Joe, don't bother waking up. There's not a damned thing happening."

The Navy operated two signal stations in conjunction with the harbor entrance control post. These concrete two-story structures, equipped with signal devices, stood on Bonita Ridge at Fort Barry and in front of the Toll Plaza at the Golden Gate Bridge. When the HECP so ordered, the twenty-four hour Navy crew of the signal station challenged incoming ships with blinker, flag hoists, or radio signal (using call letters WUQ.) Eleven artillery observation stations and command posts, in addition to regular duties with their assigned batteries, phoned sightings of new vessels to the HECP. The Navy kept a moving plot of all ships on a large magnetic wall map depicting the coastal area between Point Reyes and Monterey. Ships entering the harbor through the Main Channel first encountered two Navy entrance vessels stationed off Cutfish Rock Buoy. The guard

The nerve center of HDSF: camouflaged main command post and HECP visible as two L-shaped patches behind the Fort Scott barracks. 6-inch and 12-inch gun batteries farther seaward lack camouflage in this early 1942 Navy photo. (K. Cooper, Jr.)

vessels reported the new arrival to the HECP. When the command post returned an acknowledgment, the ship proceeded through the Main Channel. Inside the bay, one-quarter mile seaward of the submarine net, a Navy destroyer moored to a huge buoy. Assigned to the HECP, the destroyer was on call at all times, steamed up and ready for any emergency.

Lieutenant Ralph DeMoisy, the 56th Coast Artillery officer who heard General Stockton's December 7th radio announcement in far-away Washington D.C., arrived in San Francisco after a four-day cross-country car trip. He found the city blacked out at night. From his apartment in town, DeMoisy saw the light from an open blind, then the shout from an air raid warden in the street; "Shut off the light!" After the first blackout, San Francisco settled into wartime conditions. During the first six months of war, alerts were called approximately two dozen times in the Bay region; about eight resulted in full blackouts. The cause, so the authorities routinely informed the newspapers, was unidentified planes that later proved to be friendly. When aerial targets appeared on radar screens, 4th Interceptor Command flashed progressive alerts; Yellow meant the targets were twenty-three minutes away. Blue signified fifteen minutes. When the targets were eight minutes out, the Red alert was flashed, triggering a blackout. As air raid sirens sounded in the city, residents closed windows, pulled shades, and turned off lights. Block air raid wardens with flashlights patrolled their routes making certain the neighborhood was pitch black. Residents retreated into their hallways, which were hung with blackout curtains so a lamp could be turned on within. Families sat waiting in their blacked out homes for the all-clear siren. Outside, the city was dark and quiet.

During San Francisco's first days of war, frequent blackouts and nervousness over impending attack brought wild rumors of espionage and mysterious flashing lights. Giant swastikas were supposedly painted on house tops in North Beach, where much of the city's large Italian community lived. Floodlights, the rumor went, illuminated the markings to warn Axis planes the occupants were sympathizers.

One citizen reported flashing lights from a Marina District apartment building. Fearing a spy was signaling confederates on the Marin side, the well-intentioned citizen called police. Investigation revealed the "signaling" came from the apartment's elevator shaft as the elevator car moved between a light and the window. At Fort Scott, the harbor defense command post took calls from its own observers about mysterious signals in the night. One stormy evening, a northern station informed Captain Lehmkuhl of flashing red lights emanating from one of the civilian houses atop Wolf Ridge on the Marin side. A detail went to investigate, and found that rotating beacons of the Golden Gate Bridge shot their red beams through one window of the house. The beams reflected off panes in the house before emerging out another window, appearing as if someone was signaling out to sea.

The harbor defense posts observed blackout rules every night, whether or not a general alert for the bay region had been called. All buildings on base were light-proofed. Street lights were turned off. "Strict disciplinary action will be taken in case of violation," warned the HDSF manual to all officers. In case of an air alert, the senior officer at the H-Station notified the guard house at each sub-post to sound the alarm, while he personally activated the Scott siren "by means of the push button in the HDCP." No candlelight, flashlights, lighted matches or lit cigarettes were allowed during an alert. Vehicles pulled off the road and the riders dashed to nearby shelters or slit trenches.

Bay citizens took the blackouts in stride with a sense of humor. The nightclubs of San Francisco's International Settlement ran a topical newspaper advertisement on December 13th. "The fun's on the inside, folks," the message began, as it urged patrons to leave their blacked out homes for the watering holes between Kearny and Montgomery Streets at Pacific. "Exterior Lights may be Dark--But the Lights are Brighter than ever Inside!" as the niteries offered "fine food," "glamour," and "fun for all." The advertisement ended with the words, "Business as Usual."

Out in the waters of the harbor entrance, the Mine Battalion had worked

ceaselessly since December 7th, laying mines across the approach to the bay. "We worked night and day," recalled Frank Liwski, then commanding Battery A, 6th Coast Artillery, "cutting cables and loading mines and planting them." With eight hundred pounds of TNT in each sphere, the buoyant mines were planted one hundred feet apart, in groups of nineteen. Captain Liwski positioned the minefields in a semicircular pattern across the three navigation channels into the Golden Gate. To supplement the *Niles,* the Harbor Defenses impressed into service an emergency mineplanter. This vessel was the *El Aquario,* the 562-ton water lighter from the Army Quartermaster Department. While Liwski took his Battery A planting crew aboard the *Niles* to lay the Main and South Channel fields, Battery F and the *El Aquario* planted mines in the North Channel and Potato Patch. Corporal Charles Sullivan, temporarily serving aboard the *Niles* as a radio operator, feared the minelaying activity taking place at all hours could be seen by fishermen. But Captain Liwski was not "worried about Japanese espionage. Any vessel entering the harbor could not avoid our fields."

The end of the first week of war brought no let up to the Mine Battalion's labors. But on Sunday, December 14th, Captain Liwski and Chief Warrant Officer Carlsen, skipper of the *Niles,* decided to suspend their planting oper-

ations because a storm had made the sea too rough. However, Captain Charles Bell of Battery F believed conditions were still suitable in the North Channel for planting, and sailed there on the *El Aquario,* accompanied by the distribution box boat L-74. Arriving in the North Channel, this group belatedly found the waves too treacherous and tried to turn back.

The waves were bad enough for the 562-ton converted mineplanter, but the sixty-four foot L-74 was in danger of breaking up in the tossing seas. To make matters worse, the skipper of the *El Aquario* had little seafaring experience outside San Francisco Bay. With no time for putting a message in code, clear radio contact was established between the distressed vessels and Lieutenant Colonel Felix Usis, the Mine Battalion commander. "Go out to sea, go out to deep water," Usis told them. "Get away from the entrances altogether and ride out the storm out there where you'd be safe." Before the mine vessels had a chance to try, help came.

The *Niles,* with Captain Liwski aboard, sailed through the storm to the rescue. The *El Aquario* retreated into the calmer waters of Tennessee Cove. Meanwhile, the *Niles* would help the floundering L-74 past the rough waters to join the *El Aquario.* Chief Warrant Officer Carlsen maneuvered the *Niles* up to the distribution box boat and his crew tossed a towing rope to the smaller vessel. In choppy seas, the rope jerked the deck cleat off the bouncing L-74 and threw the small boat's skipper overboard. The *Niles* pulled the drenched man out of the sea, then helped the L-boat into Tennessee Cove where the *El Aquario* waited out the storm. Summing up the event, Lieutenant Colonel Usis called it "a bad night," but the near sinking of the L-74 on December 14th, resulted in the commanding general of the Northern California Sector of Western Defense Command calling a halt to all mineplanting at the Golden Gate until the weather improved.

A Japanese long-range submarine cruised into the area despite the storms at sea. Shortly after December 14th, the I-15 took up station off San Francisco, just west of the Farallones. The vessel belonged to a fourteen-submarine squadron designated SubRon One, which had been deployed around the Hawaiian Islands to support the Pearl Harbor attack. After sinking some merchant ships in that area, the squadron sailed to the West Coast. Like all vessels in the squadron, the submarine I-15 was designed for the lengthy mission; it could make the round trip between Japan and San Francisco without refueling. In a small hanger at the base of the conning tower, the submarine carried a tiny catapult-launched float plane. Each submarine in the squadron staked out a port from Cape Flattery in Washington to San Diego in California. "It was our job to cut off supplies and reinforcements destined for Pearl Harbor," wrote Lieutenant Zenji Orita, executive officer of the I-15. A few days after the I-15 took station off San Francisco, orders from Tokyo directed the squadron to leave their patrol areas on Christmas Day, and return to the submarine base at Kwajalein in the Marshall Islands. Before departure, the submariners were ordered to bombard the mainland with as many rounds as they could manage from their 4.7-inch deck guns.

On the night of December 17th, the I-15 surfaced to recharge its batteries. Peering through binoculars from the conning tower, Lieutenant Orita saw the glowing sky above San Francisco. "They certainly don't act like there is a war going on, allowing such illumination to silhouette their shipping along the coast," the Japanese officer thought. Orita's superiors were also on the bridge. Captain Hiroshi Imazato, the commander of the First Division of SubRon One, looked toward the coast; "If we weren't at war, this would be an excellent chance to pass in through the Golden Gate and visit that famous city of San Francisco," he said. All the officers laughed when Lieutenant Orita joked that "an excellent chance to do some sight-seeing" could be had by launching the float plane.

After ten days "in the field" with the 6-inch guns at Fort Scott, Lieutenant Tom Scally shaved, cleaned up, and reported to his new duties at the San Francisco Stock Exchange to represent HDSF at the control center of 4th Interceptor Command. A large tabletop map of the Bay Area sprawled across the Exchange auditorium. Soldiers and civilian women moved target stands around the map using long sticks as reports of aircraft sightings filtered in on the intelligence line. Looking down on this scene were military and civilian liaison people from various government agencies that might be called upon to act during an alert. Three HDSF liaison officers kept a constant presence at the center, their job to inform the Harbor Defenses of any reported aerial or naval targets approaching San Francisco. The commercial telephone line from Fort Scott to the Stock Exchange on Pine and Sansome Streets cost the government one hundred dollars a day. It became more economical to operate when the air warning center later moved to Fort Mason.

Tracking aerial contacts at 4th Interceptor Command control center, S.F. Stock Exchange. (San Francisco Archives, S.F. Public Library)

90mm antiaircraft artillery of Western Defense Command in the East Bay. (Presidio Army Museum)

Defending the skies over the Bay Area, the 216th Coast Artillery Regiment (Antiaircraft) in San Francisco and the 217th in the East Bay took orders from 4th Interceptor Command. The Harbor Defenses had separate antiaircraft protection. Battery G, 6th Coast Artillery posted platoons to fixed 3-inch AA emplacements at Cronkhite, Barry, and Funston. Battery M of the 6th CA operated searchlights and sound locators. In action, the HDSF antiaircraft guns, also controlled by 4th Interceptor Command, coordinated their fire with the two AA regiments guarding the Bay Area.

At the two harbor defense AA batteries on the Marin side, men lived in pup tents beside the guns. At Fort Funston, AA Battery No. 3 still took shelter in the dugouts constructed by Harry Payne more than a year ago. The crewmen entered through a gate and walked down underground passageways which linked living quarters to the gun pits and director well. Captain Richard Moorman, who ordered the building of the dugouts when he was in charge of the Funston AA guns, now commanded Battery G. Ready crews stayed by the guns, with full crews to follow in five minutes. The alert status in effect at all times was "Flash Green"--"Flash Green," meaning the batteries were to illuminate and fire on any aircraft not identified as friendly.

Several times during the early days of the war, aerial targets were identified as friendly only at the last moment. Once, the radar of a 216th CA battery (equipped with new 90mm guns) near the Toll Plaza of the Golden Gate Bridge picked up an incoming target. Sound locators followed the flight, but officers were puzzled by the target's slow speed and drifting movements. Antiaircraft batteries of the 216th and the Harbor Defenses began tracking. The HDSF antiaircraft guns on Wolf Ridge even had "shells in the fuse cutters within seconds of firing," remembered Richard Moorman, when searchlights illuminated the target just in time, revealing it to be a U.S. Navy blimp coming in from submarine patrol.

SS Emidio sinks after being torpedoed by Japanese submarine off Cape Mendocino on December 21, 1941. (Presidio Army Museum)

December marked heavy Japanese submarine activity off the California coast. On the 18th, a submarine attacked the tanker *Samoa* off Eureka. Three days later, another tanker, the *Emidio*, was torpedoed at Cape Mendocino. Off Long Beach, the lumber ship *Absaroka* was hit by submarine torpedoes, but the vessel's timber cargo kept it afloat. The submarine I-15 on watch near the Farallones saw no ships and made no attacks. Sometimes, the Japanese submariners could hear patrol boats in the distance and uncoded radio traffic from land. When the I-15 surfaced at night, Lieutenant Orita no longer saw the glowing sky over San Francisco. "Somehow the Americans had learned of our presence," he surmised.

Several large passenger liners, which turned back to port after Pearl Harbor, berthed at the Embarcadero and awaited their next voyages. The San Francisco waterfront had miles of docks and warehouses bustling by day with cars, vans, railroad engines, military vehicles, and gigantic lumber trucks. According to a city pictorial, "Traffic moves at a great pace, oblivious of pedestrians." But at night, waterfront activity ceased. Military guard posts were set up along the Embarcadero to stymie potential saboteurs. Troops stood two-hour guard with four hours off. On the other side of the Embarcadero, a collection of neon-lit taverns catered to waterfront denizens. With Pearl Harbor fresh in mind, patriotic feelings among

the patrons were keen, especially when soldiers came in from guard duty across the street. With "nothing too good for our servicemen" the motto of the night, longshoremen bought frequent rounds for the GI's. Four hours later, the soldiers went back to guard posts for the next watch. One night, General DeWitt of Western Defense Command inspected security along the Embarcadero and did not like what he saw at the sentry posts. On December 23rd, California Governor Culbert Olson, in compliance with General DeWitt's request, ordered the State Board of Equalization to forbid sale of liquor to persons in uniform except between the hours of 6:00 and 10:00 p.m.

Soldiers with ingenuity got around the alcohol restriction. Since the curfew only affected public drinking, the enlisted men of Battery I came from Fort Barry to downtown San Francisco, where they kept the backroom of a Maiden Lane bar as a private drinking club. For officers, the Army and Navy Club at 560 Sutter Street satisfied the law as a private establishment. The club featured a bar, a grill, a lounge, and dancing on Saturday nights. Officers of the 216th Coast Artillery Regiment (Antiaircraft) attended bridge parties here at the invitation of the regiment's commanding colonel.

In the waning hours of December 24th, just before the I-15 was scheduled to surface and shell San Francisco, orders came from Tokyo canceling the bombardment. From Cape Flattery to San Diego, every Japanese submarine of SubRon One turned about for their Kwajalein base. On the I-15, Lieutenant Orita was discouraged. Why the bombardment was canceled, he knew not, but "it was 'bows west' for the I-15 next day, without having hurt the enemy at all." Japanese admirals feared U.S. an-

Coast Guard sentry posts along the Embarcadero. (San Francisco Archives, S.F. Public Library)

tisubmarine measures had become too strong off the Pacific coast, and recalled the submarine squadron for the moment.

General Stockton's Christmas message to his harbor defensemen appeared on December 19th in the *Cronkhite Foghorn*, unit newspaper of the 56th Coast Artillery. "It is a far different holiday than was expected," wrote the HDSF commander. "You will be at your stations rather than at home with your people. I deeply regret the necessity for canceling your leaves and furloughs, but our common enemy left us no alternative. I know that each officer and enlisted man of the HDSF will render a good account of himself if our enemies are foolhardy enough to attempt to attack these fortifications."

During the first Christmas of the war, "people around San Francisco just couldn't do enough for these soldiers, especially if they found you were on antiaircraft duty," recalled Harry Freeman, who commanded Battery F of the 216th CA Regiment. Hospitable families contacted military bases, saying they could take so many officers or enlisted men as dinner guests. Freeman and some other officers in his regiment went to Christmas dinner "at some millionaire's residence" in an exclusive San Francisco neighborhood. The battery commander found the experience interesting, as he and the other officers sat and ate in the formal dining room of a "very refined family," with a quiet daughter and a twenty year-old son "who was even quieter." The young man was probably intimidated by these artillerymen, "wondering how long it would be before he was a yardbird."

No civilian Christmas dinner could outdo the holiday feast HDSF served at the battery messes. Like the elaborate Thanksgiving dinner, the Christmas menu offered choices of appetizers, entrees, deserts, and after-dinner treats, including cigars and cigarettes. The "A" Alert status complicated

Corporal Barnhart (second from right) and his crew lounge on roof of their base-end station at Drakes Bay. Note vision slit for azimuth instrument at front of structure. (D. Barnhart)

the serving of this special dinner to units in the field, but every effort was made to do so. Men on duty at their armament went back in relays to the messhalls. On remote and rain-swept Drakes Bay, the men of Battery B, 56th Coast Artillery with 155mm guns on the muddy beach, ate their holiday meal in the mess tent. But it was "not the most festive thing," thought Corporal Dale Barnhart, "slogging through the mud up to your knees" to reach the tent, while mess kits filled with rain water. "Here was all this food," Barnhart remembered, "and it rained on us while we were eating."

At Drakes Bay, rains came nearly every day. Caterpillar tractors that had moved the 155's into position were stranded in the mud. The guns stood under camouflage netting on the beach, their plotting room in a tent nearby, the battery's assigned searchlights and antiaircraft machine guns in supporting positions. Observer crews with their telephones and range scopes were positioned along the bay. Corporal Barnhart's men built a shelter over their azimuth instrument. They dug a three-foot deep pit and put a close-fitting wood and tarpaper roof over it, leaving a narrow vision slit for the telescope. For sleeping quarters, the men constructed a hut equipped with a stove. One night, a strong wind caused a down draft in the lighted stove, blowing fire onto the wood floor. As the men held onto the ridge pole to keep the hut in one piece against the howling wind, Barnhart ran outside for water to douse the flames. In the excitement, the corporal forgot where he was, and stumbled with a splash into the rain-filled station pit.

Drakes Bay had a long isolated beach with many roads leading from the shore. HDSF felt this was a potential landing site for submarines. Sometimes liaison officers from the Harbor Defenses or Western Defense Command dropped by, but the battery of four 155mm guns on the beach had a large degree of autonomy for firing on suspected targets. No other units were in the area. Lieutenant Ralph DeMoisy and his platoon fired two of the 155's. The men had nothing to do, except "wait for the Japanese to come, sit around and play cards, and see that the equipment was kept up." To keep the platoon sharp and occupied, DeMoisy conducted gun drill on his 155's. The battalion commander came down to the beach during one drill and told DeMoisy to train his guns on a rowboat in the water. DeMoisy's gunnery sergeant fished from the rowboat which he had borrowed from a farmer. "What's he doing down there?" demanded the major. "He's looking for infiltration and pretending to fish," replied DeMoisy, thinking

quickly. "How do you know he's not Japanese?" the battalion commander challenged. "He's wearing an Army uniform," the lieutenant responded. The major then inspected some equipment and found rainwater in the field phones. "That's the matter with you reserve officers," growled the major, waving his fist as he stormed down the beach. "You don't know how take care of equipment."

On Christmas Day, the troopships *Hugh L. Scott* and *President Coolidge*, carrying civilian dependents and wounded Navy personnel from Hawaii, sailed into San Francisco Bay, escorted by the cruiser *Detroit* and two destroyers. Spectators lined city hilltops to catch a glimpse of Pearl Harbor survivors. The convoy's seven-day voyage from Hawaii to San Francisco passed the gauntlet of Japanese submarines off the coast. As a sign of the dangerous times, maritime insurance rates had risen from fifty cents to forty dollars for each one thousand pounds of cargo.

By late December, observation stations of the 16-inch Cronkhite guns had received small electric batteries to power lights inside the range telescopes. At night, the lights illuminated the cross-hairs, making them "nice and red" in the darkness. The observer crews depended on the supply run conducted by Sergeant Willis Spitzer. Captain John Schonher, the Battery E commander, issued Spitzer a checkbook to buy supplies in local stores. Spitzer bought radios, cooking stoves, and other things to make less bleak the isolated life of the distant stations. He worked eighteen-hour days driving between stations north and south. A governor on the Army truck kept speeds below fifty miles an hour. To reach some of the northern stations, the sergeant drove over Mount Tamalpais, sometimes at 3:00 a.m. with blackout lights dimly illuminating uncertain back roads.

Battery E operated a northern station on Drakes Bay near the town of Olema. "There was no road out to that station," Harry Payne recalled. When the artillery engineers sent a bulldozer to make a road, the heavy machine

Sergeant Spitzer with shovel attempts to dig 4x4 truck out of the mud on road leading to Wildcat station. (W. Spitzer)

John Schonher, as group commander later in war, inspects open breech of Fort Cronkhite 16-inch rifle. (Presidio Army Museum)

sank into a bog created by the heavy rains. They did not gamble sending another tractor to pull out the stranded one, preferring to "wait a couple of months till the water drained out of the place." When battery commander John Schonher visited the Olema station, he parked his truck at the closest point and walked the half-mile in, carrying food and supplies. The station crew improvised their own transportation. Corporal Jack Wise borrowed a farmer's horse to ride into Olema for provisions.

Gun No. 1 of Battery Townsley fired 16-inch projectiles several times in December against the huge concrete blocks erected to simulate the effect of aerial bombs against various types of concrete construction. The test was originally scheduled to start following the December 6-7th weekend, but the Pearl Harbor attack put the test on hold till later in the month. Army and civilian officials gathered in a protective pillbox to observe the action. The Air Force was there also, wanting to see how this test might approximate potential damage from aerial bombs on massive metal-reinforced concrete construction like the Panama Canal. Technicians from the Lockheed Aircraft Com-

pany set up high-speed motion picture cameras to film slow-motion movie footage of the 16-inch projectiles' explosive impact.

A civilian specialist from the Ordnance Department selected various strengths of powder charges to achieve a range of muzzle velocities. To verify the estimated velocities, a special device measured the fired projectiles' actual velocities as well. An electrically charged wire was placed over the gun's muzzle. The other end of the line connected to chicken wire covering both sides of a wooden frame placed as a target on the face of each concrete block. With this device, the projectile's time of flight could be measured electrically and converted to velocity. The battery commander, Captain John Schonher, devised a way to aim a 16-inch gun like a rifle at the small targets. Schonher held up binoculars to the primer hole in the breechblock. He sighted through the hole and aimed with the cross-wires placed over the muzzle. Schonher lined up the 16-inch barrel onto the target 620 feet away. The elevation and azimuth settings were noted and used after each time the gun was loaded and ready to fire. Schonher remembered a college physics formula to determine how far the projectile would drop on its way to the target. The figure varied between sixteen and twenty inches depending on the velocity. The gun was elevated the proper amount to compensate for the projectile's drop during flight.

Gun No. 1 fired with a relay of a fraction of a second to allow the high-speed movie cameras to capture the flight and impact of the 16-inch projectiles in slow motion. The first round penetrated clear through the first test block. No data could be gotten from that. The Townsley gun then fired with a reduced charge on a second block. This round penetrated but did not go through---the desired data was obtained. But the reduced recoil of the gun, caused by the weaker charge, unexpectedly damaged the recoil mechanism and delayed continuation of the tests for several weeks. Captain Schonher saw the hollow windshields from the projectile tips lying on the ground unbent and uncrushed. Somehow, they had come off on shell impact, but were strangely undamaged.

To test the explosive effect of a shell embedded in concrete, a projectile was put in one of the shell holes and set off. "It was just like a big shotgun in reverse," Preston Cannady, the battery's range officer observed. "Fragments came out of the hole all over the place and everybody was ducking left and right." Men found pieces of shrapnel from this explosion all the way down to Fort Barry. After the tests, engineers broke up the concrete blocks and buried them where they stood. Whether the test data was ever useful in designing other concrete fortifications is not recorded; but the power of the 16-inch rifle was undeniable.

"We people in the Harbor Defenses, we were restricted. We couldn't go anywhere," remembered Tom Scally of the early war days. "We existed under blackout conditions. We ate in the rough and all that sort of thing." As enemy operations and disposition of enemy naval forces became better known by the end of December, the Harbor Defenses felt secure enough to grant leave to a small percentage of personnel in the evenings between 6 o'clock and midnight. On the 31st of December, General DeWitt of Western Defense Command informed General Stockton that invasion in force was now considered unlikely. Reinforcements to the West Coast continued, but the Army sent mainly air squadrons and antiaircraft artillery units, because the only threat now appeared to be carrier air raids. "Coast artillery actually became obsolete the day Pearl Harbor happened," believed Jack Lehmkuhl, General Stockton's aide. "No sane enemy naval officer would try to come in. They could stay out beyond our range and bomb us from aircraft carriers."

Chapter 6:

Buoyant Mines and Cracked Crab

When the storms subsided at the Golden Gate, harbor defense mineplanting operations resumed. The *Niles* and the *El Aquario* headed back out to sea, attended by the smaller L-boats and yawls of the Mine Flotilla. Similar ships operated off the entrance of many American harbors at the start of the war. "Un-armed, dumpy, and prosaic, the Army mineplanters . . . are a curious maritime phenomenon," observed *Newsweek* magazine. The *Ellery W. Niles* had been the only mineplanter at the San Francisco defenses before the war. So when the fighting started, the Army needed a second ship. HDSF brought the *El Aquario* of the Quarter-master Department into harbor defense service. This was the ship that experienced much trouble in the storm of December 14th. Built in 1919, the 162-foot *El Aquario* had been used for years in San Francisco Bay by the Quartermaster Department of the Army as a water tanker. Battery F sailed to the mine-fields aboard the *El Aquario*, while Battery A went out most of the time on the *Niles*. New, more maneuverable mineplanters were months away.

Newsweek called Army mineplanters "sea-going ships with soldier crews." "Under control of the Coast Artillery, their skippers (in charge of the ship itself) are khaki-clad warrant

The USAMP Niles, one planter not fitting Newsweek's description of "dumpy and prosaic." (D. Grover)

officers." Six warrant officers commanded for-ty-one crewmen aboard each planter. Officers and men were members of the U.S. Army Mineplanter Service, a part of the Coast Ar-tillery Corps. They lived aboard the planters which berthed at HDSF docks in Sausalito or Horseshoe Bay. Planter crews worked aboard their ships; they could not be used ashore by the harbor defense command for parade cere-monies or duties on post. The master of the planter was the ship's senior officer, stationed in the pilot house and in charge of all shipboard operations. Two junior warrant officers assisted the master. They supervised the deck crew. Below decks, the Chief Engineer and three assistant engineers handled the vessel's machinery. Sergeants headed up the deck, engine, and steward's departments with enlisted men assigned to each section. Warrant officers and enlisted men wore regular Army uniforms; except the former had stripes on their cuffs---like the stripes worn by the Merchant Marine---to denote their rank, accompanied by an anchor insignia for deck officers, and a propeller insignia for engineering officers. Enlisted mineplanter men carried the Coast Artillery Corps' crossed cannons over a mine as their collar insignia.

Though HDSF sometimes loaned the *Niles* to other ports, or sent it to the open sea to lay cable, the normal routine of a planter usually took the crew "only 4 or 5 miles from shore. They stay out for periods varying from a few hours to a few days--never more," wrote *Newsweek*. Like all military personnel at sea, the mineplanter crew rated one and one-half rations in cash from the Army. The mess sergeant purchased food from any source, frequently from the Fort Scott or Treasure Island commissaries, where he obtained a bulk supply of food for a good price. When a planter towed practice targets, an officer from the

firing battery went aboard to supervise safety. "And that was where I found out how well you ate on those mineplanters," recalled Frank Mahoney, a lieutenant from a 6-inch gun battery. The food was good and plentiful, he recalled; "If you didn't watch the porthole, it didn't bother you." Though *Newsweek* called these Army vessels prosaic, the magazine admitted mineplanters had an important mission. Their "movements and the location of the mines they plant interest enemy spies as much as a warship's sailing date."

The ships sailed out to the minefields with the commanding officer and the planting detail from the mine battery aboard. The planting crew, headed by a senior NCO, comprised port, starboard, and afterdeck details who handled the mines and lowered them beneath the waves. The mine battery commander supervised the planting operation, supporting boats, and shore parties. The battery commander told the master of the vessel when and where to sail. The master, who was a Chief Warrant Officer, commanded the ship and the ship's crew. Mutual respect between battery commander and the ship's master was necessary for good working relations.

The early wartime minefields consisted of buoyant type mines, planted in groups of nineteen. To start, three buoys were placed in the water on a straight line marking the group. A thirty-ton L-boat took position facing the center of this line, its stern towards the Golden Gate. Planting was done on a flood tide to maintain this

Mine crew aboard outbound HDSF planter prepare cast-iron mine anchors for lowering over the side. Golden Gate Bridge in background. (Presidio Army Museum)

position. A heavy distribution box, containing a watertight mine selector with electric receptacles for nineteen mines, lay on the L-boat's foredeck. The planter started planting at one end of the line, with the vessel's skipper estimating distance and the battery commander ordering mines and their heavy cast-iron anchors lowered into the water at one-hundred foot intervals. On each side of the vessel, the port and starboard mineplanting crews alternately dropped mines or manhandled them onto davits. As the crew planted each mine, the mineplanter brought the electric cable up to the waiting L-boat and passed the line to the smaller vessel for attachment to the distribution box.

In the meantime, two-man mine yawls motored up to wooden markers floating above each mine. The crew lifted the wooden buoys for the battery's shore stations to observe, allowing the stations to plot the specific location of each mine. Aboard the L-boat, nineteen cables from the mines had been plugged into the watertight mine selector in the distribution box. Special waterproofing tape wrapped around and sealed the connections. Using the crane on the L-boat's foredeck, the crew lowered the connected distribution box into the water. The box was always planted inshore of its line of mines so no hostile ship could grapple for it without first crossing the field. Finally, the L-boat brought a single conductor cable from the distribution box toward shore. In the shallower water, a mine yawl took over, leading the cable up to the beach, where battery men dragged it to the cable hut for connection to a distant mine casemate. Later, five-conductor and nineteen-conductor cable reduced the separate lines of cable coming to shore.

In planning location of the fields, mine officers consulted nautical charts bought from

Planting crew lowers anchor and attached buoyant mine. Distribution box boat in background. (Presidio Army Museum)

local ship chandlers. The charts gave hydrographic data on currents, ocean depths, firmness of the sea floor, and existence of pipelines and commercial cable. The location of observing stations, searchlights, and rapid-fire batteries covering the water areas also influenced minefield placement. At the start of war, Captain Frank Liwski of Battery A arranged the San Francisco submarine minefields in a semicircle across the harbor entrance. The mines began at Ocean Beach, ran through the South Channel and the south patch---curved north across the Main Channel---then bent back toward the Marin side, through Potato Patch and the North Channel to Rodeo Beach. Liwski ordered a double line of mines to be used throughout, except through Potato Patch and the South Channel, where the water was only eleven feet deep. Captain Liwski put a single line through these areas, feeling assured "submarines could not possibly come through that." A final line of mines stretched across the inner Gate, between Mile Rock and Point Bonita.

Minefield fire control operated from both sides of the Gate---the mine casemate at Fort Barry fired mines in the North Channel and Potato Patch, and the mine casemate on Baker Beach at Fort Scott fired the mine groups of the Main and South Channels. The concrete casemates housed control panels for the mine groups and drew municipal electric power from the city to energize the mine circuits. Diesel generators were on hand in case the city grid shut down. From outside, the mine casemates appeared as low earthen mounds topped by ventilators. A concrete entrance faced inland. On Baker Beach, two concentric circles of barbed-wire surrounded the vital structure, with sentries patrolling the perimeter.

The buoyant type mine was a large metal sphere floating fifteen feet below the water's surface. Wire rope and cable tied to a cast-iron anchor moored the mine to the sea floor. At San Francisco, each buoyant mine carried eight hundred pounds of granular TNT

as a standard explosive charge. An open electric circuit of 110 volts ran from the mine casemate on shore, through the cables and distribution boxes, into each mine in the water. When a ship struck a mine and tipped it at least twenty-five degrees from the vertical position, a ball in the mine's arming mechanism rolled to one side or the other. This closed the electric circuit which activated a light on the control panel in the casemate. On the panel were rows of lights, each representing a particular mine. When one lit up, the bumping vessel and its location in the minefield could be pinpointed. Once the H-Station ordered him to fire, the mine officer had several ways to explode the mine, according to HDSF's Standing Operating Procedure. Contact fire "insures explosion on direct contact" with the ship. Delayed contact fire waited for the mine to be drawn directly under the hull of the target before the mine was exploded, "obtaining greater damage to the vessel." In both cases, the operator pulled the switch to close the circuit, increasing power to six hundred volts, which overrode the forty-eight hundred-ohm resistor in front of the detonator to explode the mine.

Though HDSF mine officers realized enemy submarines would be their most probable targets, they maintained observation posts and plotting boards for firing on surface vessels. If mine officers desired to attack one vessel of a group and let the others pass, or if blown mines left a gap in the field, observers telephoned range data to the casemate plotting board. Based on the vessel's course and speed, the mine nearest the vessel's predicted crossing of the field could then be exploded "near enough to a vessel's course to gain destructive effect." While observation fire was useless against unseen targets like submarines, observation stations and plotting rooms stayed busy spotting

Seaweed-covered mine is hauled out of the water for maintenance. (Presidio Army Museum)

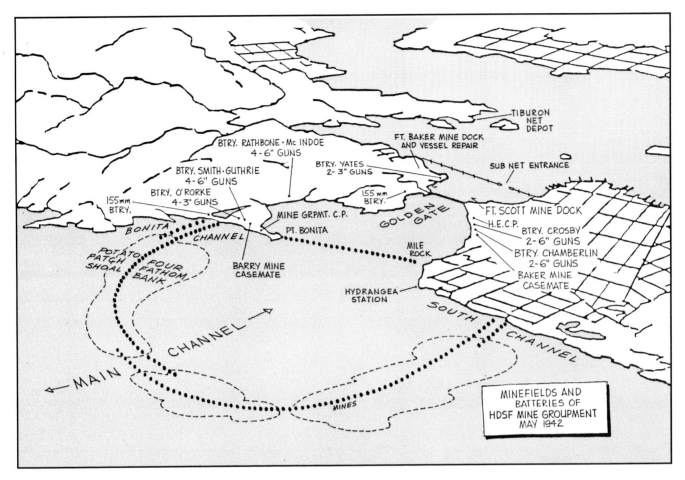

MINEFIELDS AND
BATTERIES OF
HDSF MINE GROUPMENT
MAY 1942

mines as they were planted or taken out for repairs. Regardless of the tactical situation, observation stations kept watch on the mine-fields around the clock.

While Batteries A and F of the 6th Coast Artillery planted, maintained, and operated the mine defenses, the Mine Flotilla, comprised of detachments from both batteries, cared for and manned the L-boats and mine yawls. The two batteries and the flotilla formed the HDSF Mine Battalion. (The mineplanter ships worked with the battalion, but were independent units under the harbor defense commander.) Above battalion level came the Mine Groupment, which grouped the minefields under covering fire of 6-inch gun batteries. One group consisted of mines in the northern waters, covered by 3-inch, 6-inch, and 155mm gun batteries around Rodeo Beach. Two 6-inch batteries at Fort Scott and a battery of 155mm guns at Kirby Cove protected another mine group in the Main Channel. The southern fields extending from Ocean Beach were guarded by 6-inch guns on the eastern heights of Fort Barry. The

Mine Groupment also controlled 3-inch guns at Fort Baker which covered the Navy's submarine net.

At Fort Barry, on Bonita Ridge, among a row of connected concrete stations built in the early 1900's, stood the Mine Groupment Command Post. The station had telephones to all batteries of the groupment, a direct intelligence line to the hydroacoustic listening post at Fort Miley, and for observation, a Lewis Depression Range Finder; it was "similar to a transit except it was graduated in mils," Frank Liwski remembered, "6400 to a circle both vertically and horizontally." An officer and three enlisted men manned the command post at all times.

"The command post was a very good one," remembered Felix Usis, who commanded the Mine Groupment soon after war began. "You could really see out in all directions." But security was a concern. A chart on the station wall "showing what we had and where it was," fell into the realm of a military secret and Usis had to put it under lock and key. An eight-foot by twelve-foot room built out of an old pumping station under a corrugated iron roof camouflaged with dirt and grass allowed the groupment commander to bunk nearby. The Mine Groupment held some lively command post exercises at night, with Lieutenant Colonel Usis, in long-johns, giving orders over the command net to illuminate the minefields. "Searchlight 7 in action!" he would say, stomping the station's wooden floor as if the searchlight on Tennessee Point could feel it. The voice on the other end of the line answered, "In action, sir!" "Out of action," countered Usis, "Searchlight 9 in action." The Bird Island light responded, "In action, sir!" Usis stomped again on the floor; "Well then, out of action. It's Searchlight 7 I wanted!"

The enemy minesweeper, a vessel equipped to remove or defuse buoyant mines posed a potential threat to minefields off the Golden Gate. Most likely, the sweeping vessels would come in at night, under cover of a smoke screen, trying to accomplish their mission before the rapid-fire guns and seacoast searchlights of the Mine Groupment found them. If the searchlights were not usable, the underwater ranging system near Sutro Baths would supply firing data. Should the hydro-coustic gear also fail, the Mine Groupment commander could order zone fire or a pre-planned barrage on the approaches to the minefields or the submarine net. Due to the potentially large expenditure of ammunition, zone fire could only be employed when the presence of enemy vessels in the area was verified.

Compared to the worst-case scenarios

put forth in HDSF battle plans, normal operations of the mine command were mundane. Observation stations kept watch over the fields day and night. Two Navy inspection vessels, anchored in front of the minefield at the Main Channel, reported to the Harbor Entrance Control Post the arrival of all ships wishing to enter port. In thick fog, when a ship bypassed the entrance vessels instead of reporting to them, the HECP could order the mine casemate to activate mines. There is no evidence this procedure was ever resorted to. There was once a report of an enemy submarine in the area, "but none ever tried to run our minefield," Frank Liwski recalled. Friendly submarines surfaced before entering the channel. "Any submerged submarine would have been blown automatically," he added.

The possible danger to friendly ships crossing a line of TNT-laden mines lurking invisibly beneath the waves worried the U.S. Navy. "At first, the Navy was a little skeptical of our fields," admitted Liwski. Whenever important ships were to pass through the Golden Gate, anxious Navy liaison officers appeared at the mine command post. To reassure them, the mine command conducted groups of naval officers through the mine casemate, demonstrating the safety of the system. After this, Liwski wrote, "the Navy cooperated very well with us."

The sudden need to expand the Mine Flotilla after Pearl Harbor sent mine officers searching among the picturesque piers of Fisherman's Wharf for vessels that could be converted into mine craft. Lieutenant Colonel Usis commandeered about sixteen crab fishing boats to supplement the ten mine yawls already on hand. The Mine Groupment commander also requisitioned the *California Bear*, a seventy-nine foot, recently-built tuna fishing boat; with the addition

The HDSF Mine Battalion commandeered a score of crab boats and a purse seiner from the fishing fleet at Fisherman's Wharf shortly after hostilities began. (San Francisco Archives, S.F. Public Library)

of davits on deck, the diesel-engined purse seiner became a junior mineplanter for mine repairs. The Harbor Defenses also had on hand several vessels used for transporting supplies, troops, and heavy equipment among the sub-posts and along any shore between Point Reyes and Half Moon Bay. Among these were the tugs *Lincoln, Mercury,* and *Josie Lena,* available to any tactical units making a request with the HDSF supply officer by 4:00 p.m. for next day service.

While men of the Mine Flotilla did ba-sic maintenance and repairs on the HDSF vessels, routine overhauls could only be accomplished in large commercial boatyards. But during wartime, commercial boatyards were swamped with other work. The harbor defenders wanted a facility of their own, where all but the large mineplanters could be han-dled. In early 1942, the Quartermaster Corps of the Army Service Forces established the Marine Repair Shop in a small building behind the Fort Baker Station Hospital on the shore of Horseshoe Bay. An old ex-Navy salt, Harry Plummer, was the shop foreman heading a two-man civilian staff. Under the expert guidance of the civilians, the Mine Flotilla de-tachments worked on the boats. A six-ton marine railway, along with some meager tools and workspace represented the start of the fledgling yard. But the line of mine craft awaiting repair at this facility soon got too long, and HDSF needed a larger repair shop.

"San Francisco's strategic waterfront districts were ordered swept clean of all enemy aliens by February 24," announced the *San Francisco Chronicle.* On January 30, 1942, U.S. Attorney General Francis Biddle issued orders banning enemy aliens from the San Francisco waterfront between China Basin and the Presidio. "No enemy alien will be per-mitted to live in a forbidden zone, to work there or even visit there," the federal order de-creed. The government "would rout approximately 1400 Italians from the 2000

men employed in San Francisco's $500,000-a-year fishing industry," estimated the *Chroni-cle.* California Governor Culbert Olson expressed the feelings of many when he announced his intention to revoke business and food-handling licenses held by enemy aliens: "If the State government is licensing aliens to do business, then we're contributing to the possibility of fifth column activity." The closure of the city's commercial crabbing in-dustry lessened the charm that had made Fisherman's Wharf famous.

Lieutenant Colonel Usis loved to eat crab, namely the delicious Dungeness variety found in the cold waters off the Northern Cali-fornia coast. When the federal edict forbade Italian crab fishermen from leaving port, Usis put the Mine Flotilla to work as a private crab fleet for the gastronomic benefit of the Harbor Defenses. The Mine Groupment commander equipped his mine yawls with crab pots ob-tained from the Coast Guard. Several recruits in the Mine Battalion had been crab fishermen in civilian life and they were now utilized by

Wooden mine yawl of HDSF Mine Flotilla with Fort Baker mine facilities on the shore. (Presidio Army Museum)

the command to do the same work in the Army. When the yawls went out in the morning to service the mines, the crews set out crab pots in the water. After the work day, mine crews hauled in the pots and headed back to the mine base at Fort Baker with their crab bounty.

They "put a submerged wooden box at the mine dock, with a little door to enter it," said HDSF officer John Schonher. The crabs were placed in the box at the Baker dock, and any battery mess could have Dungeness crab on the menu that evening. "We had all chipped in a little money for the bait, that was all," Schonher added, "just the little fringe benefits" of being with the Harbor Defenses. Though fortunate to have the delicacy in such abundance, some Midwesterners among the harbor defense personnel had no knowledge of crab cookery. One HDSF medical officer, inspecting a battery mess kitchen, saw a huge pot of cold water on the flaming stove with the cook standing over it. As crabs tried to crawl out of the pot, the cook knocked them back with a stick each time, as he patiently waited for the water to boil. The mess cook did not realize live crabs had to be dumped into already boiling water. The unofficial crabbing operation provided the featured course at "Crab Night" in the Harbor Defense Officers' Club at Fort Scott. Crab was also distributed to the higher-ups of Western Defense Command at the Presidio. This created much good will for HDSF among its superiors.

In the *Golden Gate Guardian*, the weekly newspaper of the Harbor Defenses, a close-up photograph of a crab caught by "Col. Usis' Crab Fleet" led one editorial entitled: "Stay Out of the Soup." "Here is the angle, brother---we're fighting a tight war under tight conditions," the *Guardian* reminded its readers. "We're a fighting force assembled to blast the Axis. Because we eat, sleep, and fight alongside each other, we must get along . . . Why be a grouch, a bully, or crab? Save all that pent up nasty energy for the enemy . . . it doesn't pay to be a crab---you invariably end up in the soup."

Colonel Felix M. Usis as a regimental commander with sample of 19-conductor mine cable on his desk. Regimental colors of 6th Coast Artillery at right. (Presidio Army Museum)

Chapter 7:

They Shall Not Pass

By January 1942, American fear of a West Coast invasion by Japan had subsided. But the wave of Japanese conquest against Allied domains rolled onward in the Far East. In the Philippines, Japanese forces took Manila on January 2nd as American and Filipino defenders retreated into the Bataan Peninsula. In Malaya, the Japanese proved themselves adept at infiltration and flanking maneuvers, forcing British forces to retreat ever backward on Burma and Singapore; Japan's relentless southern invasion pushed toward the oil and rubber riches of the Dutch East Indies.

Though direction of Japanese offensives pointed elsewhere, the men of the Harbor Defenses of San Francisco did not let down their guard. The command maintained twenty-four hour alert and busily improved fortifications. Neither did the grim situation in the Pacific dampen the harbor defensemen's sense of humor. In January, an inspector general from Western Defense Command was to pay an official visit on Battery C, 6th Coast Artillery and their 16-inch guns at Fort Funston. Upon learning the inspector general was an old cavalryman, Captain Arthur Kramer, the battery commander, added a new twist to the inspection of a seacoast artillery battery. Battery C had a bugler on its roster, a Private Denver McQuiston. Kramer had the bugler precede the official party and blow "Attention" at every stop in the inspection. To call the troops to man the 16-inchers, McQuiston blew "Call to

Harbor defensemen on Marin side pose in morale-boosting photo for Golden Gate Guardian. (Presidio Army Museum)

Arms" plus three additional blasts signifying the guns. As an old horse-soldier, the inspector general was impressed. "That old boy was tickled to death," Kramer recalled years later. "He thought it was wonderful that we used bugles to signal."

Due to wartime rationing of tires and gasoline, civilian automobile traffic across the Golden Gate Bridge declined. But the bridge ends bustled with military activity. 150 California State Guardsmen housed in barracks near both ends of the span furnished bridge security. Down the road from the Toll Plaza, a battery from the 216th Coast Artillery manned 90mm AA guns in emplacements disguised as houses. Next to the Toll Plaza, 37mm automatic weapons and .50 caliber machine guns of Battery F, 216th CA Regiment, protected the bridge itself.

Assigned there without armament days before Pearl Harbor, Battery F stood by for several weeks until equipped. "We got the latest and the best," stated the battery commander, Harry Freeman. Battery F received eight 37mm automatic weapons that spewed 120 rounds-per-minute at an effective range of five to six hundred yards. The director, a separate control unit, guided the fire of these weapons. Trained on the moving target by its two operators, the director calculated speed and range; the 37mm weapons moved in accordance automatically, firing clips of shells fed by the gun crews. Battery F emplaced four of the 37mm's at the top of Lime Point for a good field of fire overlooking the bridge's north tower. On the San Francisco side, west of the Toll Plaza, Battery F sandbagged and camouflaged another four 37mm's.

In practice, low-flying planes gave little warning of approach and flew quickly out of range; the gunners would have only seconds of firing time. Captain Freeman sited a number of .50 caliber antiaircraft machine guns around the bridge to bolster the 37mm weapons. To give his defenses "a little more reach," Captain Freeman sandbagged two .50's on both sides of the bridge's roadway. He even thought of mounting machine guns on the tower tops to fire above the low summer fog. But the bridge maintenance foreman warned that during construction of the towers, steel workers sometimes became "cloud happy" in the high altitude, overcome with the hallucinatory urge to step into the fog. Not easily dissuaded, Captain Freeman went up to the top of one tower. He looked over the railing to the water 746 feet below and recognized the folly of tower top machine guns. "The truth of the matter was," Freeman later said, "I wasn't

about to ever come up there again."

Battery F found ideal living quarters in the tunnels of deactivated emplacements lining the bluffs on either side of the Gate. The chambers were dry and comfortable. The men's heaters drew power from the existing generators. The magazines of old Battery Lancaster, which the Toll Plaza partially covered, served as battery headquarters, messhall, and kitchen. A smaller chamber with a fireplace became the officers' mess for Freeman and his two lieutenants. The messhall fare was prepared with fresh ingredients; canned food went overseas.

To extend the range of antiaircraft protection on the bay, Battery F placed weapons on several San Francisco landmarks. On the roofs of the Embarcadero docks nearest Fisherman's Wharf, Captain Freeman set up several .50 caliber machine guns. The machine gun squads experienced pleasant duty; when not on alert, they fished from the piers. More dramatic surroundings became the backdrop for 40mm weapons and machine guns that Captain Freeman transported by barge to Alcatraz. Civilian contractors hoisted the armament onto prepared positions atop the cellblock and the prison staff apartment building. For the first several months, detached crews from Battery F commuted to Alcatraz daily on the prison launch. Later, a different unit lived permanently on the island.

"A humble Oakland garbage boat is believed to have lived up to the highest traditions of the sea in ramming a Japanese submarine within sight of the Golden Gate on December 20," reported the *Chronicle* on January 27, 1942. The *Tahoe*, an Oakland Scavenger Company garbage scow, was inbound in broad daylight nine miles southwest of the Farallones when Captain William Vartnaw spotted dead ahead what appeared to be a periscope and part of a conning tower. There was no time to slow down or alter course; seconds later, the scow hit and scraped over the object. Eleven crewmen ran over to the stern of the *Tahoe* to see what had happened, but found nothing.

In drydock sometime later, the garbage scow revealed an eighty-foot gash in the hull. "No doubt the Tahoe struck a steel object," stated the insurance underwriter's report. The ship's owners received two thousand dollars in damages. The Oakland Scavenger Company released details of the accident in a news conference on January 26th. Rear Admiral John W. Greenslade of the 12th Naval District discounted the story when reporters asked him why the Navy did not make public this incident. Without independent corroboration of the event, Greenslade explained, "actual credence of ramming and possible sinking could not be accepted." The *Chronicle* did not comment on the admiral's statement except to remind readers that a tanker was torpedoed off Santa Cruz on the same day as the *Tahoe* incident, inferring an enemy submarine had been in the vicinity. A few weeks later, *Collier's* magazine published their version of the story, claiming the incident was well-known to Pacific Coast reporters, though some journalists claimed "it was just some more Orson Welles stuff." "It's publication would have given a lift to a slightly bewildered Pacific coast public," *Collier's* contended in good humor, chiding military officials for staying mum; "Army and Navy are both working like beavers to make the Coast impregnable--but they can't tell people what they're doing."

Two months after Pearl Harbor, the War Department felt enough had already been done to strengthen the Pacific coast. The deployment of Army units to guard the coastline interfered with their training for offensive operations. On February 4th, testifying before a Senate subcommittee considering plans for added military strength on the West Coast, Brigadier General Mark W. Clark played down invasion jitters. After inspecting Western Defense Command, General Clark admitted coast defenses were not adequate to prevent air and naval raids---but he thought the likelihood of an invasion in force was small. In coming months, as Japanese offensives in the Pacific ebbed, the War Department began reducing stateside defenses.

After one month in the mud of Drakes Bay, Battery B of the 56th Coast Artillery towed their 155mm guns back to Fort Cronkhite in mid-January amid rumors that some elements of the regiment were headed overseas. A preliminary check of personnel records found 250 men of the regiment skilled in language or key military specialties. "I had one year of French in college," recounted Dale Barnhart, "and the fact that I was working on the base-end stations made it possible for me to be included in that group." In preparation for overseas duty, the chosen men took a series of inoculations, but a defective serum batch sent several dozen of them to the Fort Baker Station Hospital. There they lay for some time, losing weight and suffering from yellow jaundice. From the initial selection of 250, the Army formed three twenty-seven men detachments for sending to unknown destinations.

The first group said farewell to loved ones as they left the Harbor Defenses on February 17th. A captain, a lieutenant, and twenty-five enlisted men comprised Shipment No. 9098-B. They called themselves the "Secret" 9098-B. The detachment was taken to the Port of Embarkation at Fort Mason on February 18th, their ultimate destination still undisclosed. The next morning, Shipment No. 9098-B boarded the *Etolin*, an ex-passenger liner turned Army transport. Immediately, the vessel got under way. "Going underneath the Golden Gate Bridge, I saw my wife and several people waving goodbye to us," recalled Ralph DeMoisy, the group's lieutenant. "They knew

"Secret" 9098-B arrives aboard transport Etolin at their secret destination on March 15, 1942. Escorting cruiser USS Concord in background. (D. Barnhart)

The 54th Coast Artillery Regiment, firing 155mm seacoast guns, was part of HDSF for a short time in 1942. (Presidio Army Museum)

where we were going, but we didn't know." The detachment had not been told when they were sailing, but DeMoisy figured that informal chat among the wives at the Harbor Defense Officers' Club had bested military security.

Outside the Gate, the old swayback Navy cruiser *Concord* joined the *Etolin.* Together, the two ships, accompanied by a Navy blimp, sailed south along the California coast. In the hold of the *Etolin,* the men found full battle equipment for a tractor-drawn coast artillery battalion; sixteen 155mm guns with their prime movers, searchlights, and .50-caliber machine guns. "We knew we were taking all the key people and we were going to fill in with other troops," DeMoisy remembered, but not until the ships reached the open sea did the commanding colonel gather the detachment on deck to reveal their destination.

The detachment headed for Chile, where offshore Axis submarines threatened ships carrying copper nitrate between that South American country and the U.S. Four batteries of 155mm guns were to be established on the lengthy Chilean coast, and a Chilean coast artillery battalion would be trained by the American detachment to man the guns. The American coast artillerymen also had a diplomatic mission. The U.S. State Department wanted to counter the influence of German and Japanese consular officials in neutral Chile. The American soldiers would act as "eyes and ears" on Axis intentions,

Lieutenant DeMoisy was informed---as regular artillerymen, they were "less suspect." For some of the men, this promised to be the adventure of their lives. "It was terrific," recalled Dale Barnhart, "because I knew that the other guys left behind were going to be shipped to the Aleutians. And I didn't want to go to Alaska."

During the sea voyage, the men gathered on deck to learn Spanish with the Hispanic members of the detachment. Off San Pedro, California, the Navy blimp quit the ships, leaving the cruiser *Concord* as sole escort. After a stop in Panama to take on ammunition and firing charts, the ships continued to Chile, arriving without incident at Tocopilla harbor on March 15th. The detachment spent an interesting year in Chile, their special wartime adventures filled with romance, ceremony, and political intrigue. Two other units detached from the 56th Coast Artillery went to Peru and Venezuela on similar missions.

As "Secret" 9098-B sailed through Southern California waters, they missed the Japanese submarine I-17, which lurked into the Santa Barbara Channel on the early evening of February 23rd. The submarine surfaced and shelled the Signal Oil and Gas petroleum field at Ellwood, east of Santa Barbara. The shelling slightly damaged an oil well pump and some structures before the I-17 submerged and left the area. The next day, newspapers noted the attack as the first bombardment of the American coast since the War of 1812. The *Chronicle* dismissed the shelling, saying it had scared nobody. But "the next one may be worse," the editorial warned. "We must expect substantial property damage or loss of life," but we must not take the "advice of shore-minded holdovers from prewar isolationism" by curtailing offensive operations in reaction to nuisance raids.

To replace the 155mm guns taken to Chile, the all-black 54th Coast Artillery Reg-

.30 caliber machine gunner on "A" alert for low-flying enemy planes at Fort Scott. (Presidio Army Museum)

iment from Camp Davis, North Carolina came to Fort Cronkhite on the 28th of February. They manned guard posts and beach defenses at the fort, as well as using their 155mm guns to support the concrete artillery.

The emergency after Pearl Harbor was over, wrote an HDSF correspondent in March to the *Coast Artillery Journal*. He blamed faulty intelligence methods for causing exaggerated claims of enemy activity off California. But now "the presence of actual enemy vessels is being predicted with great accuracy." "Though no enemy fire has penetrated the Harbor Defenses of San Francisco and the waters have not brought the foe to these shores," the correspondent continued, "all through these defenses there is offensive action." But the troops could not be kept permanently on constant alert. "To prevent undue fatigue of personnel and to conserve the strength and morale of the command," HDSF's Standing Operating Procedure established four levels of readiness; "A" Alert meant instant action, with all personnel bivouacked at their batteries. "B" allowed the men to stay in barracks if they could reach the seacoast guns in fifteen minutes. Slower manning times of one to four

Roll-away roof reveals .30 caliber machine gun on antiaircraft mount and three-man crew who have entered position through connecting trench. (Presidio Army Museum)

.30 caliber machine gunner on "A" alert for low-flying enemy planes at Fort Scott. (Presidio Army Museum)

hours were possible if the tactical situation permitted.

On some duties, "A" alert status was always in force. On the theory that nuisance air raids presented the most probable form of attack, HDSF kept anti-aircraft machine guns and their crews "ready for instant repeat instant action." The Standing Operating Procedure ordered machine gun hoses attached, water jackets filled, and one belt loaded so firing could be commenced without delay. One man with a whistle around his neck, stood behind the machine gun trigger at all times, scanning the skies for low-flying planes. The two other crewmen bivouacked close by in foxholes and slit trenches. If an enemy plane was "engaged in hostile action" against his position, the lone man could open fire without waiting for the rest of the gun crew.

The H-Station and all command posts of groupments, groups, and batteries operated around the clock in three shifts with at least one officer on duty at all times. One man acted as air observer, constantly peering out the vision slit for low-flying aircraft. Doors and hatch covers to each command post were locked from the inside. Soldiers stood guard in foxholes outside, not only to prevent the enemy from sneaking up on the command post, but to prevent unauthorized entry or exit by

HDSF personnel. "No person will be allowed to enter or leave any of the stations, batteries, or other installations of these harbor defenses without a proper pass or the correct password," warned the Standing Operating Procedure. Western Defense Command sometimes tested the vigilance of the defenders by sending teams of red-uniformed "infiltrators" to see how local commanders reacted to saboteurs and small landing groups.

"Day and night a constant vigil is kept from every observing station and gun battery to warn of any suspicious action on land, sea or in the air," an HDSF writer proclaimed in the *Coast Artillery Journal.* "It is the firm determination of every man in these defenses, regardless of personal sacrifice, to allow NO ENEMY SHIPS TO PASS THROUGH THE GOLDEN GATE." Battle plans of the Harbor Defenses envisioned five attack scenarios with plans to deal with each. Naval feints or reconnaissance raids attempting to probe the defenses would be fired upon by only those batteries probably known to the enemy. In this scenario, searchlights illuminated as little as possible for fear of revealing themselves to future attack. Unless a good chance existed of sinking the attackers, a minimum of guns was to be employed to keep the enemy at a distance. On the other hand, an enemy naval bombardment called for full reply from all HDSF guns, with secondary batteries concen-

trating their fire on enemy smoke-laying vessels. In the case of attempted "run-bys"---a quick dash through the Gate by enemy vessels---the HDSF battle plan demanded maximum effort by all defense guns to target and destroy the leading ship and successive vessels as they came in range. If the enemy tried to block the harbor entrance by scuttling their own ship in the channel, shore batteries were to destroy the blocking vessel before it reached the desired location. Minefields and rapid-fire batteries would fire on enemy torpedoes launched into the harbor from outside the Gate, though HDSF deemed this form of attack "highly improbable." But under no event should the harbor defenders leave their guns in the face of naval attack in order to resist an enemy landing. Except under an extreme emergency, the seacoast mission had to be carried out simultaneously with land defense.

In early 1942, Standing Operating Procedure No. 3 arranged seacoast batteries in three tactical groups. The Mine Groupment concentrated on the harbor entrance, and contained the minefields and all 3 and 6-inch rapid-fire batteries. Funston Groupment covered the waters south of the Main Channel with Batteries Howe (12-inch mortars,) Davis (16-inch guns,) Bluff (155mm guns,) and Chester (12-inch guns.) Group 1 protected the northern waters with Batteries Wallace (12-inch guns,) Mendell (12-inch guns,) and Townsley (16-inch guns.) The long-range armament of Group 1 and Funston Groupment made up "the Harbor Defense Commander's reserve," stated the Standing Operating Procedure, and "as such, he will determine when they will open fire." Planned in advance were "Battle Orders," a set of clear directives issued by the H-Station during combat to subordinate commanders. They ranged from Action 1---"Withhold fire, but assign

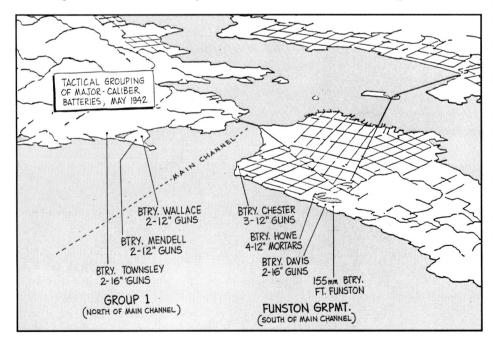

TACTICAL GROUPING
OF MAJOR-CALIBER
BATTERIES, MAY 1942

MAIN CHANNEL

BTRY. WALLACE
2-12" GUNS

BTRY. MENDELL
2-12" GUNS

BTRY. TOWNSLEY
2-16" GUNS

GROUP 1
(NORTH OF MAIN CHANNEL)

BTRY. CHESTER
3-12" GUNS

BTRY. HOWE
4-12" MORTARS

BTRY. DAVIS
2-16" GUNS

155mm BTRY.
FT. FUNSTON

FUNSTON GRPMT.
(SOUTH OF MAIN CHANNEL)

HDSF officers outside Harbor Defense Officers' Club at Fort Scott. Colonel Usis in center, with Major Arthur Kramer on extreme left and Major John Schonher on left end of back row. (Presidio Army Museum)

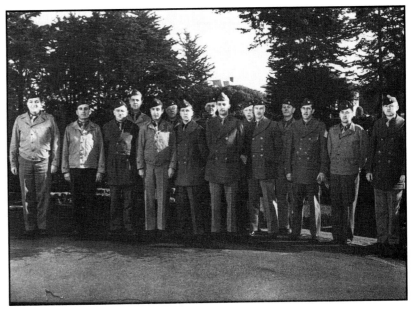

targets for tracking," to Action 2--"Employ minimum number of appropriate batteries to accomplish required effect," to Action 4--"open destruction fire with every available gun," to Action 5--fire on "loaded transports and small boats approaching the beaches."

The Harbor Defenses maintained strict security in its territory. Password usage was the order of the day and passwords were changed daily. Guards had orders to shoot if their challenges went unanswered. A soldier on guard duty atop the Cronkhite 16-inch emplacement challenged an intruder in the fog. When the intruder did not reply, the sentry fired. His bullet struck with a loud and hollow ringing sound---but the intruder did not fall. Upon closer inspection, the guard found he had just hit the bell of the improvised gas alarm. One of the hollow cone-shaped windshields that fell off a 16-inch projectile during the concrete block tests of December had been saved and mounted atop a post to be rung in the event of gas attack. The cone, "standing on top of the post on a foggy night looked like a person," battery commander John Schonher remembered.

Several other instances occurred of guards firing shots. A sergeant of Battery E, 6th Coast Artillery, returning to Battery Townsley from a six-hour pass near midnight, drove his auto past a radar van at Fort Cronkhite. The sergeant had his windows rolled up against the cold wind. He did not see the guard or hear the guard's challenge, and continued driving. As the car went through the checkpoint without stopping, the guard whirled around and fired. The rifle bullet went through the back of the vehicle and exited through the dashboard. The driver halted and gave the password.

At the Fort Baker mine compound, HDSF artillery engineers established a lumber yard. Unauthorized nighttime foraging expeditions from various batteries came by truck and helped themselves to the lumber. Major Frank Liwski, Mine Battalion commander, ordered the guard not to let anyone remove lumber from the yard without written permission from Colonel George Burr, the artillery engineer. One night, a Captain Tilson and his men entered the yard; in plain sight of the sentry, they commenced to pile lumber into the truck. On the way out, the guard halted the truck and asked if they had written permission to remove the wood. When Captain Tilson replied they had none, the guard refused to let the truck pass. The annoyed Tilson asked why he was allowed to load up when he could not depart with the material. "Sir, my orders don't say anything about loading a truck," the sentinel replied. "They just say you can't take the lumber out." The chagrined captain had to order his men to unload the truck.

By the spring of 1942, life at the Harbor Defenses had settled into the routine of a wartime Army post. The 6th Coast Artillery Band played regularly for Saturday night dinner dances at the Fort Scott Officers' Club. Officers' wives participated in bridge clubs, volunteered for Red Cross work, and joined other war-related charities. Post chaplains oversaw religious activity, and transportation was provided for men from distant outposts to attend religious functions. But the alert status prevented the Harbor Defenses from holding many military ceremonies on the parade ground.

Leaves and furloughs for officers and men were not routinely granted, "except in cases of extreme emergencies," stated the Standing Operating Procedure, "and in all cases must be approved by Harbor Defense Headquarters." When the "tactical efficiency" of the command allowed, passes were issued. Generally, passes were good for six hours, but HDSF could call for Pass Status No. 1, which meant no passes at all, to Status No. 8, allowing fifteen percent of the men to be away for twenty-four hours, and another three percent for three days. Before going on pass, all personnel signed a departure book, leaving an address and phone number "to summon quickly to their battle stations men on pass in event of an emergency." "No enlisted man will be allowed to leave his organization who does not present a superior appearance," HDSF Headquarters warned. An officer or experienced NCO inspected each man, checking for "appearance, cleanliness and complete and proper uniform." The Standing Operating Procedure emphatically stated: "THE CLASS A UNIFORM ONLY WILL BE WORN ON PASS."

At Battery I, manning 6-inch guns at Fort Barry, the men lived in long wooden barracks under the hill behind the emplacement. Judy, the battery's lion cub mascot stayed with the men. The cub liked to come up behind and grab the legs of men walking on the battery parade behind the guns. At other times, the lion cub became moody and stayed by itself, preferring to crouch low in the tall brush surrounding the emplacement. Once, it disappeared for several days. Lieutenant Daniel Cook offered a three-day pass to anyone who could find the cub, but beating the surrounding brush failed to uncover the animal. Coming back from guard post inspection one foggy evening, Lieutenant Cook and his reconnaissance car driver saw in their headlights, a speeding blur that streaked across the road. The driver stopped immediately; they were in front of the post warehouse. Cook, wearing a heavy mackinaw coat, shined his flashlight as he walked toward the warehouse dock. The Battery I mascot was under the building, crouched and growling as Cook's

light found it. The cub started to swing its paws as the lieutenant quickly bundled it in his mackinaw and put it in the truck.

Judy showed up during an inspection visit by General DeWitt of Western Defense Command. DeWitt, along with General Stockton and Major Liwski, was discussing some matter on the concrete pad behind the 6-inch guns. The two HDSF officers knew about the lion cub, but General DeWitt did not. As they conversed, DeWitt suddenly felt something around his legs. "Imagine his feelings when he looked down," Liwski wrote, "and saw a half-grown lion rubbing against him." The battery mascot had emerged from its hiding place in the low brush. After General DeWitt "recovered his surprise and composure," continued Liwski, "he took the incident very gracefully. General Stockton and I got a big kick out of it."

Battery G of the 6th Coast Artillery, manning the harbor defense antiaircraft guns, was a large unit. Captain Richard Moorman, the commanding officer, drew up a new Table of Organization and Equipment. He came up with a personnel count of 375 men, about three times more men than an average gun battery. When HDSF Headquarters saw the document Moorman submitted to them, they decided to form a new unit; on April 1, 1942, the 130th Coast Artillery Battalion was activated as the antiaircraft artillery component of the Harbor Defenses. The battalion consisted of one searchlight battery and three batteries firing 3-inch fixed AA guns. Most Battery G personnel transferred to the battalion, including Moorman, who was promoted to major and assigned to the new unit as executive officer. Lieutenant Colonel Benjamin Hawkins, late of the 216th Coast Artillery Regiment, headed the battalion.

By spring, the antiaircraft batteries had left their pup tents for life underground. At the AA positions on Barry Ridge, tunnels connected the messhall and the underground quarters. Sliding panels made of netting covered the gun pits. An empty subterranean water tank, with a ladder leading down into it, became the battery command post. At the Wolf Ridge battery, engineers buried and outfitted a quonset hut as crew quarters. At one end, stairs led up from the underground command post to the concrete director pit covered by a sliding metal roof. The men named the position "Battery B on the Ridge," 720 feet above sea level, offering an unobstructed view of San Francisco and beyond, with the rocky coast at Devils Slide visible on a clear day. But the heights were also windy, cold, and desolate; one recruit, upon arrival at his new post, looked around and asked, "What town is this?" "It didn't take him long to find out he landed in a so called dead end street," wrote the *Golden Gate Guardian*, "especially when the fog rolls in." "It was a dreary spot," remembered battalion executive Richard Moorman. "Even though winter in San Francisco is the rainy season, the men were healthy and had very few colds until after we got the buried quonset huts."

The AA battalion's searchlight battery deployed fifteen lights in a wide area. Each gun battery had five assigned searchlights. Each light was paired with a sound locator--giant "mechanical ears" that detected the

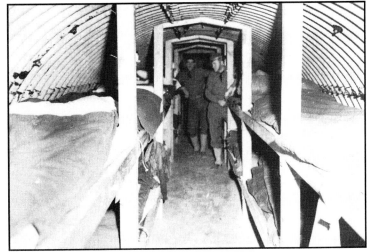

Underground quonset hut used as living quarters by antiaircraft gun crew on Wolf Ridge, March 12, 1942. (Presidio Army Museum)

sound of aircraft engines in the dark sky. Two specially-trained operators with acute hearing followed the engine sound through the "ears," and directed the searchlight onto the target. When on target, the 60-inch light sent a beam thirty-five thousand feet into the clear night sky. The gun and searchlight crews sometimes practiced with flying targets. Army planes flew "around and over the defenses" to give the AA crews on the ground a feeling for the real thing. The battalion executive rode along on one mission and "got sick as a dog" when the pilot put the aircraft into a dive over the batteries.

From the signal station next to the Toll Plaza, one could see warships and military convoys steaming out the Golden Gate. An old Navy chief petty officer in charge of the station kept watch on the maritime traffic, "logging them in and logging them out." Captain Harry Freeman of the neighboring 37mm AA battery liked to converse with the Navy man. As the two men chatted, troop transports with secret destinations passed under the Golden Gate Bridge. Ship decks teemed with soldiers "in their khaki uniforms, getting their last look at the United States." The harbor defenders on the bluffs sometimes saw history in the making, but never knew it at the time.

On April 1, 1942, at the Alameda Naval Air Station, cranes hoisted sixteen B-25 twin-engined Army bombers onto the flight deck of the Navy carrier USS *Hornet*. The ol-

Battery M, 6th CA, the HDSF antiaircraft searchlight battery training with sound locators at Oakland Municipal Airport. (Presidio Army Museum)

ive-drab planes, too big to store below, looked even bigger as they crowded the flight deck of the carrier. At 3:00 p.m., the *Hornet* moved out into the middle of San Francisco Bay and dropped anchor. That evening, the Army fliers enjoyed the night life of the city, but with some apprehension. "I hope they rounded up all the Japanese spies," thought one of the pilots. "If they didn't I hope they think those planes are just being transported to Hawaii."

The Navy notified the Harbor Defense Command Post that a carrier group was leaving the harbor on the morning of April 2nd. Captain Jack Lehmkuhl went up to the bridge of the H-Station at dawn. Under a bright sun and poor visibility, he saw the escorting ships of TF-16.2 steam out the harbor entrance. The cruisers *Nashville* and *Vincennes* led the task force, followed by the oiler *Cimarron*, and the four destroyers, *Gwin*, *Meredith*, *Monssen*, and *Grayson*. Captain Freeman, while visiting the chief petty officer at the signal station at 11:48 a.m., saw the carrier *Hornet* sail under the Golden Gate Bridge with the sixteen B-25's on deck. The two men surmised the carrier was delivering bombers to Pearl Harbor. At the H-Station, Captain Lehmkuhl watched the *Hornet* with its unusual cargo moving out to

join the escorts. Lehmkuhl thought in amazement, "My God, those planes look too big to be on an aircraft carrier!" He too, guessed Hawaii as their final destination. This event was forgotten by the following week, when on April 9th, the American and Filipino defenders of Bataan surrendered; many at HDSF took that news glumly, for it meant the island fortress of Corregidor in Manila Bay would be next. Several former HDSF officers were among the doomed defenders. But spirits heightened on April 18th when news of the American bombing raid on Tokyo by B-25's made the headlines. Where the bombers came from, press accounts would not disclose, but those who saw the *Hornet*, loaded with Army bombers as it steamed out the Golden Gate, felt they knew the answer.

After temporary duty at the Harbor Defenses, the all-black 54th Coast Artillery moved to Fort Ord on April 5th. From there, the 155mm gun regiment fanned out to defend various locations along the Central California coast; a battery of 155's to Morro Bay, two 75mm field guns to Estero Bay, another pair to Pismo Beach, and other detachments to Capitola, Santa Cruz, and Pacific Grove. Asking for the cooperation of the public, Major General Walter K. Wilson commanding the Northern California Sector of Western Defense Command told the press, "Along the Pacific Coast it is necessary to move units from place to place, and the arrival and emplacement of artillery or other units in your locality is a matter which should be kept quiet."

An Army observation plane, with Captain Jack Lehmkuhl aboard as passenger, cruised low over the water off Ocean Beach. The pilot came "right down on the deck" to avoid what he considered "trigger-happy" harbor defense AA gunners. The plane headed back to Crissy Field after flying Lehmkuhl over the harbor forts. General Stockton had ordered the mission to see if camouflage put up in the autumn might need alteration for spring colors. As the low-flying plane turned toward the Golden Gate, it headed between Lands End

A 60-inch searchlight used at HDSF in antiaircraft role. (Presidio Army Museum)

and the Mile Rock lighthouse. Rising out of the surf one thousand yards north of Lands End, the lighthouse also watched for enemy motor-torpedo boats trying to sneak in during fogs. A recently-installed telephone line extended out to the lighthouse, but Lehmkuhl's pilot was unaware of it. As the observation plane passed between Lands End and Mile Rock, it struck the wire. For a moment, the aircraft seemed to come to a complete stop as Lehmkuhl looked below and thought, "there was going to be an awful cool swim in from here." The plane managed to limp in under the bridge to an emergency landing at Crissy Field.

HDSF artillery engineers also used spotter planes to check camouflage, flying three or four passes over areas under observation. But Navy blimps proved more efficient, because they hovered slowly over an installation, allowing the engineers to carefully study and photograph the camouflage effect. At Moffett Field, where the Navy had a one-quarter mile long dirigible hanger, Captain Harry Payne, assistant artillery engineer, borrowed blimps for the camouflage missions. Other harbor defense officers sometimes went along on the ride to study the camouflage over their own batteries. "The camouflage really looked pretty good," recalled HDSF officer John Schonher. "To the casual observer, you wouldn't notice there was an emplacement from that height." But Schonher found more interesting the slow ride over San Francisco. He never suspected the city had so many backyards.

On the night of May 6, 1942, General Walter K. Wilson of the Northern California Sector sat before studio microphones of San Francisco radio station KGEI, from which short wave signals reached American forces in the Philippines. After a month-long bombardment from Japanese artillery on the Bataan peninsula, the island fortress of Corregidor and the island sub-posts which made up the Harbor Defenses of Manila Bay, were on the verge of surrendering to the enemy. General Wilson, who commanded those defenses the year be-

February 1942 aerial photo shows 12-inch Battery Wallace (left) at Fort Barry with no camouflage on emplacement or road leading to it. Foxholes and field fortifications appear around the two gun pads. Deactivated 12-inch mortar battery is adjacent right. (K. Cooper, Jr.)

fore, read a farewell message to his former comrades: "America is proud of you as valiant soldiers. Those of us who know you personally are proud of you as friends. In order to let you know that your relatives are well, KGEI has very generously agreed to send this broadcast." The fall of Corregidor weighed heavily on San Francisco harbor defensemen. The previous year, several HDSF officers were transferred to the Philippines. Among them were Major Joe C. East, a former battery commander at Fort Baker and Captain Samuel M. McReynolds, who commanded Battery Wallace during its well-photographed target shoot in 1941. HDSF officers remembered the big farewell party held at the Fort Scott Officers' Club when the men left for the Philippines. Now they fondly recalled how the 9th Coast Artillery District commander, General Henry T. Burgin, complained when the party got too noisy.

The Corregidor surrender affected one HDSF officer personally. Colonel Karl F. Baldwin, Fort Scott post commander and former CO of the 6th Coast Artillery, served a shift at the H-Station the night Corregidor surrendered. Charles Sullivan, a radio operator at the H-Station, remembered the senior officer sympathetically: "It was a bad night for Baldwin. He was quite elderly . . . he was sweating it out." The colonel's son, Captain Lawrence C. Baldwin, was a coast artillery officer on Corregidor. Ironically, the younger Baldwin was born in Japan, when the father served as military attache in Tokyo during the 1920's.

Springtime brought annual target practice. Battery C at Fort Funston received notice on April 22nd that a shoot with their 16-inch guns would be conducted on May 9th. First Lieutenant Kenneth Cooper, the battery commander, instituted two hours of daily gun drill. "This worked out very well for everyone except the observers," Cooper reported, since fog kept the observers from tracking the towed target. Battery C had two 75mm guns mounted on pedestals as excaliber pieces outside the casemates. Using these weapons, the gun crews fired over one hundred rounds at a range of seventeen thousand yards. To simulate working under gas conditions, the men sometimes wore gas masks during the firing.

Ever since his days as Harbor Defense Ordnance Officer, Arthur Kramer sought ways to improve the accuracy of the 16-inch seacoast guns. From his study of target practice results at Battery Hatch in Hawaii and Battery Townsley at HDSF, Kramer found the distance between splashes of the initial rounds sometimes amounted to a difference of three thousand yards. This was known in the Navy as "cold gun effect," when gun crews were supposedly less sharp at the start of the shoot, and only became more accurate as they "warmed up." Kramer attributed this problem to faulty ramming of the shell into the breech. Reports from the Hawaiian battery showed the depth of seating into the chamber for each projectile could deviate by three inches, depending on the skill of the ramming operator. "Training with dummy projectiles cannot really remedy this fault," Kramer wrote in 1942. When Kramer had earlier commanded the Funston 16-inch guns, he made ramming more uniform by painting marks on the loading table to help the operator stop the forward ramming motion at a certain point, allowing the projectile to proceed on inertia and seat itself in the

breech. In the spring of 1942, Kramer was a major in command of the tactical group consisting of the two HDSF 16-inch batteries. He was anxious to solve the "cold gun effect." Kramer thought the rammer operator, who needed "the finesse of a concert violinist," was the key to the solution.

On May 9th, the day of the 16-inch practice, the H-Station transmitted a meteorological message to the battery at 6:49 a.m. The Ordnance Department inspected the Navy Model 1919 M1 guns. To prevent cut-off, their motors were warmed one-half hour before firing. Breechblocks were washed with solvent and dried. Firing circuits were checked for shorts. Since no scales were available, the projectiles were assumed to weigh 2100-pounds apiece. To save wear on the guns, rounds would be fired with two-thirds the normal powder charge (approximately 440-pounds of powder.) Target practice permitted four sensing rounds before firing for the record. Instead of both guns firing two rounds apiece and adjusting fire on the remaining two shots, Kramer and Lieutenant Cooper, the battery commander, intended to fire all sensing rounds from one gun---thereby having three shots to adjust on after the first round.

At the battery commander's station near the emplacement, Colonel Felix Usis and Colonel William F. LaFrenz, the harbor defense executive officer, looked on as Lieutenant Cooper awaited the command to commence firing. Cooper instructed the telephone operators in the station not to interrupt him "for any reason" once firing started. From another location, Major Kramer assigned the target and the battery jumped into action. Since only ten percent of the crews had ever fired big guns before, "everyone was gun shy," the after-action report observed. On No. 1 Gun, the apprehensive rammer operator stopped the forward motion of the rammer one foot short of seating the projectile. He then had to repeat the operation. Four minutes after the firing order, the 16-inch rifle fired its first ranging round. The towed pyramidal target was moving seaward at 18,600 yards when the sensing shot landed short 130 yards. The next round hit 120 yards over. Just then, the battery commander's station was notified by tele-

Battery C, 6th CA range section in plotting room of Funston 16-inch guns. (San Francisco Archives, S.F. Public Library)

phone that a naval convoy was about to emerge from the harbor. "Davis is already firing. To hell with the convoy, we'll be finished in a few minutes," came the reply from the station, as the operator later claimed. Then the third and fourth ranging shots quickly followed, 140 and 220 yards short of the target.

While the range crew made corrections for center of impact, Lieutenant Cooper reminded the station operators to let no telephone calls interrupt the firing. Then "fire for effect" commenced with both guns firing twice, resulting in splashes 190 yards short, 520 over, 230 over, and 510 short. To measure the consistency of projectile ramming, Major Kramer called time out between rounds to measure deviation in the depth of seating. Though three inches had been normal previously, Kramer found the maximum deviation this time to be only one-eighth of an inch. The center of impact between splashes of the previous salvos were considered close, so the range officer made no corrections as the 16-inch guns prepared to fire their remaining six rounds. Just then, a radio message from the H-Station ordered cease firing for the passing convoy. Battery C suspended practice for the day. They removed powder and primers, but left projectiles loaded in the breeches.

Immediately after the day's practice, Funston Groupment asked Lieutenant Cooper to explain why he did not cease firing when first warned of the convoy. Cooper responded in writing, confirming that no officers answered the telephone during the target practice. And in reference to the station telephone operator's statement, Cooper did "not recall telling the officer at Funston Groupment to 'stop the convoy'." Cooper could not explain why calls to the battery commander's station were not answered during the practice. "No reason for this failure of communication can be given," the lieutenant admitted.

The next day, Battery C resumed target practice with even better results. The first two salvos hit 280 yards short, 110 short, 110 over, and 40 yards over. No corrections were made before the last salvo was fired. The final two shells landed 150 yards and 70 yards short. Several weeks later, Major Kramer commended Battery C in an indorsement to General Stockton. The major observed that no delays or breakdowns interrupted the practice, due to "the careful preparation of the guns and accessory mechanisms." The quick lapse of time (3.55 minutes) between "Commence Firing" and the first round "is considered to be a further indication of the excellent state of training of this organization." Colonel J.C. Ruddell, regimental commander of the 6th Coast Artillery, recommended an "Excellent" rating be awarded the battery, and General Stockton did so on June 11th, saying for the record: "The Commanding General is pleased to forward this rating and congratulate the officers and men of Battery C, 6th Coast Artillery on their excellent performance."

Another Funston unit held Record Target Practice three days after the 16-inch shoot. On May 12th, the four 12-inch seacoast mortars of Battery Howe fired for the last time as first-line armament. Battery E of the 18th Coast Artillery earned a "Very Good" rating for the practice. Barely two months later, HDSF designated the mortars surplus armament and Battery E of the 18th became an antiaircraft weapons unit assigned to outlying positions in the Golden Gate defenses. They fired 37mm and 40mm automatic weapons, and twin and single .50 caliber machine guns.

After the B-25 raid on Tokyo, Western Defense Command worried that Japan would retaliate on the West Coast. Since May 14th, American code-breakers, able to decipher coded Japanese messages, detected groups of Japanese ships leaving port. On May 27th, the War Department put Western Defense Command on special alert. Army intelligence officers expected the Japanese to attack the West Coast with hit-and-run raids. Reading the same intercepted code, the U.S. Navy thought the Japanese thrust was pointed at Midway Island north of Hawaii and also at Dutch Harbor in the Aleutians. As a precaution, the Navy advised the Army to expect attack from Alaska to Southern California by low-flying aircraft, airborne assault, and shore landings.

On May 28th, from Pearl Harbor sailed three American carrier task groups toward the suspected Japanese target: Midway. Three days later, the old battleships *Colorado* and *Maryland* emerged from San Francisco harbor to form a last line of defense. On June 2nd, hoping to lure the U.S. Navy away from Midway, the Japanese attacked Dutch Harbor in the Aleutians with carrier aircraft. The *San Francisco Chronicle* urged readers to look at the danger coming from the north, and revealed that Army forces on the West Coast had been put on twenty-four hour alert with all leaves canceled. Western Defense Command asked citizens to report any Japanese in GI uniform. Japanese-Americans in the service had already been transferred from Western Defense Command, except for three individuals at Fort Ord, the *Chronicle* revealed.

As opposing naval forces gathered for a showdown at Midway, a small drama occurred on June 3rd at the Golden Gate. At four o'clock in the morning, the *Bunting*, a Navy coastal minesweeper collided with the Navy patrol craft PC-569 off Point Diablo, just two thousand yards west of the Golden Gate Bridge. The *Bunting*, an ex-tuna fishing boat, began to sink. Speeding to the stricken Navy

vessel was another former purse seiner, the *California Bear*, a junior mineplanter with the Harbor Defenses. The *California Bear*, under its skipper Sergeant William Kilcourse, maneuvered into position to rescue fourteen officers and men before the *Bunting* sank. For his skill in effecting the rescue, Sergeant Kilcourse won the Legion of Merit.

Major Arthur Kramer was the senior Army officer on duty one night at the H-Station when a coded message came in. After deciphering the code, Kramer read the message and realized a more senior officer should see its contents right away. The major called Colonel William LaFrenz and suggested he come to the command post to read a message that could not, for security reasons, be relayed over the telephone. LaFrenz quickly arrived at the H-Station and read the good news---the big enemy carrier force that Western Defense Command thought might raid the West Coast, was destroyed by U.S. Navy air power near Midway.

Despite their losses at Midway, the Japanese decoy forces in the Aleutians played out their assigned task on June 6th with unopposed landings at Attu and Kiska. Thanks to the intercept of Japanese coded messages, the American military knew of the feint and were not overly concerned. Even San Francisco newspapers reacted calmly, treating the event with minor interest on the editorial page. On June 8th, Western Defense Command called off the alert that had been in force since late May.

Compared to the significant American victory at Midway, the shelling of Fort Stevens at the mouth of the Columbia River in Oregon was anticlimactic. The last Japanese shelling of the West Coast during the war occurred at midnight, June 21st, when the submarine I-25 dropped a few deck rounds on the main post of the Harbor Defenses of the Columbia River. The shore batteries there did not fire back. The defenders did not wish to reveal their positions in a vain attempt to hit a lone submarine that seemed out of range. Since these defenses were in the purview of the 9th Coast Artillery District, several HDSF officers, including Lieutenant Colonel Usis traveled north to investigate the matter. The investigation turned out to be a reunion of sorts as the man in charge of the Columbia River defenses was Colonel Carl S. Doney, former HDSF executive officer and 6th Coast Artillery commander.

After planting submarine minefields, the HDSF Mine Battalion maintained them and on occasion, rounded up stray mines that broke loose. The buoyant mines were designed to stay put in a four-knot current. But at the Golden Gate, the Main Channel had a flow of six knots and also had a sandy bottom. The swirling sand and the swaying of mines in the rapid current caused grinding on the mooring ropes where they attached to the cast-iron anchors resting on the sea floor. Several buoyant mines broke loose in this way, and depending on the current, floated north or south. The Mine Battalion recovered all of them. They found one buoyant mine adrift south of Mile Rock. As the mine crew dragged the errant sphere onto the beach, a large crowd of onlookers gathered to watch. "One of my sergeants decided to be funny," Frank Liwski recalled, "and said in a loud voice, 'I hope this mine doesn't explode'." The crowd disappeared as quickly as it had gathered.

"In order to prevent entry into the harbor of undetected surface vessels or submarines, mines in the North and South Channels were placed on contact power during periods of reduced visibility and after dark," stated the official history of Western Defense Command. The report claimed the mines were put on contact power beginning in May 1942 until the practice ceased a year later. There is doubt whether the minefields at the Golden Gate were so freely put in the armed position in times of low visibility, though the mines were designed with that option. The May 1942 Standing Operating Procedure listed this measure as a tactic to be imple-mented only under personal order of the harbor defense commander. In operation, a controlled minefield on contact power was dangerous to friendly vessels unfamiliar with the area. With six hundred volts going through the open circuit, a twenty-five degree tilt on a mine caused by a lost vessel bumping it in the fog, would close the electric circuit, exploding the mine.

Writing in the *Coast Artillery Journal*, Major Roger W. Chickering, an HDSF staff officer, described the wearisome routine of field duty at remote base-end stations, searchlights, and gun batteries in 1942. "The opportunities for recreation and entertainment are extremely limited," he wrote. After awhile, "a man's ingenuity in thinking up new ways to pass the time between hours of duty becomes sterile." After six months, the major continued, "morale takes a nose dive." To "give the troops from the outposts a complete change of scene," the Harbor Defenses devised the Special Training Program.

Two batteries at a time came from their field positions to live for one week in the permanent barracks at Fort Scott. "For the first time in months," Major Chickering wrote, "they can eat off china, take a good hot shower, buck up their equipment, and have full use of a complete day room." On the parade ground was set up a bayonet course and an obstacle course nicknamed "Little David."

"Little David," the Fort Scott obstacle course devised for the Special Training Program. (Presidio Army Museum)

The program was designed to get battery personnel, who had been living in far-flung positions remote from one another, to feel once again like a single unit. The coast artillerymen ran infantry drills; they practiced counter-infiltration and anti-paratroop tactics at a brisk trot with plenty of dropping to the prone position as riflemen. Of "Little David," the 150-yard obstacle course, only ten percent of several thousand men could successfully run its fifteen obstructions in under a minute. Four times over the week, formal retreat parades served to reacquaint the men with parade ground formations. For the sake of healthy competition, the best battery in each day's program won the colors. On Saturday, the troops went on ten-mile hikes over unfamiliar terrain. The day also included full field inspections when the men pitched tents and displayed equipment before regimental or HDSF Headquarters officers.

When coast artillerymen could not leave their alert stations, entertainment and post exchange services went to them. Two Fort Scott Post Exchange mobile canteens traveled to scattered outposts, bringing harbor defensemen the candy, sundries, and toilet articles of the typical PX. The rolling canteens visited most of the larger detachments five times a week, but the trucks seldom reached outlying positions in the East Bay and San Mateo County. The 6th Coast Artillery Band gave

concerts at some batteries. If the GI audience did not care for marches and classical music, the military band played "enough well arranged popular numbers to catch the fancy of even the most indifferent," wrote a Fort Scott battery commander.

By arrangement with the HDSF Special Services office, a Red Cross Cookie Brigade truck regularly visited the restricted military areas, bringing cakes, candy, cigarettes, and refreshments to the artillerymen on alert. "Today, beautiful USO and Red Cross girls bring cake to your door with a song," commented Colonel Usis to the post newspaper, as he compared his days at the Military Academy to the life of 1942 GI's. The Red Cross brought entertainers, usually local talent, for song, dance, and comedy. Sometimes, the entire cast from a city nightclub brought "a sparkling review of a gag-lined show" to the batteries. After the performance, the audience showed appreciation by inviting the cast to lunch at the battery mess. To amuse the men of the antiaircraft battery on Wolf Ridge, the Red Cross Cookie Brigade brought along Mr. Rhine, a San Francisco real estate salesman. As the AA men gathered , Mr. Rhine began "shuffling a deck of cards with one hand and producing a straight flush from every jeep's pocket on Wolf Ridge," wrote a correspondent from the *Golden Gate Guardian*. While the amazed gunners and all the senior officers of the 130th Coast Artillery Battalion looked on, the real estate man did "every trick in the book except climb a hypnotized rope and saw one of the pretty Red Cross ladies in half." "Black jack snorters and poker scions watched those five of a kind come up in Mr. Rhine's hand," reported the *Guardian*, "like a kid watches chocolate cookies on a pantry shelf."

USO-Camp Shows, Inc. made appearances at some batteries as well, but during 1942

Red Cross Cookie Brigade visits Battery D, 6th CA on Baker Beach. (Presidio Army Museum)

Singer Kitty Carlisle entertains harbor defenders at Fort Barry 6-inch gun battery. (Presidio Army Museum)

these visits were infrequent. The latest feature films played nightly at the Funston, Scott, Baker, and Barry post theatres. Dances for enlisted men were held as often as possible. For men going into town on pass, the Special Services officer distributed free tickets for radio shows produced by the Blue Network in San Francisco. Tickets for stage performances at the Curran Theatre and to sporting events such as football's East-West Shrine Game, became available in mid-1942 to HDSF men.

Friendly rivalries between harbor defense units provided good copy for the large sports section of the post newspaper. Batteries formed teams for hotly contested intramural games of baseball, basketball, and bowling. Special Services officers arranged "box tournaments" in these sports, with no set schedule except at the convenience of both batteries. Awards of show and coupon books went to outstanding players, while triumphant teams took plaques or trophy cups back to their batteries. Units adopted team names, such as the Fort Scott Gunners who were challenged for the title of "top keglers" by the Fort Baker Medics in a bowling tourney the *Golden Gate Guardian* predicted would "create smoke in HDSF circles." Fort Baker spent four hundred dollars to install automatic pin setters and recondition the post's two-lane bowling alley. A full-time attendant worked at the lanes, so the battery personnel and station hospital staff "can stay home and bowl at 10 cents a line." Human pin setters still arranged the pins at the Fort Scott lanes, charging four cents per set-up. "Teams are getting smart and are bringing their own pin setters," added the *Guardian* cheekily.

Battery B of the 6th Coast Artillery above Baker Beach demonstrated the coast artillerymen's ingenuity in making a home of their concrete emplacement. Under the cam-ouflage nets of the fifteen-foot by two-hundred foot concrete parade behind the 6-inch guns, the men played sports when the area was not used for official business. "Practically any unoccupied moment of the day finds a pitcher's duel raging along the battery parade," wrote battery commander Boyd Pulley. Several Battery B men played on the Fort Scott baseball team and honed their pitching arms during the long hours on alert. On one end of the parade, they installed a basketball hoop against the emplacement wall. On the two horseshoe courts at the other end, soldiers pitched horseshoes for bottles of soda pop thrown in as side-bets for high scores. In 1942, the Fort Scott library underwent reorganization and could not provide much service to individual units in the Harbor Defenses. Battery B owned some books, but not many. Several subscriptions to daily newspapers and magazines kept the men serving the 6-inch guns well informed.

During the early-war alert status at the Harbor Defenses, a formal ceremony of the command signified an important event. On July 13, 1942, officers and men of HDSF lined Kobbe Avenue, the main street leading out of Fort Scott. Brigadier General Edward A. Stockton, followed by his aide Major Jack Lehmkuhl, walked down Kobbe Avenue, shaking hands in farewell with every officer of the command. Then the two men, who were instrumental in the buildup of the Golden Gate defenses, boarded their command car and proceeded past as unit guidons dipped in salute. From there, General Stockton and his aide proceeded to Camp Wallace, Texas, an antiaircraft replacement training center. Brigadier General Ralph E. Haines arrived to take command of the Harbor Defenses two months later. Haines, a University of California graduate, had previously commanded the Harbor Defenses of Narragansett Bay, Rhode Island.

The reassuring sight of U.S. Navy blimps hovering lazily on submarine patrol greeted maritime traffic at the Golden Gate. At the beginning of the year, when the transport *Etolin* left port with the special detachment of the 56th Coast Artillery bound for Chile, a

blimp served as escort. Later, a Navy airship, the L-8, brought supplies onto the bomber-laden flight deck of the carrier *Hornet* as the vessel steamed into the open ocean just outside San Francisco. On June 29th, another blimp reported enemy mines in the water west of the Main Channel; a minesweep turned up nothing, but maritime traffic was halted for five hours.

On August 16, 1942, the airship L-8 rose from Treasure Island at 6:03 in the morning. Part of Navy Airship Squadron 32, the L-8 flew a routine patrol over the harbor entrance to the Farallones, then north to Point Reyes, where the blimp turned south to Montara, finally circling back over the Golden Gate Bridge. The L-8 had a crew of two that morning--a lieutenant junior grade and an ensign as observer. At 7:38 a.m., the airship crew radioed the presence of an oil slick four miles east of the Farallones. Wing Control at Moffett Field later grew concerned when no further reports came from the L-8; airships and scout planes took off to search for the missing blimp. At 11:15 a.m., bathers on the beach of the Olympic Club golf course saw the L-8 drift in from the ocean and hit the beach twice at Fort Funston, the second bounce shaking loose a depth bomb. Rising again, the lightened blimp drifted to its final rest on a residential street in Daly City, just south of San Francisco.

Captain Kenneth Cooper and other har-

(Above) Guidon bearers from HDSF units bid farewell to General Stockton and Major Lehmkuhl as they leave the command, July 13, 1942. (Presidio Army Museum)

(Right) November 1942 review of the trroops by new HDSF commander Brigadier General Ralph E. Haines at Fort Scott. Colonel Usis, 6th CA commander accompanies Haines. Battalion commanders John Schonher and Frank Liwski at end of line. (M.L. Usis)

bor defensemen at Fort Funston rushed over to the neighboring town to view the wreck. The Army spectators found local police and firemen at the cordoned crash site waiting for Navy investigators from Moffett Field. The gondola of the deflated L-8 rested against a telephone pole while the collapsed gasbag covered several parked cars on the street. There was no sign of the two-man crew. Inside the gondola, Navy men found the engine switches still on, the radios working and tuned to proper frequencies. On the cabin's window ledge rested an officer's cap, but two life belts were missing. Investigators took note of the gondola door, fastened in its open position, with a headset microphone dangling from a cord over the sill. The two crewmen were never found. The Navy could only conclude a freak accident had occurred in which one crewman followed the other out the door to their undetermined fates.

By August 1942, the war in the Pacific had tipped against the Japanese. American and Australian offensives on Guadalcanal and New Guinea signified the initiative now lay with the Allies. Despite the substantial movement of troops to the Southwest Pacific and to a lesser degree, to Great Britain and Iceland, until mid-1942, three-fourths of the Army's combat troops served in defense of the Western Hemisphere. Not until home territory was secure, did the War Department move its forces to Pacific and Atlantic war fronts.

Navy airship L-8 at crash site on Bellevue Avenue, Daly City. Two HDSF enlisted men stand at left sidewalk. (Presidio Army Museum)

Starting in the fall of 1942, the Army began removing harbor defense and antiaircraft artillery troops from positions along the East and West Coasts and sent them overseas. This was a calculated risk, the War Department realized, for even "moderately successful nuisance raids" by the enemy "might influence uninformed Congress and an uninformed press" to demand American forces be withdrawn for home defense. In November, the Operations Division of the Army weighed in with their opinion: "The existence of the defense commands creates in the public mind a false sense of security." Even small enemy nuisance raids would embarrass the Army. Citizens "will believe that the enemy's successes were made possible by military inefficiency. The Army will lose

HDSF families and members of HDSF headquarters staff observe troop review for General Haines. (M.L. Usis)

highly valuable public confidence." For this reason, the Operations Division urged abandonment of the defenses altogether. This never came to pass at the Golden Gate, but as the war progressed, the Harbor Defenses deployed additional guns to counter nuisance raids by aircraft, submarines, and motor torpedo boats.

The crabbing industry returned to Fisherman's Wharf on November 5th, as the federal government lifted restrictions on Italian aliens. Prominent San Francisco Italians lobbied the government for nearly a year before the ban gave way. This allowed "200 to 300 Italian fishermen to take out about 30 vessels," estimated the *San Francisco Chronicle*, "which have been tied up since a few days after Pearl Harbor." Now every man who put to sea with the crab fleet carried an identification card issued by the Captain of the Port; the boat skipper or fifty percent of the crew had to be U.S. citizens.

At Fort Cronkhite during the first Thanksgiving of the war, officers and their wives ate the traditional feast in the battery messhall with the enlisted men. "Messhall atmospheres were suddenly hushed," reported the *Golden Gate Guardian*, "table manners were amazingly super-duper." In San Francisco at the Thanksgiving Night Ball for Servicemen at the Civic Center, one harbor defense private reported, "entertainment delightful; orchestra tuneful; evening gowns entrancing; but only 2000 girls instead of the announced 6000." The private said more young ladies were needed, because there were "at least 10,000 sailors present."

What official ceremonies might have been held at the Harbor Defenses on the anniversary of the Pearl Harbor attack is not known, but December 7, 1942 was also the day renowned billiards champion Willie Hoppe showed off his skills before an enthusiastic audience of harbor defensemen at the Fort Scott gymnasium. The diminutive Hoppe, "demon of the green felt and chalked cue," played the towering commander of the 130th Coast Artillery Battalion, Lieutenant Colonel Ben Hawkins, who the *Golden Gate Guardian*

described as the "one officer in these defenses brave enough to challenge the champ in a three cushion exhibition game." Hawkins, a tall, barrel-chested National Guard antiaircraft artillery officer from Minnesota, owned a "first class billiard and bowling establishment in Red Wing, Minn." In that line of work, the colonel and Hoppe had met over the pool table before the war. Billiards is "a sensible sport for the soldier," the 130th CA Battalion commander told the *Guardian*. The game taught "coordination, patience, quick thinking." However, the colonel had never won a game against Willie Hoppe; and this match in front of the men of the Harbor Defenses was no upset; Hoppe bested Hawkins by a 50 to 16 score. "No excuses," the colonel said afterwards, "Willie wields a mean cue. But I can still trim him on the bowling alleys."

"Christmas Menu For Khakimen of the Harbor Defenses of San Francisco: Roast Turkey an' all the Trimmin's," read the boxed announcement encircled by a border of holly leaves in the December 25th issue of the post newspaper. Every battery in the command had their Christmas trees decorated by the Camp and Hospitality Council of the Red Cross, and the Cookie Brigade brought individual presents to all the men. Proclaiming "No White Christmas" at the defenses, the *Golden Gate Guardian* photographed a soldier patrolling a barbed wire-strewn beach at twilight: "On the Pacific sands of a San Francisco beach, a sentry walks his post. One of thousands, he foregoes a White Christmas, determined that NO ENEMY SHIPS SHALL PASS THROUGH THE GOLDEN GATE." Said HDSF commander Brigadier General Ralph E. Haines to his troops on the limited pass privileges granted during the holidays, "there can, of course, be no relaxation during the Christmas season." On a note reflecting the direction of the war by year's end, Colonel Felix Usis, now commanding the 6th Coast Artillery, predicted, "it is only a matter of time when our soldiers will try 'apfelstrudels' in Berlin and 'Sukiyaki' in Tokyo, American style."

Chapter 8:

War City on the Bay

"Come out here before it's too dark to observe the military secrets," said a friend beckoning John Dos Passos to the apartment balcony. The famous novelist walked out onto the terrace and saw before him the vast harbor under a dark sky. "Everything was drowned in transparent indigo," observed Dos Passos, as he took in the breathtaking view from the balcony of a friend's home on a San Francisco hillside. On the bay, ship convoys rode at anchor. "That's the Golden Gate," exclaimed Dos Passos' host, pointing to the harbor entrance. "That's the spout our supplies are pumped through into the Pacific. Even if we wanted to keep it secret we couldn't," confided the friend. "From Telegraph Hill a sightseer (or a spy) can look down on whatever units . . . are in the harbor," claimed *Life* magazine in 1943, "San Francisco is once again the greatest Western port, the key to Pacific communications."

Over 1.6 million Army personnel and twenty-three million tons of materiel sailed out the Golden Gate in World War II. The bay waters and the surrounding shores became a vast staging ground. Not only were Navy fa-

Troops wait out the rain at Pier 15 on the Embarcadero as taken over by U.S. Army Transportation Corps. (San Francisco Archives, S.F. Public Library)

cilities numerous, the U.S. Army operated a network of transit installations on the bay, collectively called the San Francisco Port of Embarkation. The four-mile length of the city's Embarcadero served only military purposes now. Over 120 piers in the East Bay, encompassing the Oakland Army Base, the Alameda and Richmond Piers, and the Emeryville Ordnance Shops, funneled Army troops and supplies onto ships and planes bound for the

July 20, 1942: 387th Quartermaster Battalion arrives by horse trailer at Pier 45 to board SS Boschfontain. (Presidio Army Museum)

housed motor inspection facilities which gave military vehicles in transit a final check before loading them on ships. Fort Mason was dubbed the "home base of the troops overseas" because its Army postal operation funneled mail to and from GI's serving in Asia and the Pacific. "This port has one main commodity to send abroad," declared the *New York Times Magazine*. "It is exporting war."

From the balcony of his friend's home, author John Dos Passos not only saw freighters "being loaded and unloaded clear round the clock," but looking past the hoists and cranes along the Embarcadero, he noted that "a shipyard glowed like a forest fire" across the bay. The Mare Island yard on the north shore of San Pablo Bay built scores of Navy ships and submarines. Mare Island assembled new destroyer escorts with prefabricated sections brought in from as far away as Denver, Colorado. Warships damaged in battle were repaired and refitted here as well. In San Francisco, the Navy had a major repair base with huge drydocks at Hunters Point. And the Bethlehem Steel shipyards, formerly the old Union Iron Works, long active as a Pacific coast warship producer, repaired and refitted more ships than any other privately owned yard in the nation. But the majority of vessels produced in the Bay Area came down the ways at Marinship in Sausalito and Kaiser Shipyards in Richmond. The two yards produced over one thousand vessels, mainly transports. At their peak, Kaiser and Marinship employed about ninety thousand workers.

Pacific. Situated on the upper bay, through the Carquinez Straits and the San Joaquin River leading to the delta, Army ports like the Benicia Arsenal, Camp Stoneman troop staging area, and the Stockton Piers seventy miles east of San Francisco, played their roles in the vast logistical war waged at the Golden Gate.

At the heart of the San Francisco Port of Embarkation was Fort Mason, a Transportation Corps post of the Army Service Forces. Troops and supplies came by rail from interior zones of the country, then processed through Fort Mason for shipment overseas. Aside from docks and waterfront terminals, Fort Mason

In 1943, six hundred members of the Women's Army Corps were stationed at San Francisco Port of Embarkation, Fort Mason. These WAC's are participating in flag retreat ceremony. (San Francisco Archives, S.F. Public Library)

(Top Right) Small warships, transports, and submarines at Bay Area shipyard, possibly Hunters Point. (Presidio Army Museum) (Below Right) Line of buses deliver defense workers to their shift at Mare Island Naval Shipyard. (Presidio Army Museum)

"San Francisco has not been a really peaceful place" since the Spaniards sent an expedition north and discovered a "fabled bay that opened from the Pacific between two rocky headlands," explained *Life* magazine in 1943. After a history of "gold rush, booms, brawls, violence and vigilantes," San Francisco felt smug after 1906 and the Great War, "until Southern California ports threatened its shipping supremacy. Then this war came to disturb the city again and take away whatever peace it thought it had." Amid anchored convoys awaiting sailing orders in the bay, tugs, barges, minesweepers, "bobtailed, oddly contoured craft, hybrids of wartime needs," went about their mundane business. A writer for *Travel* magazine described the entrance to the submarine net, portraying the gate vessels as "two black watch dogs which hold the sub nets, smoke curling from their stacks." The writer hinted of silent warships at rest in the harbor. "Everyone knows--they're not supposed to but they do--that on the darkened bay a monstrous convoy is in the making."

Because of the coastal defenses, San Francisco's famed 49-Mile Drive was off-limits to touring motorists. "You go by way of town now," disclosed *National Geographic*, "perhaps past Sea Cliff with its beautiful homes boarded up or blacked out." The blackout dimmed such coastal attractions as the Cliff House where author William Saroyan once wrote that he could "sit at a table for a cup of coffee and from high up look out at the great, magnificent, lonely, lovely Pacific." Now the Cliff House windows were blacked out at night and one could not see the crashing waves on Seal Rocks below. Along Ocean Beach, at the Playland amusement park, the Army dim-out rendered the rides and midway "ghostly in their abandonment," *National Geographic* opined, "and still worse, the huge Ferris wheel moves around silently without lights." Black paint covered tops and seaward faces of glass-globed street lamps in the city's seaside districts. Sodium lights with dimout shades added their diffused orange glow. "There are no practice blackouts in San Francisco," revealed the *Geographic*, "when the sirens wail, it means 'Unidentified Planes!'---and business."

In the wartime city, men and women in military uniform swarmed abundantly in public places. In restaurants, officers eating a last stateside meal, carried their kits "which can only be for overseas duty," surmised one reporter, "but you would not suspect it was a farewell party to watch their faces." The downtown streets teemed with military people, especially Navy ones, noted *Life*, "spending money on their last soda or last drink or last date, full of the wonderful happy-sad feeling of being off to war." On a less lofty aside, the magazine added, "The boys have no trouble, however, picking up 'sea gulls' who work streets."

Among the civilian canteens that offered free or inexpensive distractions to servicemen in the city, the newest in 1943 was the Pepsi Cola Center. For the benefit of all "men and women in the uniform of the United Nations," Pepsi Cola, in cooperation with the Hospitality House Committee, opened the center in an eight-story building at 948 Market Street in downtown San Francisco. Dedication ceremonies took place on March 6, 1943, presided by Mayor Angelo Rossi and soft drink company president Walter S. Mack. Local military officials, including General Haines of the Harbor Defenses, attended the dedication as invited guests. After the speeches, all were treated to "Pepsi-Cola and other refreshments on the house." Guests toured the checkrooms, showers, dressing rooms, and telephone facilities. For servicewomen, the center had two special rooms, noted the *Chronicle*: "The Eleanor Roosevelt lounge and the Madame

Co-eds pose atop air raid siren at City College of San Francisco, August 27, 1943. (San Francisco Archives, S.F. Public Library)

Chiang Kai-Shek parlor--for the ladies."

Twenty days later, on March 26th, Madame Chiang Kai-Shek arrived to adoring fanfare in the bay city. Enormous popularity attended the Wellesley-educated Madame Chiang, wife of Generalissimo Chiang Kai-Shek, leader of China's Nationalist government. A celebrity in her own right, Madame Chiang had been *Time* magazine's Woman of the Year. She was idolized in America as a symbol of the Westernized, but still mysterious Orient. Her visit to San Francisco during a lengthy stay in the United States was the crowning jewel of the local social season. City and military dignitaries greeted her arrival at the Embarcadero and gave a parade in her honor at the Civic Center. The Chamber of Commerce hosted a Palace Hotel banquet that evening for their very distinguished visitor, with California Governor Earl Warren, Mayor Rossi, and General DeWitt among the VIP guests. On Saturday night, with an Army regimental band providing music and with Governor Warren and Mayor Rossi making presentations, China's "First Lady" delivered a speech at the Civic Center Auditorium. The next morning, final ceremonies took Madame Chiang to Chinatown. At St. Mary's Square, she laid a wreath of bows and gardenias at the foot of the steel and concrete statue of Dr. Sun Yat-Sen, founder of modern China. Said the *Chronicle* in the typical journalistic prose accorded Madame Chiang at every step of her U.S. tour, "She tottered a brief instant and then, her

San Francisco downtown at Market and Jones Streets during dim-out on November 21, 1943. (San Francisco Archives, S.F. Public Library)

Madame Chiang Kai-shek during ceremonies at St. Mary's Square, Chinatown on Sunday, March 28, 1943. (R. Gyn)

face an ivory mask, she descended the sloping greensward to stand at the base of the gleaming image of China's George Washington."

Press plaudits for the Golden Gate harbor defenders were no less stinting of enthusiasm, but military secrecy prevented reporters from revealing more than colorful descriptions. La Verne Bradley of *National Geographic* described "the magnitude of San Francisco's Harbor Defenses" in March 1943. On a nighttime tour, HDSF officers escorted Bradley past a succession of security check points, finally reaching a "strange troglodyte world of life underground," filled with barracks, offices, and store rooms. The writer crawled through "damp 3-foot square tunnels revetted and lined with burlap." The escorted tour came upon a command post "in a dugout no bigger than a dinette," where the men on duty managed to set up shop with "desks, bunks, a complicated communications board, and powerful telescopic equipment." Impressed by what was shown, Bradley proclaimed, "The city's magnificent, wave-washed Golden Gate is the most strongly fortified spot in America." Strongly fortified perhaps, but according to the Army's Deputy Chief of Staff in March, radar and aircraft now eclipsed mines and seacoast artillery in coastal defense. Barring the remote possibility of carrier raids, the West Coast was secure, the Deputy Chief thought, with radar and bombing planes replacing "to a large extent our present outmoded system of coast artillery defense."

Operating between the rosy publicity of *National Geographic* and the talk of obsolescence fostered by the Deputy Chief of Staff, harbor defensemen diligently maintained watch at the Golden Gate. At Fort Barry, a road leading past the old dirigible hangar ascended the hill to a row of four 6-inch guns shared by Batteries G and H of the 6th Coast Artillery. In the guard shack at the foot of the hill, Battery H installed a "squawk-box" intercom so the

guard could warn the hilltop defenders of vehicles headed their way. A receiving intercom went into the battery commander's station atop the emplacement. When inspections were imminent, the men listened intently for the guard below to announce: "Brass coming."'

During the early part of 1943, Colonel Felix Usis, as regimental commander, made frequent inspections of the batteries. The West Pointer had a reputation for being "a very particular inspector," to quote Daniel Cook, commanding Battery H. Next door, Battery G had a messhall built into the hill near the emplacement. Their first sergeant threw his empty liquor bottles under a certain floorboard of the building. Colonel Usis inspected the messhall, looking closely at the dishes and utensils, unable to find fault with anything. Then with practiced ease, he reached down and pulled up the wooden floorboard, uncovering the sergeant's cache of empty liquor bottles. The colonel's responding words, recalled Daniel Cook, were "really rough." But thorough inspections kept the batteries alert. Usis' nightly forays turned up lax sentries reading magazines at their posts. "I took it seriously," said Usis of his activities, "I worked at it, inspecting every night between two and four in the morning."

By 1943, Japanese defeats and the U.S. Navy's rising strength in the Pacific reduced the possibility of enemy capital ships challenging seacoast artillery off the West

Coast. The War Department concluded the most likely threat would now be enemy motor torpedo boats making a surprise dash into the harbor. Tests conducted at Fort Monroe's Coast Artillery School found the 90mm antiaircraft gun, because of its quick traverse and rapid rate of fire, the best existing weapon against speed boats. But antiaircraft units had priority on all 90mm guns then being manufactured. To fill the gap, HDSF used their existing 155mm batteries and also moved some 3-inch seacoast guns to temporary positions at Kirby Beach. A version of the 90mm gun with protective shield became available in 1943 for seacoast defense and HDSF emplaced the new gun, usually in tandem with smaller 37mm weapons, at numerous shoreline locations. On the Marin side, one such combination was set up at Kirby Beach. The Army also sited two 37mm weapons below the Point Bonita lighthouse. At Fort Baker, a 37mm weapon on the mine wharf and another on Point Cavallo could fire on any motor torpedo boats that got past the bridge. On the San Francisco side of the defenses, 90mm seacoast batteries were emplaced at Baker Beach and Lands End. Detached platoons from existing units of the Harbor Defenses manned the new positions.

Even the pre-Civil War battlements of Fort Point under the archway of the Golden Gate Bridge saw duty in the newest defenses of the waterway. Captain Harry Payne of the ar-

tillery engineers cleaned out the old fort and prepared positions for anti-motor torpedo boat (AMTB) defenses. To the right of the sortie gate, at the top of the cast-iron staircase, Payne had barracks built, consisting of quarters, kitchen, showers, and latrines. In some of the old galleries, he established an engineer supply dump to store sandbags and camouflage netting. On the fort's top deck, engineers poured concrete foundations on the seaward side and installed two 3-inch guns from Kirby Beach, naming the emplacement Battery Point. Battery Gate, a pair of 3-inch guns on the top tier's west side, pointed into the bay, its mission to fire on vessels making for the submarine net. The 3-inch guns had a high muzzle velocity that fired a fifteen-pound projectile on a flat trajectory. At four to five thousand yards, if the guns were elevated an extra mil, the shot traveled an additional eight hundred yards. When the 3-inchers fired, "the crack was deafening," wrote a battery commander, "amplified by the sounding box of the old fort's open parade behind them and the deck of the bridge above them."

To exercise the new rapid-fire batteries, Colonel Usis ordered special targets built. He "believes the big time gunners in these fortifications need something a bit tougher to shoot at than a slow-moving pyramidal target," to quote the *Golden Gate Guardian*. Captain M.L. Berry, the boat operations expert at HDSF, scrounged Navy salvage yards in the bay and found aircraft pontoons from planes destroyed in the Pearl Harbor attack. The floats were patched up and turned into a "snappily fashioned blitz target" towed by speed boat at forty knots. Speed craft built specifically for target practice, thirty-five foot JR-boats soon came into service with the Coast Artillery. These wooden, two-man boats could also be controlled by

HDSF built high-speed targets for practice firing of AMTB batteries. Pontoons with patched holes came from Navy planes destroyed during Pearl Harbor attack. (Presidio Army Museum)

USAMP Horace F. Spurgin at Sausalito dock. (R. Palihnich)

radio. Powered by a 550-horsepower gasoline engine, "it went forty-five knots--fastest thing on water at that time," Usis recalled. "They were built as targets to shoot at, knowing that no one would ever hit them."

At Marietta Manufacturing of Point Pleasant, West Virginia, ship builders put final touches on the last vessels of a new Army mineplanter class. "While having beautiful lines," the new design "is of a decidedly competent character for the work to which these vessels will be assigned," wrote the *Coast Artillery Journal*. The new 189-foot vessels of welded steel construction carried three complete mine groups; two on deck and a third group in the hold. Mine davit electric hoists lifted two tons at the push of a button. For cable laying operations, a steam-driven reel mounted on the forecastle head handled fifty tons of cable. The ship's galley, of all-stainless steel construction, was "a mess sergeant's dream." Propelled by two steam uniflow engines, the new planters attained 13.5 knots. One of the vessels from this class, the USAMP *General Samuel M. Mills*, had already been built and delivered to the San Francisco defenses in 1942.

In early 1943, the fourteenth mineplanter of this class of sixteen vessels, the USAMP *Colonel Horace F. Spurgin*, was ready to leave the builder's yard when Rudy Palih-nich, a newly commissioned junior engineering officer, came aboard. He started the war an enlisted man on the Boston mineplanter *General Absalom Baird*, and subsequently made sergeant, instructing engine room trainees. When his promotion to junior warrant officer came through, Palihnich joined the new planter at the Point Pleasant, West Virginia shipyard. From there began US-AMP *Spurgin's* meandering journey to the Golden Gate.

The mineplanter sailed west on the Ohio River. The shipbuilder had omitted the planter's two yardarms to allow the vessel to go under bridges during normal water levels. But in 1943, the Ohio River was heavily swollen by spring rains. At Cincinnati, Ohio, the *Spurgin* halted, unable to go under a bridge because the river was too high. Twenty days later, the water level subsided, and the *Spurgin* went through. At Louisville, Kentucky, the ship again encountered high waters and a low bridge. The mineplanter waited three days for the river level to drop. Days later, reaching Cairo at the southern tip of Illinois, the incident was repeated a third time; but once the Ohio River joined the wide Mississippi, the *Spurgin* had clear sailing to New Orleans. In that port, two yardarms were installed, and a 75mm field piece of First World War vintage was mounted on board to supplement the vessel's .50 caliber machine guns.

From New Orleans, the *Spurgin* proceeded south to the Panama Canal. Trying the gun on the open sea, the crew discovered the 75mm gun to "be as useless as useless could be." In comparison to the ship's speed, the old field piece had slow elevation and traverse. For Junior Warrant Officer Palihnich, "it was nothing more than a fake gun." At Panama, the San Francisco-bound planter was held up for a final time. Because the local mine defenses lacked enough planters, the *Spurgin* and its crew stayed in Panama for six months, working the minefields on both sides of the canal.

At the Golden Gate, a small wooden freighter had somehow broken apart in the Main Channel on April 5, 1943. While maritime traffic switched to the North Channel, Lieutenant Colonel Frank Liwski, the Mine Groupment commander, sailed with the mineplanter *Niles* to the stricken freighter. After placing a buoyant mine next to the freighter, the *Niles* drew away five hundred yards. From that distance, the mine crew detonated the mine with a storage battery. The explosion "blew the freighter to pieces and cleared the channel." Another minefield mishap occurred when a freighter became tangled on the cable of a buoyant mine. Again, the *Niles* went to the rescue. The planter crew grappled for, and located the line. As the cable was held back, the freighter reversed its propeller and cleared the attached mine. The crew hoisted the loose buoyant mine aboard the *Niles* and brought it back to port.

By the middle of the war, the buoyant mine's defects had become apparent. Deep-draft vessels hit the mines floating so close to the surface. Powerful currents, like those at the Golden Gate, broke mines loose from their moorings. On the East Coast, German submarines sowed their own mines near American minefields, and the minesweeping operations that ensued cleared enemy, as well as friendly mines. Then too, submarines, with their narrow hull widths, could pass through the one hundred-foot interval between buoyant mines without touching the spheres. The buoyant mine's drawbacks were known to the Army before the war. Since May 1941, development moved ahead on a new mine that

solved these problems.

When the new M3A1 ground mine came to San Francisco in mid-1943, Lieutenant Colonel Liwski took General Haines and other officers aboard the *Niles* to a location just south of the Main Channel to test the weapon. The M3A1 was a squat, cylindrical capsule seventy-two inches tall and ninety inches in diameter. Three hundred pounds of TNT, 1500 pounds of weight, and the detonating mechanism were packed into the flat-bottomed mine case which rested on the sea floor down to depths of one hundred feet. Unlike the floating buoyant type mines, the ground mines could not be swept by minesweepers. The heavy weight, flat-bottomed design, and low center of gravity suited this new mine for the rough currents at San Francisco. The magnetic-electric arming device within the mine sensed the magnetic field of an approaching vessel up to one hundred feet away, activating lights in the mine casemate. With General Haines and other officers looking on, the test mine was lowered into the water. When the *Niles* had retreated a safe distance, Liwski ordered the M3A1 exploded "to see what would happen." The detonated mine "threw up a huge column of water," and everyone aboard was satisfied. Before long, the Mine Battalion replanted all the fields with M3A1 ground mines in the same semicircular pattern as the previous buoyant mines. The ground mines were planted in groups of thirteen. The mine command instituted a new planting procedure; the observing stations from shore sighted through their range instruments and guided the mineplanter by radio to the exact location for dropping each mine.

If mine warfare devices fared well in the extreme underwater conditions of the Golden Gate, they could survive anything. So went the reasoning that sent most of the Army's experimental mine gear out to the San Francisco defenses for a trial run. Soon after the establishment of ground mines, Bell Laboratories came to HDSF with an underwater sound detection system it had developed. With the aid of the mine command, Bell technicians placed thirteen underwater microphones in front of an outer group of thirteen mines. Lead

(Right) HDSF officers aboard mineplanter Niles to test new M3Al ground mine. Colonel Usis and Lieutenant Colonel Liwski second and third from left. General Haines third from right. At right edge is Major Fred C. Weyand, HDSF adjutant, later to become Army Chief of Staff.
(Below) HDSF commander Brigadier General Ralph E. Haines aboard Niles at Horseshoe Cove, Fort Baker. Note north anchorage of bridge in background. (Presidio Army Museum)

cable connected the microphones to the mine casemate, where the microphones were hooked up to a special panel with thirteen rows of lights, each row representing one mine. The lights acted as an audiometer, visually indicating the distance of a target by the strength of the sound-levels picked up on the microphones. An amplifier brought the actual engine noise of the target into the casemate. When a ship approached, the casemate operator decreased the sound-level so that only the microphone closest to the ship would detect any sound and activate only the lights for that mine. "It worked very nicely," recalled Frank Liwski, the Mine Groupment commander. With a range of five hundred feet to two miles depending on hydrographic conditions, the Bell detector reported eighty-seven out of ninety-two submarine test crossings. As a boon to Army-Navy relations in defending the Golden Gate, the microphones enabled the mine casemate to warn Navy picket ships of approaching vessels in low-visibility and what type of vessels they were. The device tested at San Francisco was standardized in July 1943 as the audio detection system MI, and used till war's end.

USAMP *Horace F. Spurgin* would convert to a cable-layer, heard the crew, as the new mineplanter sailed into San Francisco Bay after six months in Panama. But "it seemed that nobody knew anything about us," said junior engineering officer Rudy Palihnich. A sister ship, the *Samuel M. Miles* was already with the Defenses, and together with the venerable *Niles*, the two planters easily handled routine

mine duties once the fevered activity of the early war days had passed. When Western Defense Command desired one of Lieutenant Colonel Liwski's mineplanters as a cable vessel, the Mine Groupment commander thought the oldest ship was the most expendable. "The *Niles* was a little bit top-heavy," reasoned Liwski, "whereas the *Spurgin* was smoother running." He gave Western Defense Command the *Niles*, but exchanged skippers of the two planters, keeping Chief Warrant Officer Richard Carlsen with the Harbor Defenses---"For which the Department of the Army got a little bit mad at me," Liwski admitted later.

Since the founding of the Marine Repair Shop at Fort Baker the previous year, HDSF sought a larger and better facility for maintaining the mine flotilla. Major Frederick Insinger, head of the Post Quartermaster at Fort Scott secured funds for shop improvements. By the summer of 1943, the expanded Marine Repair Shop was finished and awaiting formal dedication by General Haines. The boatyard now had two launchways. Beside the original six-ton way, a new launchway, 240-feet long with a one hundred-ton capacity, had been constructed. The new launchways accommodated all but the large mineplanters, which continued to have their hulls scraped at commercial drydocks. To keep the undertows of the Golden Gate from damaging the ways and docks, a breakwater of rock and landfill was built at the entrance to Horseshoe Cove. Because of wartime priorities, modern repair equipment could not be gotten, so shop foreman Harry Plummer did the next best thing. At salvage bases in Oakland, Plummer found damaged or abandoned equipment from Pacific war zones. His staff repaired them, "and today their shops house some of the best marine repair tools in the Army," boasted the *Golden Gate Guardian*. The repair shop staff had increased to eleven civilian employees, including several mechanics, boatwrights, and pipefitters. A large sign hung over the newly completed yard reading, "Property of the Post Quartermaster." The night before General Haines' dedication of the new facility, without telling the Post Quartermaster, the mine command added their own sign directly under the first one: "Subsidiary of the Harbor Defenses of San Francisco."

Second Lieutenant Leo Murphy, the new Special Services officer at Fort Scott, sat munching doughnuts and drinking coffee in the post exchange. A San Franciscan, Murphy joined the Harbor Defenses only recently and felt left out of the circle of officers who had been with the organization for some time. How was he going to "get anywhere with the headquarters?" Lieutenant Murphy wondered. Then he heard a voice behind him exclaim, "I'm so sick and tired of the doughnuts we're having." Murphy looked around and saw General Haines telling Colonel LaFrenz, "I just wish we could get a good doughnut." This gave the new Special Services officer an idea.

Later that day, Murphy called LaFrenz and invited him to the Special Services building the next morning for coffee. Murphy asked LaFrenz to bring the general along. Next morning, Murphy bought a batch of "the best doughnuts around" from a Marina district bakery, and with a big pot of fresh coffee, he set up for business in the Special Services building. "This is great," said General Haines upon seeing Murphy's handiwork. "I want you to have this for me every morning." For the rest of the day, the Special Services lieutenant took calls "from all the other brass," who asked to be included in the new coffee and doughnuts routine with the harbor defense commander. This was Murphy's big break, an acceptance into the daily life and hierarchy of HDSF. Every morning from then on, over a dozen top officers gathered over the coffee service he had initiated. To quote Leo Murphy later, "It shows you how breaks get you into a place."

The men that fired the big 16-inch guns at Funston had a popular battery mess. Just inside the security fence gate, Battery C of the 6th Coast Artillery burrowed a messhall into the hillside. A tree grew through the roof. Not wanting to destroy the tree, the men had built the kitchen around the trunk. The underground messhall resembled a diner accommodating thirty

The large oakwood grill pit in Battery C kitchen. (L. Kanof)

(Right) Uphill ramp leading to a Devils Slide base-end station of Funston 16-inch battery. (L. Kanof)
(Below) Station atop ramp belonged to Battery C, 6th Coast Artillery. Many steel-domed stations at HDSF were camouflaged with rock to break their outlines. (L. Kanof)

or so men on four-man tables, with the officers' mess in the kitchen. The mess sergeant wanted to become a baker after the war, so he spent his off-duty time on the night shift at a San Francisco bakery. Battery C breakfast featured a variety of baked goods the mess sergeant brought back from his night work. A Chinese recruit from San Francisco was one of the battery cooks. One day a week, the messhall served a Chinese meal with locally purchased ingredients. Wednesday lunch consisted of grilled steak, and Sunday supper featured cold cuts and beer.

Forest rangers allowed the Battery C observation crew stationed near Mount Tamalpais to shoot deer. A steady supply of deer carcasses hung in the battery's walk-in reefers on the lower post at Funston. At the underground messhall, Livermore Valley oak wood fed the flame of an eight-foot long grill pit in the kitchen. On Wednesday nights, venison roasted over the pit. Before long, officers and men from other units of the Harbor Defenses "just happened to drop by" at dinner time. It seemed to Battery C range officer Lee Kanof that "every Wednesday, half the harbor defense ate in our messhall." Battery C commander Kenneth Cooper finally thwarted the uninvited guests by ordering Vienna sausage served on two Wednesdays in a row, and the extraneous diners "got the hint." From then on, "we only had those people we invited," Kanof recalled.

Battery C's outlying observation crews loved their duty which entitled them to one and one-half rations in cash. The twenty men on observation details pooled the money together, decided what food they wanted, and had the mess sergeant make the purchases.

The crews pocketed the remaining cash, and the mess sergeant got his cut as incentive for economical shopping. The food was delivered daily to each distant observation station, where the men did their own cooking on camping stoves. The battery range officer tried to inspect each crew and station every other day, "just to check if they were awake."

When Lieutenant Lee Kanof's friend, a naval reserve officer, came to port every three months, the two men visited the Bethlehem shipyards where spacious ocean liners were being converted into troopships. Workers pulled rugs, berths, and luxurious fittings out of the passenger liners, and left them on the dock. Kanof got permission for his battery to haul away items they could use at Fort Funston. Battery C put the booty to comfortable use in the tunnel between their 16-inch guns. They installed thick rugs and wide, soft beds which made the concrete corridor more livable. The officers might even have been

Interior of Battery C station at Devils Slide with M1 Depression Position Finder at the view slit. (L. Kanof)

gun. The first ranging salvo went off 4.23 minutes after "commence firing" was ordered. After several rounds were fired, the target's tow line broke. The battery postponed firing. Practice continued to conclusion the following day. Firing results were roughly similar to Battery C's excellent effort the year before--but with a new crew, it took more rounds to range in consistently on the target. In July, Captain Cooper, the battery commander, was notified Battery C would use radar in a target practice on October 5th. But the Funston 16-inch guns would not be the first at HDSF to fire by radar. That honor went the 6-inch battery on Baker Beach.

Before the war, the Coast Artillery asked the Signal Corps to develop radar as gun-laying equipment for seacoast armament. The Signal Corps' resulting effort was the SCR-296, a radar service-tested and ready for Coast Artillery use by late 1941. The unit was very sensitive; even ocean waves registered on the radar screen, so an actual target had to be very large and distinct on the water's surface. The SCR-296 determined range and direction of the target and fed the information directly to the guns' pointer dials, making the job of range-finding nearly automatic. Initially, the Coast Artillery ordered twenty sets. After the beginning of hostilities, with the War Department fearing attacks on American harbors by "forays of deadly torpedo boats or submarines," the order for the SCR-296 was increased to 176 sets. Deliveries of the new radar began slowly. The San Francisco defenses received their first sets in the spring of 1943.

"We didn't call it radar. We called it special equipment," revealed Charles Sullivan, a member of the first SCR-296 training class at the Signal Corps School at Camp Murphy, Florida in late 1942. Radar was new and top-secret. When officers took the radar course at the Coast Artillery School in Fort Monroe, Virginia, they could not bring pens or pencils to class. Sergeant Sullivan worked for the HDSF

envious of the enlisted men. Officers slept in a room adjacent to the emplacement's four diesel generators with two of the generator exhaust fans in the officers' quarters. "Needless to say," remembered Lee Kanof, "uninterrupted sleep was a rarity."

Before the war, the Army allowed the city of San Francisco to build a police department pistol range at Fort Funston. When the war made the fort a restricted zone, the pistol range and its adjoining clubhouse could not be used by the police. Battery C converted the abandoned building, which resembled a hunting lodge, into a dayroom. The battery hosted dances there once a month and invited women from the military services and civic groups. Because the alert status of the defenses often prevented the men from going on pass to the bright lights of town so visible from the fort, the clubhouse dances lifted battery morale.

For many of the men, their stay at Battery C ended in April 1943 with routine mass transfers from the unit five days before a scheduled target practice with the 16-inch guns. Then followed nine weeks of working up a new crew before the group commander felt the battery was ready for target practice. Once again, the battery fired excaliber 75mm guns to give observation crews experience in tracking and adjusting on towed targets. June 29th became the new date of Battery C's target shoot. With the "warming up effect" discounted by experience in the previous year's practice, the battery fired two sensing rounds from each 16-inch gun instead of all four rounds from one

Radar Officer, Major Charles Ottinger in the Harbor Defense Headquarters building at Fort Scott. Five hundred feet north of Battery Chamberlin on Baker Beach, HDSF radar technicians installed the first SCR-296 set. The radar antenna, hidden in a dummy water tower, rose twenty-five feet above the trees on a sandy hill, with power generator and operating room next to it. The station had one or two officers, a maintenance staff sergeant, an operations sergeant, and several radar operators. Other than the crew, few people had clearance to enter the installation. Even Colonel Usis, whose men guarded the station, could not enter the operating room. But under the escort of General Haines, Usis went in once and saw the blips moving on the radar screen.

The radar operators were attached to Battery D, 6th Coast Artillery, the outfit firing the 6-inch guns for HDSF's first radar-guided target shoot. Battery D's first sergeant, a career soldier named Harry Wright, did not like having special duty personnel assigned to his battery. The radar men consumed food and supplies, but the senior NCO could not put them on any duties. Sergeant Wright considered the attached radar crew a drain to the unit---until the day of the radar-guided target practice. At Treasure Island, Sergeant Charles Sullivan supervised construction of a big metal chicken wire target mounted on a raft. The target had to be metal so it would register on radar. The Navy brought the completed raft to Fort Scott. An HDSF mineplanter towed the metal target for the firing of the radar-directed 6-inch guns at Baker Beach. "We really knocked that target all to hell," recalled Sullivan of the practice outcome. Radar had shown what it could do. Now First Sergeant Harry Wright could not help beaming at the specialists in his care, proudly calling the radar men, "my boys, my boys."

By mid-1943, ten SCR-296 radar installations served the seacoast armament at the Harbor Defenses. Artillery engineers erected them on Army property where observation stations existed. In the north, this included Wildcat Ridge, Bolinas Point, and Hill 640 above Stinson Beach. The SCR-296 also stood at Fort Cronkhite on Wolf Ridge and behind the Mine Groupment Command Post at Point Bon-ita. On the San Francisco shore, radar towers were positioned at Baker Beach and Fort Funston. Supposedly, General George C. Marshall, the Army Chief of Staff, climbed to the top of the one-hundred foot SCR-296 tower at Fort Miley, followed by two radar sergeants and "nine thousand officers," while a visiting Latin American general looked on from the ground. Further south, HDSF sited radar stations at Devils Slide, Milagra Knob, and Pillar Point, the last location being a tip of high ground jutting into the northern end of Half Moon Bay. The Harbor Defenses also used the long-range SCR-532, an early detection radar which provided general surveillance of maritime traffic. For coverage, two of these units sufficed, one at Pillar Point and the other at Fort Cronkhite.

In preparation for the upcoming radar-directed target shoot of the Funston 16-inch guns, battery commander Captain Kenneth Cooper wrote a letter on July 26th to the Commanding General, HDSF. Citing his long experience with gunnery and fire control at Battery C, Cooper expressed a desire to learn more about gunlaying radar: "It is felt that observation of these new position finding instruments in action would be beneficial," he wrote. Cooper requested permission to "make an inspection tour of the coastal defenses of England. The primary purpose of such an inspection would be to study the tactical and technical employment of radars and computors [sic] with . . . major caliber weapons." The enterprising Captain Cooper felt the trip could be made easily "by Army plane." "If granted," he added, "it is believed that this inspection tour will be for the benefit of the government." In a first indorsement dated August 5th, Lieutenant Colonel Richard Moorman, now commanding the 2nd Battalion of the 18th Coast Artillery at Funston, added his approval of Cooper's plan. "This officer is a well-informed man," wrote Moorman. "He will gain much valuable experience for future instruction purposes." Then the letter went through channels to Captain Cooper's own regimental commander, Colonel J.C. Hutson. The new CO of the 6th Coast Artillery was hardly enthused by the proposed trip. "Considering background of this officer it is not believed that sufficient benefit would be derived by the government to warrant such a tour as requested," Hutson replied. General Haines agreed, and through Colonel LaFrenz, the HDSF commander turned down Cooper's British trip on August 9th.

A blind radar firing of the Funston 16-inch battery did occur later in the war. New synchronous motor-controlled dials were added to the 16-inch battery's gunlaying equipment. The range settings determined by radar were transmitted electrically to the gun dials where the crew adjusted azimuth and elevation by matching pointers. This eliminated the older method of fire control in which aiming data was transmitted by telephone and usable only on periodic bell signals. The guns could now be fired when ready, and not be required to wait for the next ring of the bell . The day of the Funston 16-inch practice with radar was foggy with no seaward visibility. The weather would not affect accuracy of the firing since radar determined range to the target. But the fog obscured the mineplanter towing the practice target, and the safety officer wanted to maintain a safe angle of firing between the flight of the projectile, the towline, and the towing vessel. As usual, the target tug sailed right to left through the battery's field of fire. When the guns fired dead ahead, a round landing beyond the target would not put the towing vessel in danger. But as the guns traversed to their extreme left to fire on a target moving away, a shot beyond the target brought a splash down closer to the towline or the towing vessel. Even if the round did not land beyond the target, a ricochet on the water might skip dangerously close to the vessel. In fog, the desired safe angle was hard to monitor. On this particular radar-guided practice, Group Commander John Schonher acted as safety officer. He recalled the splash of one 16-inch round "was uncomfortably close to an unsafe angle" but not close enough to be dangerous to the towing vessel. The captain of the mineplanter towing the target felt otherwise, and protested. "Fortunately," Schonher remembered, "it was the last round to be fired after a short delay in the firing practice."

After college ROTC at the University of San Francisco, Frank Mahoney enlisted in the Army and attended Officers' Candidate School at Fort Monroe. Eight months later, he returned to his home town as a second lieutenant with Battery F, 18th Coast Artillery. By autumn 1943, this battery had exchanged their 12-inch guns at Fort Miley for a pair of 6-inch Navy guns mounted on Point Lobos. Battery F constructed the Lobos emplacement under the supervision of HDSF ordnance and artillery engineers. Second Lieutenant Mahoney, who had recently married, liked the location of Battery Lobos; "It just happened that my new mother-in-law lived four doors down from Clement Street on 42nd Avenue," Mahoney later reminisced. After doing his duty for the day at Battery Lobos, the second lieutenant walked across the street from Fort Miley to his house. All went well until Mahoney and his wife attended an officers' reception in General Haines' home at Fort Scott. Being an out-going San Franciscan, Mahoney's wife knew all the wives of the officers, which annoyed Mahoney's captain. "Where are you living?" testily demanded the captain of his junior officer, to which Mahoney could only reply, "at my mother-in-law's down the street." "Get your stuff up immediately," the Battery F commander ordered. From then on, Mahoney lived at Fort Miley in the Bachelor Officers' Quarters of the hospital.

The two Point Lobos 6-inch guns were long-retired Navy models. So old that no firing tables existed for them, the armament had six to twelve inches of whiplash in the muzzles when fired. One night when Battery F took its turn as the examination battery for the H-Station, an unidentified ship approached the harbor entrance. The Navy signal stations used semaphores and blinkers, but no reply came from the vessel. The Harbor Entrance Control Post ordered the examination battery to challenge the vessel with a single round over and ahead. One of the Lobos guns fired. The muzzle whiplashed; the shot landed on line but short of the target. It was lucky, recalled Frank Mahoney, that the shell did not skip across the water and hit the ship. After one shot, the vessel quickly hoisted signal flags, revealing itself to be a Navy supply ship with no lookouts on deck.

Battery F manned the Lobos guns and

awaited construction of their permanent armament, a new type of 6-inch emplacement directly behind Battery Chester at Fort Miley. Started in January 1943, Construction 243 featured two guns enclosed in armored shields with a one hundred-foot magazine and power room tunnel separating the pair. Along with the casemated 16-inch guns, Construction 243 and another one like it on Milagra Knob would represent the newest generation of seacoast artillery at the Golden Gate.

General Eurico Gaspar Dutra, Brazil's Minister of War, and the Joint U.S.-Brazilian Defense Commission landed at the San Francisco airport on September 7, 1943. General DeWitt and an honor guard from Western Defense Command greeted the foreign dignitaries who arrived on Brazil's independence day. After brief ceremonies, "5 carloads of officers, assorted jeeps and other army equipment drove rapidly into San Francisco," reported the *Chronicle*, to an independence day reception hosted by the Brazilian consul general at the Bohemian Club in honor of General Dutra and his entourage. General Haines and his wife attended the reception. Haines would reciprocate the next day by giving the Brazilians a special tour of the Harbor Defenses.

In August 1942, Brazil had declared war against Japan. She also permitted establishment of American air and naval bases on her northeast coast; this action brought German submarine attacks on Brazilian shipping. There was even talk of sending a Brazilian military force to Europe. Brazil wanted to be more than a regional power. Remembered Vernon A. Walters, then a young Army captain accompanying the Dutra mission as War Department liaison officer, "For political as well as military reasons it was important that the largest nation in South America take an active part in the war against Germany."

The War Department created the Joint U.S.-Brazilian Defense Commission to bring Dutra, a reputed admirer of Germany, to "an ever more friendly position toward the United States and its war effort." The War Department guided the Brazilians on a whirlwind tour of Army bases, to "impress General Dutra with the seriousness, the determination and capability of the United States to conduct the war to a victorious conclusion," to quote Vernon Walters. The Brazilian war minister and his party reviewed American infantry divisions at Southern training camps. Then in visits to Fort Knox and Fort Sill, the Brazilians saw tanks and artillery in action. In California, the commission toured the desert warfare center at Indio before heading north to the cooler climate of San Francisco.

On Wednesday morning, September 8th, Minister of War Dutra and his party were chauffeured from the St. Francis Hotel to the Presidio. In front of Western Defense Command Headquarters at nine o'clock, General Dutra received a nineteen-gun salute and other ceremonies. The VIP's then boarded eight shiny HDSF limousines. General Haines installed Colonel LaFrenz and other members of the headquarters staff as guides in each car. Top local Army commanders also joined the procession, including General Wilson of the Northern California Sector, and Generals DeWitt and Delos C. Emmons, the out-going and in-coming Western Defense Command chiefs.

With motorcycle escort in the lead flying the U.S. and Brazilian national colors,

(Above) S.F. North Beach residents read about Italian surrender outside newspaper office of Giornale L'Italia, morning September 8, 1943. (San Francisco Archives, S.F. Public Library)

HDSF motorcade carrying War Minister Dutra of Brazil and his delegation approach the south entrance to Fort Scott after visiting Funston, Miley, and Baker Beach, September 8, 1943. (Presidio Army Museum)

mine casemate on Baker Beach. The Brazilian war minister was allowed to operate the mine control board in the casemate before proceeding to the H-Station. The tour stopped for a luncheon hosted by General Haines at the Harbor Defense Officers' Club where additional Army brass joined the party.

At 2:30 in the afternoon, the limousines drove onto the Scott mine wharf where all boarded the USAMP *Spurgin* for a trip across the Golden Gate. On the way over, yawls and L-boats of the Mine Flotilla staged a procession on the bay for the Brazilians. The limousines rejoined the entourage at the Fort Baker dock. The officers rode up the hill to uncompleted Battery 129. Along the coast road to the hilltop fortification, General Dutra spotted a female surveyor dressed for the job in pegged pants and high tops. Dutra said something in Portuguese to his American interpreter, Lieutenant Clark D. Burton. "The

the eight limousines headed for Fort Funston by way of 19th Avenue. At 10:00 a.m., the entourage, with Army and civilian newsmen in tow, inspected the fort's 16-inch casemated guns. Informed by a reporter of Allied landings in Italy, Minister Dutra turned and bowed in congratulations to General DeWitt, the ranking American officer. "I expected Italy to succumb, but not so soon nor so completely," Dutra told the press. When asked for his opinion on the refusal of U.S. Lend-Lease aid to Brazil's rival, Argentina, Dutra diplomatically parried, "That's politics--I'm a soldier."

Emerging from the impromptu news conference in the battery tunnel, the official party moved on to Fort Miley, then to the

Luncheon at Harbor Defense Officers' Club for the Brazilians, left to right: MG Walter K. Wilson, CG 9th Corps Sector, WDC; BG James W. Barnett, CS of WDC and 4th Army; MG Eurico Gaspar Dutra, Minister of War, Brazil; Lt Gen John L. DeWitt, CG WDC and 4th Army; BG Claude Adams, U.S. Military Attache to Brazil; MG Leitao de Carvalho and MG J.G. Ord, Joint U.S.-Brazil Defense Commission; General Haines; MG Fulton Gardner, CG 4th AA Cmd.; Lt Gen Delos C. Emmons. (Presidio Army Museum)

Inspection of Fort Scott mine dock by Brazilian War Minister Dutra prior to boarding mineplanter Spurgin for trip to Fort Baker. (Presidio Army Museum)

General is pleased with what meets the eye," translated the lieutenant to reporters, "even in the remotest places, in these impressive defenses."

After seeing the weaponless casemates of Battery 129, the tour closed with War Minister Dutra praising his HDSF hosts: "Witnessing these defenses and all its magnificent equipment and efficient personnel, gives one a sense of security." By four o'clock in the afternoon, the South Americans had returned to their suites at the St. Francis Hotel. After San Francisco, the Brazilians traveled through the Midwest, inspecting heavy industries and armament plants. General Dutra made his last stop in Washington D.C., where President Roosevelt received him in the Oval Office. American efforts to court the Brazilians paid dividends the next year when Brazil sent sizable land and air forces to Italy.

On September 16th, the Combined Chiefs of Staff recommended putting the East and West Coasts on Category A---"coastal frontiers that probably will be free from attack, but for which a nominal defense must be provided for political reasons." Minimal forces were to be kept stateside for repelling submarine or surface vessels "operating by stealth or stratagem or isolated raids by aircraft operating chiefly for morale effect." At the end of October, the Army canceled Western Defense Command's theatre of war status and ordered the command put on a "strictly nominal defense basis" within six months.

Wartime Army priorities favored tanks and field artillery over the huge seacoast guns which took so much steel to build. The new 6-inch batteries at Fort Miley and Milagra Knob had cast armored shields but lacked guns, because field artillery production had priority. The casemates and 16-inch gun barrels of Battery 129 at Fort Baker awaited gun carriages which never arrived---steel was needed for tanks, not seacoast artillery. With the de-creasing likelihood of enemy battleships appearing off the Pacific coast, the Army suspended work on Battery 129 on November 26th. The only modernization of seacoast guns brought to fruition at the Harbor Defenses during the war was the casemating of 12-inch Battery Wallace at Fort Barry. This conversion of the open barbette emplacement had started sometime after March 1942. During construction, Battery K of the 6th Coast Artillery continued manning the guns; the artillery engineers worked on one casemate at a time, leaving one 12-inch rifle always ready for action. By late autumn 1943, Battery Wallace was back in business with both guns.

Besides serving as military protectors of the Golden Gate, harbor defense troops, as part of the Bay Area community, participated in the community war effort. The Third War Loan Drive came to San Francisco in the fall of 1943, and HDSF sent the 6th Coast Artillery Band under the direction of Chief Warrant Officer William K. Hershenow, to lead a parade down Market Street on September 9th. The *Golden Gate Guardian*, a partial observer, called the regimental band "the snappiest, most colorful band in the parade." Later, at the City of Paris department store on the corner of Stockton and Geary Streets, the military musicians gave a sidewalk concert. Performing before the store's Louis XVI window frames of white enamel and carved gilded wood, the harbor defense band inspired the sidewalk au-

Army equipment, including a Lockheed P-38 fighter, were displayed at San Francisco's Union Square during 3rd War Loan Drive in Bay Area, September 17, 1943. (San Francisco Archives, S.F. Public Library)

dience to purchase thirty thousand dollars in war bonds. Mrs. M. Laugesen, chairwoman of the bond drive at the City of Paris "greatly attributes this record one day sale to the assistance of W.O. Hershenow and his music makers," reported the post newspaper. Meanwhile at the nearby White House department store, the Harbor Defenses staged an indoor display of coast artillery projectiles, which the *Guardian* claimed "attracted young and old alike and gave Bond Buyers a good hunch as to where their Bond money was going."

Movie personalities from Hollywood arrived at the Southern Pacific depot at Third and Townsend Streets on the morning of September 25th to do their bit in the city's war loan drive. Mayor Rossi greeted Greer Garson, James Cagney, and several other movie stars at the station. The celebrities then boarded jeeps driven by military policemen from Western Defense Command. They paraded down Market Street and through Chinatown. Then the Hollywood jeep cavalcade climbed Nob Hill, with a stream of Chinatown youngsters trailing after them all the way to the Fairmont Hotel lobby. In the evening, a Civic Auditorium audience, who paid for seats with war bonds as legal tender, saw a celebrity-filled performance headlined by Harpo Marx, Judy Garland, Lucille Ball, Betty Hutton, and Kathryn Grayson.

The *Golden Gate Guardian* sponsored group blood donations with all HDSF units giving to the Red Cross Blood Procurement Center on Jones and Chestnut Streets in the city. Harbor defense batteries vied with one another to offer more donors than called for. Between April and September, one thousand pints of blood had been donated. Harbor defensemen responded so readily, the Red Cross blood bank set aside Thursday afternoons as "HDSF Time." On one occasion, Fort Scott M.P.'s, including the provost marshal, donated fifty pints of blood. In September, the gratified Red Cross issued a certificate to the Harbor Defenses "for outstanding cooperation." The award presentation was broadcasted over the radio from the blood center. Mrs. Gardiner Dailey, chairwoman of the area's blood banks, said during the presentation that only

Lieutenant Colonel Arthur Kramer (left) mans HDSF projectile exhibit at Union Square. (Presidio Army Museum)

WDC M.P.'s drive Greer Garson, James Cagney, and other stars of Hollywood Bond Cavalcade from Southern Pacific Depot to downtown San Francisco, September 25, 1943. (San Francisco Archives, S.F. Public Library)

five certificates of this kind had ever been awarded in San Francisco. Accepting accolades for his men, General Haines addressed the radio audience: "I am proud of the men in my command for the way in which they have responded to this splendid work. We shall cherish this certificate as a token of service to our country."

Like civilians did at home, harbor defensemen on post collected scrap for the war effort. Not only did they consign obsolete seacoast weapons, such as the 12-inch rifles of Battery Mendell, to the scrap drives of 1943, the troops also recycled hundreds of tons of metal, paper, kitchen grease, tin cans, bones, meat trimmings, textiles, and shoes. Old ceremonial cannon found on post became scrap as well. The *Coast Artillery Journal* estimated that metal collected by the Harbor Defenses in 1943 equaled 250 two-ton bombs.

"Fastidious and careless eating habits of the past are gone for the duration," proclaimed the post newspaper. The *Golden Gate Guardian* urged men to eat at the barracks before going to town on pass. "If this procedure were followed," preached the *Guardian*, "San Francisco restaurants would not be jammed with servicemen who take seats from civilians. GI's could eat just as well in their own mess hall-- and get better and more food, all for nix." The mess sergeant ordered food by counting every man on the battery roster, and

"an empty plate at suppertime means that one more plateful of chow goes to waste." During a six-month period under the food conservation program, the Harbor Defenses saved an estimated four hundred tons of vital edibles without affecting the amount of food needed to feed the troops.

The joint Army-Navy Harbor Entrance Control Post at the Fort Scott H-Station functioned continuously since its inception in

40mm AA gun on exhibit in downtown San Francisco. (San Francisco Archives, S.F. Public Library)

1941. Work progressed on a new, heavily re-inforced H-Station casemate in front of the old structure; but it would not be ready for use until January 1944. Meanwhile, the Harbor Defenses made do with the old station. Since both the Army and Navy staffed the command post, HECP toilet doors bore both words "latrine" and "head." Women personnel of the Army and Navy serving at the command center required their own toilets, and perhaps further signs.

The Navy had equipped their HECP coffee room "first class," with refrigerators, decorations on the wall, and big stainless steel coffee machines. The Army's coffee room, outfitted with a glass pot and two-burner hot plate "was very primitive," to quote Harry Payne, an HDSF assistant artillery engineer who did his share of late-night duty in the H-Station. The Navy always had doughnuts and pastries to go with the coffee and soft drinks, a courtesy especially welcomed by the night shift. The Army enlisted men on duty at the H-Station made friends with the sailors. Before long, soldiers took coffee breaks on the Navy side. "Why doesn't the Army build a nice coffee shop like we've got," a Navy lieutenant commander kidded Harry Payne. "Your guys are over here drinking our coffee and eating our doughnuts and filling up the room all the time." In response, Payne asked for funds through channels to set up a better Army coffee room. HDSF Headquarters turned down the request. Several weeks later, a gray Navy truck pulled up to the H-Station with a large coffee system and the Navy crew to install it. The Army finally had a nice coffee room, courtesy of the Navy lieutenant commander. "I'll always remember how the Navy could get anything they wanted," said Payne later. But "it made the rapport a lot better" between the two services in the command post. On October 16th, General Haines invited all naval officers of the HECP for an October 23rd dinner dance at the Fort Scott Officers' Club "to promote social contacts between Army and Navy officers on duty with the Harbor Defenses of San Francisco."

Men serving with the seacoast batteries found a convenient pastime in fishing. "The fish around here are getting bigger and better than ever, and the boys are having good luck in landing them," wrote a corporal from an anti-motor torpedo boat weapons battery at Kirby Beach. In the narrows of the Gate, the men hooked sea bass that weighed between ten and twenty pounds. With battery funds, GI's manning 6-inch guns above Baker Beach in San Francisco bought six sets of poles and tackle for surf fishing. Captain Boyd Pulley, the battery commander, put a limit on sets bought, fearing the men might someday lose interest in fishing. The troops made their own sinkers and other tackle. Those who broke fishing equipment paid for replacements out of their own pockets. Said the captain, "Soldiers have a healthier respect for materials with a pocketbook value." On one memorable day at Baker Beach, the men had a two-hour run on striped bass. The battery mess cooked the fish, and "because battery personnel made a sport of getting it, the savory flavor was enhanced."

Three different lion cubs reigned in succession over the years as mascot for Battery I, 6th Coast Artillery at Fort Barry. The original mascot was Judy, followed by another cub when Judy outgrew the keepers. Punchy was the third feline, but this "rapidly growing cub" also got "transferred to his original outfit, a lion farm near Los Angeles," reported the post newspaper. Until the sergeant trainer brought a smaller lion back from furlough, Battery I adopted a young raccoon named "Cecilia," who amused the defensemen by washing her hands and food before dining. At Cronkhite, Battery E, 6th Coast Artillery, owned two cats named "Breechblock" and "Head Space" who wandered up the hill to the Wolf Ridge AA positions and never came back. Some time later, the antiaircraft battery sent down two offspring which the 16-inch gun crew dubbed "Switchboard" and "Caliber." Aware of the wild cats that prowled Wolf Ridge, the crew thought the kittens looked like "bobcats for sure."

The staples of Army recreation on post, such as drama clubs and hobby workshops, were not established at the Harbor Defenses. These amenities graced the big, well-established bases like the Presidio. Fort Scott and the coast artillery sub-posts around the Golden Gate existed to serve the seacoast defenses---

(Above) A Bob Hope radio broadcast performed before GI audience at Presidio post theatre. (Presidio Army Museum)

(Right) Bob Hope and Army private rehearsing for radio show at Presidio. (Presidio Army Museum)

and to do so as secretly and quietly as possible. Whatever recreational outlets HDSF had were due mainly to the Special Services officers and the ingenuity of the troops themselves. Fort Barry had a service club near the Mendell PX, which a fire destroyed. During the autumn of 1943, Battery K, 6th Coast Artillery, scrounged nearby structures for timber and supplied carpenters to build a new clubhouse for parties and dances. The interior featured a large hardwood dance floor with a small stage and a dressing room at one end, plus eight spacious windows to give a panoramic view of the Golden Gate and the city beyond. The new Mendell Service Club stood with a group of wooden buildings in front of Battery K's casemated 12-inch rifles. The big guns wreaked havoc with the buildings during target practice, breaking dishes, shattering windows, and blowing in walls.

USO celebrity tours did not play at the Harbor Defenses. Celebrities touring stateside military camps usually went to large training facilities like Fort Ord. But comedian Bob Hope entertained the troops several times at

the Presidio's big theatre and also at Fort Barry. In early October 1943, movie actor Pat O'Brien performed at Forts Baker, Barry, and Scott. He also "ate at one of the batteries," and entertained at the Harbor Defense Officers' Club. One officer recalled Pat O'Brien used "blue material" in his stage act, which did not mesh with the actor's straight-laced screen persona. Other Hollywood names that played the HDSF venue in 1943 were Allen Jenkins at Fort Scott and Jane Withers at the Funston theatre. By the end of the year, a large group including Mickey Rooney, George Burns, Gracie Allen, Anne Baxter, Phil Silvers, and Porter Hall, toured the batteries and outposts. Singer Ginny Sims performed for patients at the Fort Baker Station Hospital. Appearing with her was Raffles, a talking mynah bird. Concert violinist Isaac Stern and a USO-Camp Shows presentation entitled "Let's Go," also entertained at the defenses in 1943. But Special Services and Red Cross entertainment could not reach every location. This prompted Lieutenant Colonel Richard Moorman at Fort Funston to book his own "discovery." Moorman patronized a San Francisco nightclub, the Music Box on lower O'Farrell Street, where he met vocalist Nino Milo. Eventually, Moorman arranged for Milo to perform for the men at Funston. But at the last moment, Milo's agent made the singer cancel the performance.

During the Christmas season, four HDSF trucks journeyed to Lake County, one hundred miles north of the bay, to harvest Christmas trees at a government reserve. The Harbor Defenses brought four truckloads of trees back to San Francisco. "The brass got the best," remembered Special Services officer Leo Murphy. High-ranking officers at the Presidio received the choice trees. This put General Haines in good standing with Western Defense Command and 4th Army. All HDSF batteries and the families of HDSF personnel received the rest of the Christmas trees. For the distant outposts, trimmings and ornaments for the trees came from the Red Cross, who solicited the public for donation of used Christmas decorations.

Since the enemy might be tempted to attack during the winter holidays, the Harbor Defenses did not let many officers and men leave the post. Christmas dinner invitations from the public were kindly refused because the defenses could not afford to be caught short. But if one had family living in nearby bay communities, a pass was usually granted. From the men of the H-Station came this holiday message; "Let's all hope to remember Christmas 1943 as the last Christmas during World War II."

Chapter 9:

Wide Awake and on the Job

Carrying his repair kit, a technical sergeant knocked on the door of General Haines' Fort Scott home. The sergeant's superior had sent him there to fix a broken radio. Mrs. Haines let the sergeant in and led him into a room where a big console radio stood against the wall. Mrs. Haines excused herself and left the room while the NCO set down his repair kit and took out the tube-checker. In order to get to the vacuum tubes inside the radio, the sergeant pulled the big cabinet away from the wall. When he did so, he found the radio had been unplugged all along. "By God, what an opportunity," the sergeant said to himself. Then, he pretended to work on the set. Twenty minutes later, he plugged the radio back into the electric outlet. After telling Mrs. Haines the set was fixed, the sergeant left the general's house. The next day, General Haines telephoned the sergeant's superior at the radio shack. The harbor defense commander was very happy with the repaired radio and wanted to know the name of the man responsible so that he could remember it.

Lieutenant Colonel Arthur Kramer's wife telephoned her husband's sergeant major with a problem. She had just dented the fender of the family car, and did not want her husband to find out. The sergeant major reassured Mrs. Kramer that help was on the way. A short time later, the sergeant major told Mrs. Kramer to take the car to the Presidio and see a man who would repair the dent. She was even advised how much money to give the moonlighting soldier for his trouble. That afternoon the dented fender was fixed without Lieutenant Colonel Kramer suspecting anything had been amiss---and the efficient sergeant major never let on.

On Monday nights, HDSF executive Colonel William LaFrenz played poker with a group of officers, mostly graduates of one local university. "They were very self-conscious of their own group," one junior officer recalled. "But I was one of them, I suppose," he continued, recounting that when transfers out of

Colonel LaFrenz, General Haines, Captain G.C. McClellan, the general's aide, emerge from HDSF Headquarters, Fort Scott. (Presidio Army Museum)

Captain Kenneth Cooper, Battery C, 6th CA, at wheel of jeep during inspection of his observation stations on Marin coast. (K. Cooper, Jr.)

HDSF were in the wind, Colonel LaFrenz always insisted, "we can't let Murphy go. We get those doughnuts every morning."

"Truly, the time spent with Battery 'C' was the most pleasant and profitable of my life," wrote Captain Kenneth Cooper on January 1, 1944. "Through the constant flow of personnel, both enlisted men and officers, it was my experience to serve under the most capable predecessors in command, and with the finest organization of enlisted men in the army," Captain Cooper proclaimed in a heartfelt farewell after serving three years and three months as officer and commanding officer with the Funston 16-inch guns of Battery C, 6th Coast Artillery. "Whenever your name is mentioned it will quicken the pulse," Cooper continued, "and send a thrill of joy and comradeship through the heart of him who once had the honor and pleasure of commanding you and serving in your organization." The captain, who came to HDSF as a Thomason Act officer in 1940, had been transferred to the 2nd Battalion of the 18th CA as a tactical group commander at Fort Miley. This sentimental letter to his former battery revealed the close attachments formed in harbor defense units which served long periods of time in the same place. "Certainly many hard days of fighting lie ahead in the present struggle," Cooper predicted. "Some of you, no doubt, will see enemy action. Others will not be so fortunate but must be content to maintain homeland installations and train others for their part in the task of overcoming the present enemy." Striking the theme prevalent at stateside commands as the action moved far from domestic shores, Cooper concluded: "Whatever your assignment might be, it will be your contribution toward winning the war."

By early 1944, the Allies pushed the fighting ever closer to the enemy's doorstep. In the Southwest Pacific, American and Australian forces erased Japanese gains made in New Guinea and the Bismarck Archipelago. In the central Pacific, the U.S. Navy continued driving toward Japan with landings on the Marshall and Caroline Islands. Allied air forces over Europe bombed targets day and night to cripple German war industries and to prepare the way for the invasion of France. The Allied offensive stalled on the Italian peninsula, but the January 22nd landings at Anzio showed the Allies maintained the initiative everywhere. The daily headlines announcing battle news from Europe and the Pacific caused some harbor defenders at the Golden Gate to feel left out of the action.

"I was able to get home every night," remembered John Taheny, a lieutenant with the seacoast searchlight battery. "My folks lived out in the Richmond District and I could walk from Battery N to my home." The University of San Francisco ROTC graduate went from officer training at Fort Monroe directly to HDSF. But three months into his duties, Second Lieutenant Taheny found inspecting seacoast searchlight positions not his idea of excitement. So when an Army recruiter from the Office of Strategic Services (OSS) visited the Harbor Defenses, Taheny became hopeful for a change of scene. "They must have alerted all the officers above the grade of second lieutenant," Taheny recalled, because he seemed to be the only one to appear for an interview. The OSS recruiter asked Taheny if he would be willing to parachute behind ene-

Seacoast searchlight installed on retracting mount that lowered into ground at Tennessee Point, Fort Cronkhite. (Presidio Army Museum)

my lines; and with this question, Taheny undauntedly expected "to be parachuted into Japan proper."

The OSS accepted the harbor defense lieutenant for training. They also told Taheny to keep his departure discreet. Not even roommate George Albers at the Fort Scott Bachelor Officers' Quarters knew Taheny was leaving. On the morning of his departure for Washington D.C., Taheny returned briefly to the BOQ to pick up his effects. Albers woke up and wanted to know what was going on. "I told him I couldn't talk about it," recalled Taheny, "because we had been instructed that it was very hush-hush." But Taheny could not resist mentioning something about his exciting assignment, and admitted that he was joining the OSS. Albers became more interested when he learned the recruiter had visited the Harbor Defenses. Eventually, the OSS sent John Taheny to Burma. "The next thing I know," remembered Taheny, "I'm overseas when George Albers shows up a couple months after I got out there."

Though theirs was a harbor defense mission, the coast artillerymen took infantry training at the Harbor Defenses. As early as 1943, the schooling of HDSF non-commissioned officers for coast artillery stressed infantry skills; bayonets, small arms, machine guns, chemical warfare, hand and rifle grenades, and several trips through the Fort Scott commando course. The men crawled through barbed-wire while live machine gun rounds whipped above their heads and controlled dynamite blasts erupted around them. Even the Ar-

my nurses stationed at the Fort Baker hospital tackled the Scott commando course as part of their training.

In the early spring of 1944, fifty chosen officers from the Army, Coast Guard, and California State Guard gathered at Fort Cronkhite under the auspices of Western Defense Command, Northern California Sector, to attend the first session of the newly created Commando School. The selectees from throughout the Pacific coast endured five weeks of rigorous training to develop combat savvy and aggressive leadership skills. The officers, picked for "outstanding mental and physical qualities," carried full packs during a week of long marches. Next came instruction in "treating the enemy rough, whether he wields a knife, bayonet, machete or billy

California State Guard in training at Fort Cronkhite commando course. (San Francisco Archives, S.F. Public Library)

club," stated the *Coast Artillery Journal*. The selected officers practiced hand-to-hand combat, swam through burning oil, climbed an emergency ladder of rifles, and bayoneted "dummies that gushed forth blood." In a mocked-up village at Cronkhite, the men evaded booby traps and electrical circuits, and learned how to silently dispose of sentries. Practice attacks on dummy pillboxes taught the latest methods of attacking fortified areas, and the steep Cronkhite hills proved useful in the mountain fighting phase of the course. The officers also went to Fleishhacker Pool in San Francisco for a cold water swim in combat gear. As a graduating exercise, the trainees came ashore at night on the San Mateo coast. Wearing red uniforms, the officers infiltrated twenty-five miles inland to "destroy" their objective. Peninsula police departments and Army units in the area acted as the defending forces.

During a war characterized by amphibious landings, the beaches on HDSF territory bristled with mines, booby traps, and barbed-wire. At the Fort Barry Land Mine School, harbor defensemen learned to make explosive devices. They planted fireworks on Rodeo Beach to simulate land mines and exploded them for the benefit of news cameramen as other troops came ashore. In the late spring of 1944, coast artillerymen staged a landing on Angel Island. Under smoke screen cover, mine yawls carried the 3rd Battalion, 6th Coast Artillery up to the shore, where several waves of harbor defensemen stormed the beach.

On March 18, 1944, a soldier missing from his battery lay at the base of a 270-foot tall shoreline cliff at Point Bonita. From the heights, no one could tell whether the soldier was dead, or injured and unconscious. Approach by sea to the cliff

base was impossible. So Captain Harley A. Stewart and Private First Class Gilbert C. Brunson, both of the mine command, started down the steep cliff on foot, without ropes or climbing aids. Reaching the bottom, they found the soldier dead. Private Brunson of Battery F stayed with the body as Captain Stewart, Battery A commander, climbed back up the cliff to call the Coast Guard. For their bravery, General Haines pinned Soldier's Medals on the two men during ceremonies on July 4, 1944.

"Those were miserable quarters most of the men had at Fort Funston," commented Frank Mahoney, a junior officer with the 2nd Battalion, 18th Coast Artillery. The men of Battery D lived in damp underground wooden boxes dubbed "rabbit huts" near the 155mm guns at the southern end of the fort. The men were a hardened bunch; some of the sergeants and corporals had served three or more years. One day, the battery commander called the first sergeant to task for allowing the men to gamble. "I want you to stop it," the captain ordered. Five hours later, the first sergeant reported back to the commander, saying: "Sir, there'll be no more gambling. Sorry it took so long. I started with five bucks, but I have all the money now."

Battery D had four Model 1918 155mm guns on Panama mounts, circular steel rails set in concrete, which allowed the guns to rapidly track moving targets. With a maximum range of 17,500 yards, these seacoast guns, emplaced and sandbagged in on a sandy bluff south of the 16-inch battery, were intended for fighting destroyers; their rate of fire was not fast enough for the motor torpedo boats

General Haines pins Soldier's Medal on PFC Gilbert C. Brunson. Captain Harley A. Stewart stands beside private, July 4, 1944. (Presidio Army Museum)

Air view of Fort Funston: From 16-inch battery casemate at right edge, road leads to Battery C perimeter fence. Empty Panama mounts of abandoned 155mm gun position on bluff at lower left, with police pistol range to its right. Among scrap heaps in upper left is 3-inch AA battery. (K. Cooper, Jr.)

which HDSF now saw as a more likely threat. Battery D held several target practices at Funston. Fire was controlled in the usual way with spotters calling in adjustments from the battery's two base-end stations. "We weren't too good one day," remembered Frank Mahoney, the range officer. "The spotters were calling in and they were missing quite a bit." One of the gunnery sergeants popped up on the parapet; "So where is that target?" he barked, looking seaward till he spotted the pyramidal shape towed by a mineplanter. The sergeant cranked the corrections on the 155, and the next round hit the mark. Battery D's veteran gunnery sergeants had a knack for it.

The guarded perimeter cutting through the middle of Funston belonged to Battery C, 6th Coast Artillery, manning the 16-inch guns. In order to pass C's sentry line, officers of the neighboring 18th Coast Artillery remembered an ever-changing list of passwords. When challenged at the guard post, the officers sometimes forgot the current password. They quickly pronounced something that sounded like "fluvium" with a lisp. Passwords with an "L" were chosen because the average Japanese soldier supposedly could not pronounce them. The mumbled approximation of the current password usually got the officers through the sentry line, especially if the guard had seen them before.

The 18th Coast Artillery manned their own guard posts and patrolled beaches from Funston south through the truck farms of today's Westlake beyond John Daly Boulevard.

Sharing the guard duties were reconnaissance squadrons from the 107th Cavalry Group, an Ohio National Guard unit, which had patrols from Eureka to Palo Alto. The harbor defensemen envied the cavalry troopers, who seemed to be jeep-mounted down to the lowliest corporal. The troopers carried a variety of weapons, from M-1 carbines and .45 caliber pistols to Browning automatic rifles and Thompson sub-machine guns. With weapons at the ready, cavalrymen challenged anyone approaching them. Frank Mahoney, inspecting sentries as officer of the day, recalled coming upon one post: "I saw this cavalryman at the same time he saw me." Mahoney remembered hearing the slide go back on the cavalryman's .45 caliber pistol and the challenge: "Halt, who goes there?" Mahoney gave the correct password, but even then, the trooper did not holster his weapon, keeping it nose up as the lieutenant passed him.

War Department policy of maintaining only a minimum force in harbor defenses took effect at San Francisco with the relieving of the 130th Coast Artillery Battalion (Antiaircraft) and the 2nd Battalion, 18th Coast Artillery from duty with HDSF. Orders issued through the Northern California Sector of Western Defense Command on April 19, 1944 directed those two battalions with all seventy officers and 1500 enlisted men to move by rail to Camp Breckenridge, Kentucky where Army Ground Forces would reassign them. The departure of the 130th Coast Artillery Battalion meant the deactivation of all fixed 3-inch anti-aircraft batteries at the Harbor Defenses. The 2nd Battalion of the 18th Coast Artillery had been there from the start of the war---activated and trained at HDSF in early 1941 with the first call-up of draftees. Longtime HDSF officers like Lieutenant Colonel Richard Moorman and Major Kenneth Cooper, who had served four to five years at San Francisco, left with their units. "We brought pool tables with us and everything to have a good time in Panama," said Frank Mahoney, a junior officer the 18th Coast Artillery. On the eastbound troop train, the men guessed that Panama would be their next assignment. But arriving at Camp Breckenridge, they learned the 130th Coast Artillery Battalion and the 2nd Battalion of the 18th Coast Artillery Regiment would disband on May 5th, with officers and men being converted to infantry and field artillery. The removal of the two battalions left the 6th Coast Artillery Regiment, in service at the Golden Gate since 1924, as the sole line unit within the Harbor Defenses of San Francisco.

A "big-time radio show, the first for the Harbor Defenses of San Francisco," according to the Coast Artillery Journal, broadcasted from the Fort Scott post theatre on May 3rd. Coca-Cola, sponsors of the "Spotlight Band" radio program, brought Hal McIntyre and his band of "solid spot music masters" to Fort Scott. "It promises to be one of the classiest HDSF sessions of all time," announced the Golden Gate Guardian. Transportation was furnished from outlying posts, and troops got first choice of seating in the theatre. "Leave your sheckels at home," the Guardian reminded the GI's, "because the shindig's for nix." Soldiers from all six coast artillery posts packed the Fort Scott Theatre. The soft drink sponsor added an extra hour of entertainment after the 6:30 p.m. national broadcast so the GI audience could hear more music and drink more free Coca-Cola.

The Fort Baker Station Hospital, originally built as the medical facility of the Harbor Defenses, now served increasing numbers of wounded GI's returning from the Pacific. The hospital prepared wounded soldiers for their return to civilian life. The rehabilitation program included supervised athletics and exercises; ambulatory patients played volleyball, ping-pong, and horseshoes. HDSF chaplains and Special Services officers, as well as the Red Cross, aided the hospital staff in their mission. The Armed Forces Entertainment Committee brought San Francisco nightclub acts from the Hurricane Club and the Dragon's Lair to entertain the recovering veterans. USO troupes also played the hospital and General Electric gave a presentation called the "House of Magic." String ensembles and community singing, plus two weekly movies provided by the Red Cross, rounded out the hospital's entertainment schedule.

Five thousand individual packets of information from the Harbor Defenses went out to prospective Women's Army Corps recruits in the spring of 1944. Pamphlets and illustrations extolled "the advantages and opportunities of serving at what has been termed the finest Army post in the country, Fort Winfield Scott." Choose this post after basic

Fort Baker Station Hospital. (San Francisco Archives, S..F. Public Library)

training, HDSF urged the women. Accompanying photographs showed the WAC barracks, post theatre, grill, and splendid surroundings, while brochures reminded women that duty at Fort Scott would develop "trades and skills which will be of great aid to them in post-war years."

"HDSF Time" at the Red Cross blood bank in San Francisco continued in 1944, with the Golden Gate defenders donating an average of thirty pints per week. Two batteries from the 6th Coast Artillery contrib-

Army transport Henry Bergh aground on Farralone Islands as viewed from deck of mineplanter Spurgin, May 31, 1944. (R. Palihnich)

uted more than their share. Battery B from Baker Beach donated blood at an eighty-five percent rate. The blood donors of Battery L at Fort Barry boasted an eighty percent participation. Battery L distinguished itself with the single largest one-time donation of sixty pints. On that memorable occasion, the *Golden Gate Guardian* observed: "There was little in sight but Army Uniforms . . . at the Red Cross Blood Bank in San Francisco as 55 men from L-6th descended on the place to make donations." The Red Cross awarded Certificates of Appreciation to Batteries B and L for their unstinting contributions.

Before dawn on the morning of May 31st, Fort Miley radar operators detected a vessel approaching the harbor entrance from the south at the outer extremity of the Golden Gate. To the radar men, the vessel seemed headed not for port, but straight toward the Farallones. The Fort Miley radar station had detected the *Henry Bergh*, a 441-foot Liberty ship carrying thirteen hundred returning sailors from the Pacific war. Fog and darkness hampered navigation as the transport plowed through choppy seas toward what it thought was the harbor entrance. The Miley radar crew reported the radar sighting to the H-Station, which in turn told the Navy. Efforts to warn the vessel of its collision course with the Farallones produced no response---radio contact was impossible in the heavy fog. The Navy, Coast Guard, and Harbor Defenses immediately dispatched rescue ships toward the Farallon Islands.

At 4:00 a.m., a call reached the US-AMP *Spurgin* at the Sausalito dock. Junior engineer officer Rudy Palihnich, officer of the day aboard the planter, immediately ordered engines steamed up and telephoned the captain, Richard T. Carlsen, and chief engineer, John B. May at their homes in Marin. The two chief warrant officers arrived in Sausalito and the *Spurgin* shoved off with only a partial crew. When the mineplanter reached the Farallones, they found the 7,191-ton *Henry Bergh* riding high on the rocks two hundred yards offshore. Some rescuing Navy vessels were already on the scene, but these ships kept their distance because they feared getting dashed on the rocks themselves. Pounding waves threatened to break the *Henry Bergh* apart. The steel hull was ruptured in several places, including the aft engine room. In abandoning ship, six hundred passengers swam to the island, or got there by life boat or breeches buoy rigged between wreck and shore. But several hundred others bobbed in the cold, choppy water or floated in motor launches. Some had swum through oily water to reach lifeboats.

The *Spurgin's* master, Chief Warrant Officer Richard Carlsen, who learned seamanship in the fjords of his native Norway, steered the Army mineplanter up close to the transport. "He was one of the best ship handlers I had ever seen," professed Rudy Palihnich, "and I have been at sea for a good many years." Oil-soaked men clambered onto the *Spurgin*, creating a greasy mess on deck. With a full load of survivors, the mineplanter set course for Treasure Island, where the rescued men were let off. The Army vessel turned about and headed back to the Farallones for a second rescue. This time, in addition to another full load of survivors, the *Spurgin* took in tow an abandoned motor

launch and several life boats. "By mid morning several hundred . . . had been brought to the receiving station at Treasure Island," reported the *San Francisco Chronicle* the following day, "One small vessel alone returned with 200 men." The local newspapers did not herald the role of the Army mineplanters in the rescue. Since the accident occurred at sea, this was a story about the Navy and the Coast Guard. After searching for mention of the *Spurgin* in the papers and finding none, Rudy Palihnich was not surprised; after all, he later said, "who knows about mineplanters?" Three days later, the *Henry Bergh* broke up and sank in the rough seas. But thanks to all those involved in the rescue, there were no fatalities as a result of the accident. Mention of the Army's role in the rescue came a month later from the *Coast Artillery Journal* when it reported the praise given to the mineplanters by the commander of the 12th Naval District.

Dramatic sea rescues did not characterize the regular mission of Army mineplanters. In day-to-day operations, the Mine Flotilla picked up old mines for maintenance and replaced them with new ones. While an accompanying L-Boat located the distribution box, the mineplanter grappled for the ground mines. At Potato Patch, the rough

(Top) Chief Warrant Officer Richard Carlsen, U.S. Army Mineplanter Service, skippered USAMP's Niles and Spurgin. (Presidio Army Museum)
(Middle Left) Henry Bergh survivors make for USAMP Spurgin. (R. Palihnich)
(Left) Rescued men clamber aboard Spurgin. (R. Palihnich)

Spurgin sister ship USAMP Samuel M. Mills joined HDSF in 1942. Two years later, vessel photographed at Sausalito dock, August 17, 1944. (R. Palihnich)

currents pitched and rolled the vessels, making the task of grappling for the mine cables especially difficult. Small octopi, startled by the sudden uprooting of their nautical roosts, clung tenaciously to the metal cases of barnacle-encrusted mines hauled out of the sea. The octopi "were small ones," remembered Rudy Palihnich, "so they didn't venture far from where they were born." As each old mine was hauled up for maintenance, the mine crew dropped a replacement mine in the water over the exact location so that no gap existed in the field. The planter shuttled back and forth between the mines and the L-boat, each time dropping the free end of a mine cable for connection to the distribution box. It took one day to replace the thirteen ground mines of a group. The planters delivered the old mines to Fort Scott, Fort Baker, or Treasure Island where the cylindrical cases were opened to check the firing mechanisms. Then the cases were scraped clean and repainted---and made ready to replace the next group of mines due for maintenance.

The mineplanters *Mills* and *Spurgin* berthed in Sausalito at a special dock south of town. The crews lived and ate aboard ship. A motor launch and two life boats rescued from the *Henry Bergh* were tied up at the dock and used as hacks by the mineplanter men. They made quick trips by motorboat into Sausalito. The men built a flight of long wooden steps leading from the wharf, up the hill to a bus stop on the road. The HDSF mine flotilla tradition of crabbing was still strong, and aside from taking the crabs found clinging to the mines, the planter crews threw a crab pot off the Sausalito dock. The men also cast heavy fishing line and tackle off the stern of their ships as they plied the outer waters, hoping to hook big cod and snapper. Nobody would "bother with the small fish," recalled Rudy Palihnich.

Business boomed at Fort Baker's Marine Repair Shop. The Army boatyard repaired all Mine Flotilla vessels, except the large mineplanters. The cost and efficiency of the civilian-supervised, Army-crewed boatyard attracted War Department attention. The Army hoped to run similar operations in other harbor defenses. Repairs at the Baker shop included painting, scraping barnacles, redesigning boats, reconditioning engines, renewing broken deck planks, and straightening propeller shafts. "Instead of waiting three weeks for a boat to return from a shipyard for a simple cleaning and painting job," crowed the *Golden Gate Guardian*, "the Baker gang can complete the task in two or three days." The Marine Repair Shop restored the deck of an L-boat for one thousand dollars; the same job would have cost five times more at a private yard. Said the shop's civilian foreman Harry Plummer: "Heck, we will save the government more than fifty thousand dollars this year."

HDSF mineplanters doubled as cable ships. A cable break midway between San Francisco and Hawaii once brought the US-AMP *Spurgin* with an escort of two destroyers and a Navy blimp out to the high seas. As the mineplanter repaired the break on deck, its naval escort sailed a wide perimeter around the Army vessel to keep other ships away from the cable's exact location. Of the three HDSF planters, the *Niles* performed most of the cable duties. This ship lay undersea communications cable connecting observation stations to the seacoast batteries; for better protection against sabotage, the telephone lines went under the ocean instead of underground. After Lieutenant Colonel Liwski turned the *Niles* over to Western Defense Command, the vessel saw considerable cable duty at various locations in the Pacific Northwest and in the Aleutian Islands, where it sailed with destroyer escort.

When an Army cable between Crissy Field and Fort Baker had been severed by a passing ship, HDSF ordered the *Niles* back to the Bay Area to repair the break. But the mineplanter could not move---it was working a large and delicate cable off Fort Worden on Washington state's Puget Sound. Major Harry Payne, supervising cable work on the *Niles*, flew back to San Francisco aboard a Navy flying boat. If HDSF could not have the *Niles*, at least they could fly the assistant artillery engineer back to devise another way to repair the broken cable. After consulting with his Fort Scott wire chief, Major Payne rented a cable barge from the Pacific Telephone and Telegraph Company. The Army drew up a $400,000 contract with the telephone company for use of the barge *Pacific* and its tugboat to

repair the severed cable. From this episode, Major Payne convinced the Harbor Defenses to engage the telephone company barge for subsequent cable operations at the Golden Gate. This freed the *Niles* for missions elsewhere.

The Navy desired to get a telephone out to the ready-duty destroyer moored by the huge buoy west of the submarine net. Major Harry Payne had to find a brand of cable durable, yet flexible enough to survive the bobbing of the buoy. Through commercial sources, the major located a nineteen-gauge copper cable encased in layers of rubber sheathing and copper mesh. The Pacific Telephone barge ran this line from shore out to the destroyer. The cable led up to the buoy and into a waterproofed box housing the telephone which was linked to the ship by means of fast-disconnect plugs. In theory, the ready-duty vessel could come and go quickly, only needing to plug in or out of the telephone system. But whenever the Harbor Entrance Control Post called, the destroyer was often in such a hurry to shove off, it ripped the telephone installation off the buoy. However, the new phone hook-up satisfied the Navy; they had the Army lay a similar cable to the nearby submarine net tender. This type of rubber-sheathed flexible cable eventually replaced existing underwater communication lines to seacoast base-end stations. The original armored telephone lines were stiff, subject to damage by the rocks and ever-powerful tides off shore. The flexible cable proved more durable, and a Treasure Island-based Coast Guard ship, the *Sequoia*, installed it.

Late in the war, Bell laboratories sent another underwater detection device to San Francisco for testing. A Signal Corps major accompanied an enormous box shipped by railroad flatcar from the East Coast. The box contained an experimental underwater ranging device, the size of a small room, with rotating arms projecting off the top of the case. One of the harbor defense mineplanters submerged the unit just outside the Gate. The project was very secret, and the Signal Corps major who fretted constantly over it, evidently pulled a lot of weight with the high command. Every time the major wanted to haul the underwater device up for adjustment, the HDSF artillery engineers had to comply. On a windy day, the telephone company barge *Pacific* and its tugboat transported the Bell device back into the harbor for yet another adjustment. Heavy winds caught the high freeboard of the barge and propelled it past the tug, which was struggling through the choppy seas. "The barge was beating us through the Golden Gate sideways," remembered Harry Payne, who was aboard the tug. Powerful winds propelled the *Pacific* with its unusual load nearly up to the submarine net before the tugboat managed to get it back under tow.

Between April and August of 1944, a group of M3A1 ground mines planted on the rocky sea floor registered constantly in the mine casemate as if submarines were disturbing their magnetic fields. The disturbance was caused by nothing more than the five-mile an hour water current at the Golden Gate. The severe undersea conditions of the Gate prompted the Coast Artillery Board to recommend that all upcoming mine developments be tested at San Francisco. However, hostilities ended by the time new mines were ready for trials.

In 1944, the Harbor Defenses became part of a friendly controversy with the Marine Corps over which organization had invented a new seacoast artillery gun mount the previous year. Colonel Peter K. Kelly, an HDSF regimental executive officer, developed a high-speed ground mount in 1943 for the 155 M1 "Long Tom" gun, enabling the Army's standard heavy artillery piece to be used against moving waterborne targets. Based on the circular Panama mount used by the older 155mm guns at Fort Funston, the steel track sections of the "Kelly mount" could be quickly assembled by gun crews of 155mm batteries employed in seacoast defense of newly captured Pacific islands. Colonel Kelly had the prototype built at Fort Scott and conducted field trials at Cronkhite and Funston. Successful tests led to furnishing these unofficial mounts to Western Defense Command-trained 155mm artillery units headed overseas. The Marine Corps commandant at San Diego sent an operations officer to San Francisco to investigate Colonel Kelly's device. The Marine officer returned to San Diego with plans and a sample mount. HDSF passed on the design specifications and a full report "through channels" to the Chief of Ordnance at the War Department. Ordnance designers "complicated it considerably with fancy hand-holds," and the "Kelly mount" was officially approved as the Mount T6EI. By the summer of 1944, the 155mm gun on rails developed at HDSF began seeing action in the Pacific. "Employment of SCA in Island Warfare," an article in the May-June 1944 edition of the *Coast Artillery Journal*, detailed the employment of 155mm seacoast artillery mounts not by the Army, but by the Marine Corps. The Marines were even credited with inventing the mount.

A reply from HDSF followed in the next edition of the *Coast Artillery Journal*. On June 15, 1944, Colonel William LaFrenz wrote a letter to the magazine expressing "the views of the officers and men of the Harbor Defenses of San Francisco." The island warfare article was "well written, and logically sound from a tactical standpoint," LaFrenz wrote, "But there alas we must stop with the plaudits and start 'griping'." The HDSF executive officer explained the Marines did not invent the "Kelly mount" as stated in the magazine. LaFrenz then recounted Colonel Kelly's story and asked the *Journal* to print a retraction "and give our good friend 'Pete' Kelly, the credit he is due." "Incidentally," LaFrenz added, "the Harbor Defenses of San Francisco would also like a good plug for itself as we pride ourselves on being wide awake and on the job."

June 1944 was a momentous month. The Allied armies entered Rome in triumph on the 5th; the next day, Allied forces landed on the Normandy coast of France. In the Pacific, the Battle the Philippine Sea in the Marianas Island Group resulted in major losses to Japanese air and naval units. Liberation for the Philippines was at hand. In anticipation of a long, bitter struggle during the invasion of Japan proposed for 1945, the War Department transferred increasing numbers of coast artillerymen to the infantry. This caused additional reduction in the Golden Gate defenses. But those who still served at HDSF carried on as they had since the war began.

The HDSF Special Services officer

Aerial danger to Bay Area officially over. Volunteers serve final shift at 4th Air Force Aircraft Warning Service in the East Bay. Center shut down by War Department on May 29, 1944. (San Francisco Archives, S.F. Public Library)

needed connections to do his job. Lieutenant Leo Murphy, a San Franciscan, was well placed for his work, with ties to Army circles and the civilian community. Being a member of the famed Olympic Club, the oldest athletic club in the country, Murphy used his contacts to obtain large blocks of tickets for live shows at the Curran and Geary Theatres. Movie houses were also generous, and Lieutenant Murphy distributed dozens of complimentary tickets to enlisted men. He saw that tickets reached "the guys way out in the sticks," so they could see a first-run show on a three-day pass. The politically savvy Lieutenant Murphy also made sure "the brass" received a share of tickets, in order to build up his "good will."

Sometimes small USO shows came to restricted areas where harbor defense troops were stationed for long periods without leave. Every few weeks, the entertainers spent two days at HDSF. Special Services officers provided the USO troupe with Army transportation through the security zone and also prepared the messhall for the performances. Two shows played at seven and nine o'clock during the evening in a messhall well light-proofed for nightly blackout conditions. Dancers, singers, and comedians gave the eighty gathered GI's a forty-five minute show; then the orchestra took over for a dance. If the men got boisterous after the dance, Lieutenant Murphy was thankful to have his driver, Ser-

geant Aurel Coutoure, at his side. "If they started something near me," Murphy recalled, "Coutoure would go after them. He had a reputation for that. I always felt well protected."

Coutoure served at the Cronkhite 16-inch battery before his assignment to regimental headquarters at Fort Scott, where he worked for Lieutenant Murphy in the Special Services office. Coutoure left the post on Friday nights to box professionally with the San Francisco club circuit in the 135-pound class. After the third fight, Murphy kiddingly asked Sergeant Coutoure if he made any money at it. "Yeah," came the reply, "thirty-five hundred bucks." As Al Coutoure's record improved week by week, the fight circuit wanted to send him to Los Angeles for the Friday night bouts there. Sergeant Coutoure "was a nice kid, and this was a chance to make some money," Murphy explained to Colonel LaFrenz. The colonel agreed under certain conditions. Coutoure could travel to Los Angeles and fight on the weekends, but only if he had a contract with the promoters that paid fifty dollars per fight and deposited Coutoure's winnings in a trust fund for his return to civilian life. Al Coutoure did well in Los Angeles, even becoming a fan favorite---until a regular medical examination discovered his blindness in the right eye. This disqualified Coutoure from boxing, and got him discharged from the service, but not until he had done well enough as a boxer to cash in a trust fund of $45,000.

Since early 1944, Brigadier General Ralph E. Haines had been serving as chief of two organizations: the Harbor Defenses of San Francisco and the Northern California Sector of Western Defense Command. As a senior officer involved in the defense of the metropolitan area, General Haines represented the Army in San Francisco civic activities. On May 13, 1944, San Francisco Archbishop John J. Mitty invited Haines and "all the officers who are under your command" to a Solemn Military Mass of Requiem for all those who have "made the supreme sacrifice of their lives in this present war." When the Board of Directors of the China War Relief Association requested the presence of an Army representative at the reviewing stand for the commemoration of the "Seventh Anniversary of China's Fight for Freedom," Major General Charles H. Bonesteel sent Haines to represent Western Defense Command for the July 6th parade in Chinatown. General Haines received many letters from civic groups and local corporations that asked for his presence at functions or thanked him for some favor done by the Harbor Defenses. He sometimes granted passes to avid saltwater anglers among the civilians he met, allowing acquaintances to fish off the restricted zone of Baker Beach. When 6th Coast Artillery Chaplain John J. Morley invited the city's Auxiliary Bishop, Reverend Thomas A. Connolly, to confer the Sacrament of Confirmation to Catholic harbor defense troops on Wednesday, September 27th, General Haines attended the ceremony. Together with the commanding colonels of HDSF, Haines reviewed the soldiers as they marched into the Fort Scott Chapel.

In the early autumn of 1944, Major General Charles H. Bonesteel, the Western Defense Command chief with the evocative name, spent two days inspecting HDSF troops. "Coast Artillery is a formidable force in the defense of these shores," he assured them; "Troops in Harbor Defense installations are performing a vital duty which must be performed well." But a long-planned Army reorganization of combat units that autumn was more cataclysmic to the Harbor Defenses than enemy battleships could have been. The Army disbanded all coast artillery regiments on October 18th; at San Francisco, this ended the 6th Coast Artillery. Its personnel went on to form four new and separate coast artillery

General Haines at post boxing tournament. Captain McClellan, the general's aide, in right foreground. (Presidio Army Museum)

battalions at HDSF.

The new battalion system simplified harbor defense organization. Previously, regiments existed to feed, clothe, and house troops, while groups and groupments controlled tactical matters. Under the new system, battalions consolidated administrative and tactical functions; and each battalion filled a specific role within the harbor defense. Antimotor torpedo boat defense was now carried out by the two batteries of the new 6th Coast Artillery Battalion, manning AMTB weapons on north and south shores. The elevation of AMTB defense to a full battalion signified the importance of automatic weapons in guarding the harbor entrance. The 174th CA Battalion maintained and operated the mine defenses with two mine batteries and a mine flotilla. The 172nd CA Battalion covered the mine-

China war relief parade on Stockton Street in Chinatown, a common sight in this S.F. community during the war years. (R. Gyn)

fields with the 6-inch guns at Point Lobos and two old 6-inch batteries on the Marin side. Long-range seacoast defense consisted of the two 16-inch batteries manned by the 173rd Coast Artillery Battalion. The three mine-planters, a separate seacoast searchlight battery, and a headquarters battery for the H-Station remained under direct control of HDSF. Purged by the streamlining were some familiar batteries of earlier days, including all 155's, fixed 3-inch antiaircraft guns, the 6-inch gun batteries along Baker Beach, and the recently casemated 12-inch guns at Fort Barry. No tradition was sacred; the ex-6th Coast Artillery Band remained at the Harbor Defenses, but was given a more generic sounding name---the 72nd Army Ground Forces Band. By early next year, this military band would be transferred out of San Francisco, "to take up its tempo" at Camp McQuaide, the Coast Artillery Replacement Center in Watsonville, California.

Though Arthur Kramer won his promotion to lieutenant colonel for having done a good job as HDSF Supply Officer, the Harbor Defenses still tapped his knowledge of gunnery. When HDSF wanted to know the range to the first ricochet of a 90mm gun at zero elevation from a site forty feet above the water, Kramer was ordered to find the answer. Employing his training in physics and ballistics, Kramer calculated the solution on paper. Then his superiors asked him to prove

it. The lieutenant colonel put a 90mm gun and crew on a suitable test site, established the base line for instrumental measurements, and conducted the firing. The live results came to "within less than 0.5%" of his paper calculations.

Eventually, Kramer left his staff assignment with HDSF Headquarters and took command of the 6th Coast Artillery Battalion, which manned the anti-motor torpedo boat defenses. Located atop Fort Point, the AMTB battalion command post directed 40mm and 90mm batteries on both sides of the harbor entrance and took orders from the H-Station. Besides staffing the command post, the battalion headquarters detachment also fired the 3-inch guns on the barbette tier of the fort.

The AMTB battalion's 90mm guns were controlled by SCR-545 radar, a type nicknamed "Mickey Mouse" because of its twin parabolic antenna. Position data from the radar fed into an M10 director, one of the first electronic fire-control directors used by the Army. Kramer conducted one target practice with a 90mm battery on the San Francisco side, intending to hit a radio-controlled JR-boat going thirty knots "on a sinuous course at 9,000 yards." Colonel LaFrenz was "convinced we couldn't do it," recalled Arthur Kramer. The two officers agreed to a wager before firing commenced. On about the seventh round, the 90mm guns hit the speeding JR-boat, and Kramer won the bet. As the mine flotilla tug towed the radio-controlled target boat back to Fort Baker, the metallic flotation tanks of the little boat collapsed from the water pressure and sank in Horseshoe Cove off the Baker dock. Too many JR-boats were being lost to AMTB target practice. The *Coast Artillery Journal* urged keeping the fast JR-boats in "optimum operating condition." "They are essentially racing boats," warned the *Journal*, "and require specialists to care for them properly."

The 40mm AMTB batteries of the 6th Coast Artillery Battalion employed director-control to guide fire up to the target. From that point, tracer rounds indicated hits and director-control was ignored. Several 40mm batteries on the northern shore fired from high bluffs. "From that height of site, shooting at a target at 3,000 yards was like shooting fish in a barrel," said Kramer years later. "We were literally looking down the target's throat." The standard 40mm target was a vertical rectangle on a towed sled as specified in dimensions by the Coast Artillery Board at Fort Monroe. Hits were counted by the number of holes piercing the rectangle. The *Redwood*, a former rum-runner, pulled the target at twenty-five knots.

When the 40mm target was smaller than specified, an allowance for the decrease was calculated into the score. If the target was three-quarters normal size, the number of hits was multiplied by the inverse, or four-thirds. This method of calculation sometimes produced strange practice scores; in one instance, the number of hits per gun per minute exceeded the number of 40mm rounds per gun per minute actually fired. After Kramer reported the results of the practice shoot, the Coast Artillery Board rejected the scores as unbelievable. But Colonel LaFrenz, the HDSF executive officer, vouched for the scores, having personally observed the actual firing. Arthur Kramer recalled this particular target practice as being "lots of fun. The number of pelicans that hit the air at the first round fired was really a sight to see."

When war began, HDSF had five batteries manning 6-inch armament. The 1944 reorganization created the 172nd Coast Artillery Battalion with three firing batteries protecting the minefields. Battery B was one of these units, and had a baseball squad called the Barry Lions, a tribute to the well-regarded battery mascot of old. Despite reorganization, business at their Fort Barry emplacement continued as it had since war started. Camouflage netting covered the position. When not in use, he four Model 1900 6-inch rifles traversed out of view under the net. From the air, one could only see two farm buildings. These were actually the messhall and latrine in disguise on the hill behind the camouflaged emplacement. Since 1941, the enlisted men lived in a wooden "railroad car" under the hill, so dubbed because of its long and narrow shape.

The captain and his lieutenants lived in the concrete emplacement amid the ammunition in a dank, airless room under the battery commander's station. When alerted, the officers quickly ran up the outside ladder steps to the constantly manned station. To First Lieutenant Mario Paolini, the battery executive officer, this arrangement was "just like a submarine, running up to the conning tower." Men assigned to the battery's observation stations came back to the battery for hot showers and to pick up the mail. Provided

General Haines at his desk. When this photo was taken, besides being HDSF commander, he was probably also Northern California Sector CG of Western Defense Command. (Presidio Army Museum)

with ration stamps and their own vehicles, the observation crews purchased food and prepared it themselves at the stations. On the road behind the battery, daily reveille took place at 6:30 in the morning. Following the maxim of "present or accounted for," the reveille was not attended by all personnel at the same time. Because of the constant alert still in effect in 1944, part of the battery was always on duty, which meant some men off-duty were asleep.

Two hundred feet down the road from Battery B stood an emplacement of 3-inch guns named Battery O'Rorke. These guns had long since stopped being a part of the tactical makeup of the Harbor Defenses. However, HDSF found a reason to fire the armament in June 1944. Beginning in that month, battery grade officers received a three-week refresher course in gunnery. The officers took two weeks of classroom study at Fort Scott, then spent a final week in the field with the 3-inch guns at Fort Barry. Neighboring Battery B furnished crews for the firing sessions as the officers practiced spotting and adjusting fire with the small seacoast guns. It seemed to Lieutenant Paolini that Battery O'Rorke "had more firing time than any other battery in the continental U.S." His gunners fired about two hundred rounds a day for the officers during training periods.

The command post for the 172nd Coast Artillery Battalion was located on Bonita Ridge in the old station of the former Mine Groupment command post. Designated GATE Station, this post controlled the 6-inch batteries protecting the minefields and aided the mine casemate and H-Station in checking harbor traffic. Like all command posts at the Harbor Defenses, GATE Station operated around the clock. The enlisted personnel came from the headquarters detachment, and the batteries of the battalion provided duty officers who put in six hour shifts. The officer with midnight to 6:00 a.m. duty arrived after evening chow carrying a good book, and settled in for the night in an alcove under the main floor of the split-level command post.

On October 20th, two days after the Harbor Defenses were reorganized, U.S. Army forces returned to the Philippines with landings on Leyte. In November, B-29 Superfortresses bombed Tokyo and other Japanese cities. In Europe, winter snow held up Allied ground advances in Italy and on the Franco-German frontier, but all anticipated that upcoming spring offensives would lead to final Allied victory. The Pacific war remained the major concern for the United States, which planned to invade the Japanese home islands in 1945 and 1946. San Francisco Bay was still the great staging base for the Pacific war. But with Japanese naval power already destroyed, would the Golden Gate still need harbor defenses?

Chapter 10:

Victory and Beyond

On January 19, 1945, the new Western Defense Command chief, Major General Henry Conger Pratt, accompanied by Brigadier General Haines, Northern California Sector commander, and Colonel LaFrenz, new HDSF commander, inspected harbor defense installations on the Marin side starting at 8:15 a.m. At Fort Baker, the officers examined mine craft, dock facilities, and several nearby searchlight positions. On Kirby Beach, they inspected AMTB batteries as a 40mm gun crew of the 6th Coast Artillery Battalion demonstrated gunnery skill by "shattering a fast-moving target" on the water. At 9:50 a.m., the commanding officers saw unfinished Battery 129 on the 800-foot heights of Fort Baker. A visit to Fort Barry followed with inspections of Batteries Rathbone and Wallace, GATE Station and the Barry mine casemate. Major General Pratt paid attention to housing, day rooms, supply rooms, troop formations, post exchanges, and "all facilities and conditions that contribute to the morale of the soldiers," to quote the *Coast Artillery Journal*. At the Mendell area, the officers visited the Orientation School for Replacement Personnel, where HDSF newcomers, mainly overseas veterans, were given a one-week introduction to seacoast gunnery and harbor defense operations. After a pause for lunch at Battery Smith-Guthrie, the officers resumed the inspection at Fort Cronkhite with a look at the 16-inch emplacement, Station QS, and the motor pool. At three o'clock, the officers returned to the Presidio by way of the Fort Barry tunnel.

As American forces advanced closer toward Japan, stories reached home of what really happened during the early days of the war. In 1945 at Fort Scott, orientation classes heard an eyewitness account of the Bataan Death March from one of its survivors, Corporal Glen Kuskie, who also lived through the torpedoing and sinking of a Japanese prison ship. The son of a civilian fireman at Fort Barry, Corporal Kuskie described his experiences to large audiences at the Scott theatre. Harbor defensemen also viewed the Army's "Why We Fight" documentary film series which explained American war aims. After each episode, local radio commentator William Winter spoke to the troops about global affairs.

In early 1945, a San Francisco newspaper instigated a new HDSF blood drive. Army, Navy, and civilian harbor defense personnel donated pints of blood to register votes in the Purple Heart Queen contest sponsored by the *San Francisco Call-Bulletin*. After six weeks of the contest, Private First Class Fannie Cox, a WAC at the Fort Baker hospital held the most votes with two hundred pints of blood donated in her honor. Thanks to newly-developed refrigerants, the blood reached the fighting front in the Philippines within forty-eight hours of donation.

On January 9th, after securing Leyte in the south, U.S. Army forces landed on Luzon, the large northern island of the Philippines. The Americans pushed toward Manila, and by the beginning of February, they reached the outskirts of the Philippine capital. Twelve hundred miles to the northeast, U.S. Navy ships and aircraft bombarded Iwo Jima as a preliminary step to invasion. Army B-24 and B-29 heavy bombers also softened the island from January 25th into the second week of February. In Europe, Soviet armies began the final drive from Warsaw to Berlin. From the west, Allied forces, having stopped the German winter offensive in the Ardennes, pushed on toward the Rhine River.

Allied victory in Europe was expected in a few months. Between February 4th and 11th, Winston Churchill of Great Britain and Joseph Stalin of the Soviet Union met with President Roosevelt at Yalta, a Crimean resort town on the Black Sea. First, the leaders agreed how to occupy Germany after her surrender. Then they discussed conditions upon which the Soviets would enter the war against Japan. Finally, they reviewed the Dumbarton Oaks Proposals, a first draft of the World Charter then being circulated for study among the forty-five states of the United Nations and Associated Nations. The Proposals envisioned an assembly of all nations guided by a council of leading states. The "Big Three" departed Yalta agreeing "that a United Nations Conference on the proposed world organization should be summoned for Wednesday, 25th April, 1945, and should be held in the United States of America."

On February 12, 1945, one day after the Yalta meeting ended, the U.S. government informed San Francisco Mayor Roger Lapham that his city was chosen as the site of the Founding Conference of the United Nations "for the maintenance of international peace and security." In the metropolis that prided itself the war center of the West Coast, the heady intoxication of playing host to this historic gathering dedicated to maintaining peace in the postwar world caused some like publisher James Delkin to proclaim, "the City by the Golden Gate is woven into a key position in the new future of the peoples of the earth." But the conflict was not yet over. In Europe, it was nearly so, but the war against Japan promised another year of hard fighting. International delegates to San Francisco could expect to find warships on the bay. "Lights glare all night long. Men and machines are at their work," observed the *New York Times Magazine* in 1945. "This port has one main commodity to send abroad. It is exporting war." As Mayor Roger Lapham would later say in apology to the international delegates regarding the simplicity of official ceremony at the United Nations Conference, "We know you realize that San Francisco is carrying a heavy responsibility as the main war port of the Pacific Coast."

After four years of war, the military atmosphere of San Francisco was no more evident than along Market Street, the city's main downtown thoroughfare. Edwin

Streetcars have stopped for a light as sailors and other pedestrians cross Market Street. (San Francisco Archives, S.F. Public Library)

Rosskam noted that Market Street sliced "through the city's plan, parallel to nothing in particular and at sharp angles to the side streets." Men and women in uniform, especially Navy uniforms, packed the downtown quarter. Market Street was boisterous and crowded, packed "with restaurants and stores of the less expensive kind. Several blocks snap with the neon signs of movies, bars and hash houses." A "Fun Center" now occupied an old Bank of America building. Men in service from all branches and Allied nations jostled shoulder to shoulder over the blinking lights and carnival bells of the pinball arcade amusements. One reporter saw "British and American sailors, arm in arm, having their picture snapped in front of a cardboard battle-wagon with a cardboard girl in a hula skirt." Outside, servicemen new to the city were startled to see Market Street trolley cars thundering by on four parallel tracks with competing cars running abreast like race horses, "which is disconcerting to the out-of-towner who sees them bearing down upon him for the first time." Women streetcar conductors became a common sight during the city's war years. "There are dozens of them," claimed the *National Geographic*, "and hundreds more in training for these jobs." Men conductors, those too old for military service, could still be seen manning the trolleys. The old motormen retained their well-known friendly "disregard for rank or station." "Climb on kids," one conductor called to two Navy captains, "let's keep this war moving."

Where Market Street ended at the Embarcadero, under the clock tower of the Ferry Building, GI's on pass signed on for twelve hours of work with maritime engineering companies which maintained and refitted transports under contract to the federal government. At midnight, company trucks took the men along the Embarcadero to ships that needed service. On these jobs, the contracting company employed as many people as possible. "You punched in, you went down, and went to sleep," revealed one GI worker, because his employer was "on a cost-plus basis with the U.S. Government. The bigger the payroll, the more they made." Shifts lasted normally eight hours with an additional four

Mare Island Naval Shipyard, April 12, 1945. (San Francisco Archives, S.F. Public Library)

hours overtime. Workers stopped for coffee or meal breaks every four hours. The job involved cleaning out the insides of transports back from war duty. The difficulty of the cleaning depended on what cargo had been carried on board during the previous voyage. But unless the deadline was pressing, the work progressed leisurely. GI's who moonlighted regularly for the same contractor, could rise to foreman in charge of a crew. "He might be a PFC and the guy working under him would be a tech sergeant," recalled one harbor defenseman who took the job. A serviceman made about twenty-nine dollars for a night's work; good pay in comparison to the fifty dollars a month he earned from the Army.

In Chinatown, shops stayed open and street lights burned brightly until the wee hours. Restaurants operated through the night for Chinese shipyard workers coming and going on their various shifts. "There are a dozen cafes in the block between Grant Ave-

Herb Caen saw "civilian patriots in saloons," buying "drink after drink for supercilious, slightly contemptuous young GI's listening with deaf ears to their self-appointed hosts' recital of their prowess in World War I."

In the black section of town, on Post and Fillmore Streets, twenty-five cents bought live music and a bottle of beer at the Club Alabam. And "if you had fifty-cents and could put your nose over the bar," recalled a harbor defense officer, "they'd serve you a drink." When servicemen patronized the club, fights sometimes broke out. The soldiers would "have a hell of a fight," and then return to the "rabbit huts" at Fort Funston "with the uniform cut when somebody went after them with a razor," reported the officer, who also witnessed the Shore Patrol charging into the fray at the Club Alabam with rifles and fixed bayonets.

Omar Khyyam's, a well-known downtown restaurant on O'Farrell Street, catered more sedately to GI's. The restaurant's owner, George Mardikian, knew a coast artilleryman of Armenian extraction from the Funston 16-inch battery. Every week, the Armenian brought three enlisted men from the battery to dine at the restaurant, and Mardikian picked up the tab. Ever the patriot, Mardikian also promoted the campaign to save food for the war effort by taking ten percent off the bill at Omar Khyyam's if the customer left a clean plate after the meal.

Not all businesses operated so honestly with servicemen. "Some restaurants sacrificed years of reputation on the altar of the quick brick," observed Herb Caen. In one of the major hotels on Nob Hill, the other employees knew the head bartender to be "a very well-to-

nue and Kearny Street," related one wartime guide book, "which serve Chinese food to Americans and American food to the Chinese." Chinatown had its share of bars, including the Twin Dragon on Waverly Place, the Club Shanghai on Grant Avenue, and the Chinese Sky Room on the corner of Grant Avenue and Pine Street. "As long as you stayed in the tourist areas you were fine," recalled one officer of the Harbor Defenses. He knew of one Chinatown alley leading into the darkness from the corner of a well-known coffee shop and bakery. "If you went in there at night, you could get into a tremendous fist fight."

The one-block concentration of nightspots on Pacific Street known as the International Settlement offered bar-hopping servicemen a choice of drinking themes that ranged from mining town saloon to prewar Parisian cafe. Goman's "Gay 90's" played to packed houses "in an atmosphere of red plush and gilt." The Hurricane, a club which sent its stage review on tour of the harbor defense outposts, featured decor with a South Seas flavor. The Hawaiian motif was so popular for San Francisco bars during the war, that "You can't pass many blocks without seeing bamboo and coconut trees behind a city door," observed the National Geographic. Columnist

do fellow." When GI customers got too inebriated to notice, the bartender filled their shot glasses only half-full, but charged them for a full drink and pocketed the difference. Sometimes a serviceman complained to hotel management. But the bartender was never fired. As Herb Caen said of incidents like this; "Not a pretty sight to see in a world-famed metropolis noted for a 'special' something."

On the lower part of Powell Street before the incline up Nob Hill, GI's found major hotels like the St. Francis and Sir Francis Drake good for "lobby dancing." Couples lingered outside hotel ballrooms, dancing and listening to the live music. This was almost as good as being inside and one did not have to pay a cover charge. "If you bought a drink once in a while," recalled a young HDSF lieutenant, "management said nothing." At the top of Nob Hill, the Fairmont Hotel attracted a different clientele. The hotel had many permanent guests and charged more for drinks. Officers frequented the Fairmont so the enlisted ranks tended to stay away. They did so because of "too much brass," to quote one Fairmont employee; the enlisted men did not "like to be seen by their superiors at times."

In May 1945, the Fairmont's new owner turned an old supper club with an indoor pool into the Tonga Room, where diners ate Polynesian cuisine aboard a "ship" in the South Seas. At the hotel's Cirque Room, many a fuzzy-cheeked Navy ensign enjoyed drinks at the black-enameled semicircular bar. The mirrored columns and intimate corner tables made the Cirque a popular club in the 1940's. Friday and Saturday night crowds got so large, man-

agement opened nearby rooms to extend the dance floor. Shore Patrol and Military Police stood at the entry to check the identification of those who appeared underaged and to prevent trouble from those who might have had too much to drink. Not all heavy imbibers were servicemen. The Navy loved to buy drinks for Father O'Malley, a priest who visited the Cirque Room during the daytime. By the end of a typical afternoon, obliging Navy ensigns carried Father O'Malley by the legs and shoulders out of the hotel.

Visiting military patrons left their hats and coats at the check stand across the red-plush corridor from the Cirque Room entry. If a soldier or sailor lost his headgear in the crowded bar, he was considered out of uniform. "Boy, that was a sad case," remembered Rose Gyn, a hat-check girl. She felt sorry for the unfortunate servicemen, because "you couldn't go back to your ship or your base without a hat." The attendants kept unclaimed hats behind the counter for any hatless soldiers or sailors who could use them.

The Fairmont, as one of the city's premier hotels, played host to famous names during the war years. James Roosevelt, one of the president's sons, visited the Cirque Room as a Marine officer. Reportedly, President Roosevelt came by the Fairmont sometimes, and even had installed a concrete ramp for his

California Street side entrance to Fairmont Hotel on Nob Hill. (San Francisco Archives, S.F. Public Library)

wheel chair that led from the curb to the Fairmont's corner entrance. Carlos P. Romulo, the noted author and spokesman for the Philippine government-in-exile, visited his countrymen who worked at the hotel. Hollywood celebrities like Greer Garson stayed at the elegant Fairmont and singer Lena Horne frequently performed there. Rose Gyn, from her vantage point at the Cirque Room hat-check stand, saw many celebrities like movie star Caesar Romero, who danced so smoothly in his military uniform and "great big boots."

As the late April United Nations Conference opening date approached, the bay metropolis rolled out the red carpet of international hospitality. At Golden Gate Park, a huge floral tapestry proclaiming "San Francisco Welcomes United Nations" rendered in red begonias, white alyssum, and blue violas, dominated the sloping lawn before the wood and glass Conservatory. "Fresh crabs and lobsters were trundled to the open-air fish markets and restaurants on Fisherman's Wharf," *Life* magazine said, forgetting that lobster was not found on the West Coast. "Historic cable cars were poised to haul delegates up and down

California and Powell Streets," *Life* continued. "The Navy was taking extraordinary measures to protect the city against a shelling by a sneak Japanese sub."

The Army reinforced their Bay Area defenses also. Lieutenant Colonel George B. Webster had returned from duty in Panama when he was assigned command of an AA group headquarters in San Diego. Then came orders to go to San Francisco and form a provisional antiaircraft artillery group with two gun battalions and at least one automatic weapons battalion. On March 27th, the San Francisco Antiaircraft Artillery Group, Provisional was activated in the bay city specifically to give antiaircraft protection to the United Nations Conference. This assignment marked a return to the Golden Gate for Webster, who as a second lieutenant in 1939-40, was the first battery commander of the Funston 16-inch seacoast guns. In the city one month before the historic gathering, the antiaircraft group positioned batteries at Golden Gate Park and "any place where there was enough room to stick a gun battery down," recalled the group commander. The mission involved protection of the Civic Center site of the convention and the big hotels where the world dignitaries would be staying. Lieutenant Colonel Webster, accompanied by a San Francisco police captain, scouted docks and rooftops as potential sites for placing automatic weapons. The Army officer had access to most buildings, though with the police captain along, nervous building inhabitants thought "they were about to be pinched for some violations." Troop support and administrative units of the provisional group set up in the red-bricked armory south of Market Street. Webster established his operations center under the concrete bleachers at Aquatic Park.

Between April 15th and 20th, several west-bound trains from the East Coast headed across the United States to San Francisco, carrying foreign delegates to the United

Mayor Roger Lapham (left) greets U.S. Secretary of State Edward R. Stettinius at S.F. Airport for opening of United Nations Conference, April 24, 1945. (San Francisco Archives, S.F. Public Library)

Nations Conference on International Organization. When the international visitors arrived in town, reporters and curious onlookers clustered in hotel lobbies, hoping to catch a glimpse of busy foreign delegates rushing by. "It was fun to see Russian generals," wrote one observer, "in their baggy pants, out in the park sunning themselves." Complimentary baskets of fruit spruced up the dignitaries' hotel rooms. Curbside limousines at hotel entrances stood ready to whisk world visitors on city tours, or on longer rides through Marin to the wine country or the redwood trees of Muir Woods. The Harbor Defenses loaned two medical officers and five technicians to the United Nations Conference for the duration of the proceedings. The HDSF medical team conducted complete physical examinations on 250 Army limousine drivers and maintained the health of these soldiers who chauffeured delegates to and from meetings.

The historic conference formally opened on April 25th, 1945. Army limousines descended on the Civic Center with their VIP passengers, taking them to the front of the San Francisco War Memorial, erected in 1932 as a tribute to the city's fallen of the Great War. Around a central court, the Memorial consisted of the Opera House and the Veterans' Building, "both of them like some marble foreign ministry, surrounded by the flashing colors of the wind-whipped flags of the forty-six nations that opened the conference," wrote one participant. The four-story Veterans' Building provided offices for the world delegates. The opening session of the conference took place in the 3500-seat Opera House. Inside, "the stage setting was right out of Maxfield Parrish," wrote Helen A. Lapham, wife of the San Francisco mayor. Four majestic garlanded pillars, representing the Four Freedoms, rose against a sky-blue background. National colors of forty-six countries lined the stage. An honor guard of American men and

(Above) Interior Opera House during first session. Military honor guard arrayed on stage during opening ceremony. (San Francisco Archives, S.F. Public Library)

women in the uniforms of all the military services initiated the ceremonies. California Governor Earl Warren and U.S. Secretary of State Edward Stettinius followed with opening addresses. Then President Harry S. Truman spoke to the assembly by telephone hook-up from Washington, asking the delegates to" rise above personal interests," and to forge a world body to "redeem the terrible sacrifices of the last six years." This was a somber and serious affair, wrote a New York Times reporter: "The mood of the assembly was so like the mood of the war . . . a war without parades . . . The fact that the opening act was simple, grave and understated added to its impressiveness."

The conferees realized, said one observer, that "the war was only half over, that out beyond the Golden Gate still lay death for . . . young men and women." Military personnel died in the line of duty even within the safety of the harbor. On May 4th at 1:00 p.m., a Navy PBY Catalina flying boat on patrol duties, crashed in heavy fog atop Wolf Ridge on property belonging to the Marin County Land and Cattle Company. "Commander, watch your airspeed," were the last words heard over headsets by the two waist-gunners aboard just before the patrol bomber hit the

Front of Opera House after opening session of UN Conference. (San Francisco Archives, S.F. Public Library)

Wolf Ridge, leading up to the burning Catalina. Eight charred bodies lay in the wreck. The dead pilot had been thrown out of the plane and lay at the edge of the burned area. A guard was posted because personal property and detached depth bombs littered the crash site. The Navy people from Treasure Island who later arrived at Wolf Ridge

fog-shrouded ridge top. The force of impact propelled the gunners through the bubble hatches on both sides of the fuselage. Staggering away from the burning plane, the two survivors made their way to a rancher. Within five minutes, Captain Charles Blaugrund, Surgeon of the 172nd Coast Artillery Battalion arrived with two enlisted medics to administer first aid before sending the Navy aircrew to Fort Baker for thorough care. The station hospital treated the gunners for shock, bruises, and third-degree burns.

Lieutenant Colonel John Schonher had seen other air mishaps over the Golden Gate during his time with the Harbor Defenses. Army fighter planes coming in from patrol sometimes flew under the Golden Gate Bridge before making the turn for Hamilton Field. Once, during an inspection of a Fort Barry base-end station, Schonher looked up and saw "somebody dangling in a parachute right over the Golden Gate." A P-39 pilot had come in too low and caught his propeller in the water, but managed to climb high enough to bail out. That incident ended happily, but the crash site which Lieutenant Colonel Schonher came upon Friday, April 5th was a different matter. A deep V-shaped groove ran along the top of

had grim faces and tear-filled eyes as they surveyed the scene where their friends and companions had died. In all, nine Navy airmen perished in the crash; four officers and five enlisted men. The next day, Navy demolitions experts detonated the depth bombs carried aboard the PBY. Since the concussion from the detonated bombs were "felt throughout Marin County," the local sheriff publicly disclosed the cause of the explosion.

Meanwhile, the meetings and social activities of the United Nations conference went on, "trying," as Herb Caen remembered, "to complete its business amid an endless round of cocktail parties." The war was being won; there was an air of optimism among the gathered delegates. The post-war world offered a fresh beginning toward international cooperation. At scattered locations around the Bay Area, each delegation hosted gatherings and put their best intentions on display for the rest of the world. "One typical afternoon started with Russian War Relief at the St. Francis," wrote Helen Lapham, where "we heard the Star-Spangled Banner played on the balalaika." The party then moved to the Panamanian delegation at the other end of town. Next, the mayor and his wife went to the

University Club for the Netherlands and to Berkeley for the Czechs. "We arrived home at 8:45," Mrs. Lapham recalled, "without having seen the Russian or Panamanian Ambassadors." International guests even visited the Harbor Defenses. Chinese naval attaches called on Colonel LaFrenz at Fort Scott. They observed the administrative organization of HDSF, then went on a tour of the installations.

The Arabian delegates in headdresses and flowing robes aroused the most interest among conference watchers. The Saudi delegation occupied an entire floor of the Fairmont Hotel. When a Saudi prince boarded the elevator, American women, whose curiosity got the better of their manners, lifted the hem of his robes. In turn, the Arabians were fascinated by flush-toilets and American gadgets. Stores were "practically bought out," claimed Helen Lapham, when the Arab delegates went on a downtown shopping spree. The Arabians did their part for international hospitality by hosting an elaborate banquet with gold service and flowing champagne at the California Palace of the Legion of Honor adjacent to Fort Miley.

Sometime in early May, Lieutenant Colonel George Webster led newspaper reporters through the provisional antiaircraft artillery group's Aquatic Park operations center. The journalists saw a target being tracked on the center's operations board and asked Webster what the sighting meant. The lieutenant colonel knew, but could not disclose that his men had spotted and were tracking a Japanese balloon bomb drifting somewhere above the Bay Area. "Gentlemen," Webster announced to the reporters, "I think you'd better leave and let these folks get on with their work." But the newshounds sensed a good story and dragged their feet about leaving. Finally, the lieutenant colonel offered to reveal the facts if the reporters promised to withhold publication until further notice. The scribes eagerly agreed, so Webster revealed the center was tracking an enemy balloon carrying one kilogram of explosives. The next morning, the story was in the paper.

The Soviet delegation did not stay in a city hotel. They lived aboard a Soviet ship berthed at the Embarcadero. Should a strafing enemy plane try to disrupt Allied wartime cooperation and cause an international incident, the San Francisco Antiaircraft Artillery Group deployed automatic weapons along the waterfront to protect the Soviet delegates. To control the fire of these weapons, the AA provisional group established an open-air command post on the roof of a nearby building. The command party was to sleep in the building's elevator machinery room. When Lieutenant Colonel Webster came up to inspect the command post, he found all the cots and bedding neatly folded and stacked. No station personnel were in sight except for the men on duty at the time. The AA group commander walked down one flight and found the off-duty men in a penthouse apartment. The soldiers relaxed in the living room, enjoying the view of the inner harbor through spacious picture windows. The "very gracious lady" who lived in the penthouse fed the men and allowed them to stay in the luxurious quarters.

High atop the Fairmont Hotel, in another luxurious penthouse apartment, the "Big Four"---China, Great Britain, the Soviet Union, and the United States guided the political reconstruction of the postwar world. This select group became five when France joined the meetings. U.S. Secretary of State Edward R. Stettinius resided in the penthouse during the two-month United Nations Conference. And since he was the ranking delegate of the host nation, his apartment became the meeting place for the informal but important sessions of the "Big Five." Reporters prowled the Fairmont's lobby, hoping to pick up tantalizing details on the ostensibly secret talks at the top-floor penthouse. As part of their political maneuverings, members of the Big Five sometimes sent agents downstairs to leak information to the press. One small room in the hotel lobby was routinely used for impromptu revelations, and became known as "The Leaker-y."

Despite amiable feelings at the founding conference, conflicting interests surfaced among the "Big Five." Much controversy involved Soviet foreign minister V. Molotov, "a blue-eyed, affable bull in a navy-blue suit," who went about San Francisco accompanied by a squad of hefty body guards. The previous year, Russian armies halted outside Warsaw, allowing the Germans to crush the Polish Home Army, which contained moderate leaders unfavorable to the Soviets. The Russians then fashioned a Polish government more to their own liking. At San Francisco, Molotov tried to gain United Nations admittance for a Poland administered by this Soviet-inspired government. Meanwhile, Latin American countries urged the U.S. to seek United Nations acceptance for Argentina, which had been sympathetic to Germany during the war. The Soviets appeared willing to accept Argentina if Poland was also admitted to the United Nations, but the Americans insisted that each case be settled independently.

Molotov made public this controversy during an open conference in the Opera House on Monday, May 7th. That day, HDSF Lieutenant Colonels Arthur Kramer and John Schonher sat in the balcony of the auditorium as Molotov spoke. The Soviet foreign minister urged delegates to investigate Argentina's profascist government and to delay a vote for that country's admittance to the United Nations. Turning to the subject of Poland, Molotov argued impassionately for her admission to the United Nations by reminding delegates that Warsaw was bombed "mercilessly" by the Nazis. "You son of a bitch," retorted Lieutenant Colonel Kramer in an audible stage-whisper from the balcony, "and who sat on the other side of the river and let them do it?" Ushers swept down the aisles looking for the speaker, but no one pointed out the Army officer who made the remark. "It would have been a damned embarrassing experience," Kramer confided years later. Afterwards, as the HDSF officers stopped for a traffic light on Van Ness Avenue, a limousine carrying Molotov and two of his body guards pulled alongside. But there was no incident. Undoubtedly, Molotov did not know who was in the Army staff car.

After sixty-two days of politics and socializing, the first United Nations conference drew to a close at noon on June 26th with all participants signing the United Nations Charter. President Truman had landed at Hamilton Field the day before. A Special Security Detachment from the Harbor Defenses fired a salute as the president descended from the plane. The overseas veterans picked for this detachment wore "service ribbons and stripes" giving "this detail a most impressive appearance," reported the *Coast* Artillery *Journal*. Northern California Sector of Western Defense Command secured the highway from Hamilton Field to the Golden Gate Bridge. Harbor defense troops lined the road and checked culverts for bombs. The provisional antiaircraft artillery group, whose men and communications were already in place by nature of their AA mission, aided the San Francisco police by watching windows and rooftops of city buildings along the president's motorcade route. "How would you like being the President des Etats Unis?" Truman wrote his mother the night before, "It's a hell of a

Soviet Foreign Minister V.M. Molotov (right) sits with Soviet Ambassador to U.S. A.A. Gromyko at opening session in Opera House, April 25, 1945. (Presidio Army Museum)

Audience for Opera House UN sessions: mid-balcony for reporters, upper balcony for spectators. (San Francisco Archives, S.F. Public Library)

life." On the eve of the final session, the president hosted a reception at the Fairmont Hotel for delegates and heads of missions.

At noon on June 26th, the United Nations charter signing took place in the auditorium of the Veterans' Building. Among the one thousand Bay Area service personnel invited to witness the historic proceedings were thirty soldiers from the Harbor Defenses. On stage, before an array of fifty national flags on gilded flagpoles, Secretary of State Stettinius reminded delegates, "When we disagreed, we tried again, and then again, until we ended by reconciling the differences among us." At center stage stood a green-baize covered circular table with two large books of hand-tooled blue leather: The Charter of the United Nations and the Statute for the Court of International Justice. Each delegation filed onto the stage and signed the documents for their countries. Signing for the United States, President Truman made note of political reality in his closing speech; "Changing world conditions will require readjustments--but they will be the readjustments of peace, and not of war."

Much had happened in the rest of the world during the San Francisco conference. On May 8th, Germany capitulated. The good news brought no delirious celebrations to San Francisco. In the Bay Area, attentions remained focused on the United Nations festivities and the heavy fighting that continued in the Pacific. Iwo Jima had been taken on March 26th; several days later began Operation Iceberg, the in-

vasion of Okinawa. The battle for that large island, 350 miles from Japan, ended on June 22nd. Not long after, the U.S. Army in the Philippines declared the Luzon campaign over. This set the stage for the invasion of Japan. At the end of June, President Truman approved plans for a two-stage invasion that

American delegation led by Truman and Stettinius watch Sen. Tom Connally sign the Charter, June 26, 1945. (San Francisco Archives, S.F. Public Library)

May 8, 1945, 3:00 p.m. in San Francisco; downtown street is quiet as soldier reads about German surrender. (San Francisco Archives, S.F. Public Library)

bombers of the Navy air group materialized in the skies over the Cronkhite hills. Aircraft flew at deceptively high angles, then suddenly reappeared in a different part of the sky, diving on the defenses. On the ground, the gunners trained their camouflaged weapons on the attacking flights. The Harbor Defenses fired no rounds, but found it useful "to know what it was like to have planes flying through the area," recalled John Schonher. After the exercises, HDSF officers went to Santa Rosa for Navy debriefing to determine how well the attacking air group had done.

In mid-1945, HDSF batteries held their last target practices of the war. It was "one of the Harbor Defenses' most successful night firing practices" for Battery B, 173rd CA Battalion, reported the *Coast Artillery Journal*. As the HDSF searchlight battery provided illumination, the 16-inch Cronkhite rifles scored hits on a Navy S-40 target four miles at sea. Then a 40mm battery of the 6th Coast Artillery Battalion fired on an AMTB target at 6300 yards with fifteen rounds finding the mark. HDSF commander Colonel LaFrenz and Colonel Kenneth Rowntree, executive officer, observed the night practice from a mineplanter. There were many within the ranks who feared these practices would be the last hurrah of the Coast Artillery.

"The outlook was most encouraging," wrote the *Coast Artillery Journal* in mid-1945, referring to Pearl Harbor and the opening shots of the war. The Japanese fleet ruled the Pacific in the early days, and it seemed "the Coast Artilleryman's dream of directly engaging the enemy would be fulfilled." But after years of

would begin on November 1st, with landings on the southern Japanese island of Kyushu. After the arrival in the Pacific of American forces from Europe, the invasion of the main island, Honshu, would start on March 1, 1946. Meanwhile, Truman received news of the successful atomic bomb tests. He hoped to use the powerful weapon to make Japan surrender without further bloodshed in a costly invasion.

In the early summer of 1945, a new Navy air group trained at Santa Rosa, thirty miles north of San Francisco, for the following year's planned invasion of Honshu. Wanting to "test tactical plans over an area comparable to that of HDSF and sub-posts," the Navy selected the rugged hills of Fort Cronkhite to simulate the mountainous terrain of Japan. "This gave a chance for our own people who had to man their machine guns and antiaircraft weapons," remembered HDSF officer John Schonher, "to see how they would react to live targets." The harbor defenders and the 122nd Reconnaissance Troop taking part in the maneuvers selected terrain for defense. They moved vehicles into position and camouflaged them. Observation posts and radio warning nets were established. Navy planes flew over Fort Cronkhite taking reconnaissance photographs in planning the practice air strikes.

One afternoon, fighters and dive-

combat on foreign shores, with armored forces, air power, and amphibious landings predominating, the defense guns of the Coast Artillery no longer had that romantic ring. "The name carries little meaning to the public," lamented the *Journal*. "It may well be that in the future army the name will be lost--but the missions will still exist."

By July 1945, HDSF activities took on the atmosphere of a farewell. More than six hundred members of the defenses, mostly veterans of Pacific fighting with enough time in service under the point system, transferred from Fort Scott in mid-month to separation centers, and then home. This was the "first mass Army release of San Francisco soldiers who have defended the city and harbor from possible enemy attack," claimed the *Coast Artillery Journal*. At the Fort Scott club, the officers of the Harbor Defenses honored Brigadier General Haines and his wife at an evening reception on Friday, July 27th. The former HDSF commander was retiring from the Army after serving as chief of the Northern California Sector of Western Defense Command. Colonel LaFrenz took over the Sector and spent time in the northern forests of the state chasing balloon bombs launched from Japan on the jet stream.

Upon his retirement, General Haines received a letter from Major General LeRoy Lutes, president of the United States Coast Artillery Corps Association. "Much of the wonderful work performed by the Coast Artillery Corps will be lost sight of around the conference table for post war organization," wrote Lutes. He urged Haines and other senior officers to "restore morale" in the ranks of coast artillerymen and publicize the role of seacoast artillery in the postwar Army. During the war, modernization of seacoast defenses in the U.S. amounted to 220 million dollars. The cost included construction of nineteen 16-inch casemated batteries

and several dozen modern 6-inch batteries. The powerful and efficient new armament enabled an overall reduction of seacoast defenses by one-half. Not wishing to give up so readily what had been accomplished at great cost, the Joint Chiefs of Staff decided to "retain and maintain in serviceable condition" all existing seacoast armament until the future dictated their replacement by newer weapons.

After he served four years at the Harbor Defenses, the Army picked Lieutenant Colonel John Schonher for a Shipment X-Ray, to board a transport with two thousand other officers headed to the South Pacific for the 1946 Honshu invasion. Schonher was packed and ready, but another lieutenant colonel "bumped" him off the list. On August 6th, the first atomic bomb fell on Hiroshima, followed days later by another on Nagasaki. Meanwhile, Soviet mechanized forces smashed through the Japanese Kwantung Army in Manchuria. On August 15th, Japan surrendered. On the same day, a troop transport carrying the two thousand officers of Shipment X-Ray sailed under the Golden Gate Bridge, headed for the South Pacific.

When the war ended, one San Francisco hotel concessionaire did not rejoice. She was stunned and incredulous. "Did you hear that?" the woman asked hotel employees on V-J Day. "The war is over!" She owned several concessions in the lobby; end of fighting

August 14, 1945: Japan surrender is more raucous in San Francisco. In celebration, mob overturns newspaper truck, with HDSF corporal looking back toward camera. (San Francisco Archives, S.F. Public Library)

meant less business from military customers. The concessionaire's attitude visibly irritated one of the hotel bartenders; "I'm gonna hit her over the head for saying things like that," he muttered angrily, his white-knuckled hands tightly gripping a bar tray.

Between V-J Day and the formal surrender aboard the USS *Missouri* on Tokyo Bay, baseball and softball teams from Army service units in the nine Western states gathered in the Bay Area for the last sports competitions of the war. After five days of elimination play at Fort Scott, the 9th Service Command baseball finals ended on August 26th. Camp Anza beat Fort Lewis 1-0 in eleven innings for the title. Teams came from Army bases as far away as Utah, Washington, and Southern California. Farther inland at the Camp Stoneman softball finals, the Fort Scott Gunners took second place and the Scott WAC team also played. The Harbor Defenses had the distinction of being the only 9th Service Command installation fielding three teams in the finals.

San Francisco's formal celebration of victory took place on September 9, 1945 as the city welcomed Lieutenant General Jonathan M. Wainwright, the "Hero of Bataan." Fort Scott M.P.'s provided escort for Wainwright and other returning officers when they landed at Hamilton Field. Twenty thousand marchers from all military services paraded down Market Street in the city's welcome to the popular military hero. The general sat in the lead car with Mayor Roger Lapham. As the procession started from the Embarcadero, Wainwright seemed nervous. After riding a small distance, the general started to smile and relax, quite moved by the tremendous reception he got from the crowds. Wainwright confided to Lapham that he expected people along the parade route would hiss him for surrendering the Philippines in 1942. Following Wainwright, the U.S. Army contingent marched down Market Street as Liberator and Superfortress bombers roared overhead. Major General Henry Conger Pratt, chief of Western Defense Command, rode in the first car, followed by Army units associated with war activities in the Bay Area; the 4th Air Force, Port of Embarkation units, military police from the 9th Service Command, and the WAC Band from Letterman Hospital. On this occasion, units of the Harbor Defenses made their last formal public appearance. Wearing Class A full-dress uniforms with combat attire, the coast artillerymen marched past the City Hall reviewing stand "with more than usual pride."

Two weeks later on September 15th, the four coast artillery battalions of the Harbor Defenses disbanded "in anticipation of reduction of personnel to peacetime strength." The *Coast Artillery Journal* announced formation of "a new streamlined HDSF regiment" composed of separate batteries manning the searchlights, minefields, AMTB weapons, Harbor Entrance Control Post, and 6-inch emplacements of Smith, Rathbone, and Lobos. Mineplanters *Niles*, *Mills*, and *Spurgin* continued their assignment at the Golden Gate. But the "streamlining" eliminated 16-inch major-caliber batteries, which reduced the Harbor Defenses to minefields and their protective armament.

HDSF Color Bearers

Proud Coast Artillerymen

HDSF participation in Wainwright parade as published in Golden Gate Guardian. (Presidio Army Museum)

Since 1941, warships sailed out of San Francisco Bay under the shield of fully-manned harbor defenses. On October 15, 1945, in a fitting end to the war years, the fighting ships returned to a Golden Gate that no longer bristled with the seacoast arms of old. The only 16-inch rifles in sight that day would be mounted in the turrets of battleships passing under the bridge. Mayor Roger Lapham, Archbishop John Mitty, and Presidio military officers waited at the Marina yacht harbor for the victorious Third Fleet. The officials looked toward the harbor entrance, but could hardly see the famous bridge hidden by thick fog. When the naval flotilla sailed through the Gate, the battleship *South Dakota*, with Admiral William F. Halsey aboard, was barely discernible in the mist, and "the other ships were mere wraiths," wrote Helen Lapham. The 680-foot battleship paused to pick up the dignitaries at the Marina, then proceeded to the Alameda anchorage where Admiral Halsey reviewed the rest of the fleet.

During the autumn of 1945, HDSF sent harbor defensemen to the Antiaircraft Training Center at Point Montara, two miles north of Half Moon Bay. Along the shore, the Navy had laid a one thousand-yard long concrete strip mounted with AA weapons of all types and calibers. Most of the HDSF men, some only recently assigned to the defenses, were awaiting discharge or had too few points to leave the service. Few had antiaircraft training. At Point Montara, they received a two-week gunnery course uninterrupted by garrison duties and details. Away from air and water traffic, the Montara range reverberated with the sound of 3 and 5-inch Navy guns, 20mm, 40mm, twin .50's, and .30-caliber automatic weapons firing simultaneously. For veteran coast artillerymen, the nimble radio-controlled miniature planes used in target practice proved more realistic than the old target sleeves. Novice AA gunners got accustomed to the noise and feel of the weapons by firing unlimited amounts of ammunition. No target practice records were kept, wrote one participant; "We can come back again and again, knowing we're improving with every belt of ammo or every clip of 40mm that passes out of the barrel." For HDSF, the value of the training

Dismantling the harbor defenses---15-ton concrete anchor lifted by Navy from submarine net across Golden Gate, September 17, 1945. (San Francisco Archives, S.F. Public Library)

lay in giving experience to officers and men thinking of staying in the peacetime Army or organized reserves; for those harbor defensemen awaiting discharge, the exercise was "an important morale factor."

"For superior performance of duty," Major General Pratt of Western Defense Command presented the Meritorious Service Unit plaque to the 4th Coast Artillery Mineplanter Battery during Fort Scott ceremonies in the fall. Captain Frank Jacott, the battery CO accepted the award on behalf of his men, the crew of the USAMP *Ellery W. Niles*. After hostilities, the HDSF planters had to dismantle the Golden Gate minefields. Unlike the urgent effort to lay the fields in December 1941, the work to dismantle them progressed languidly. Though he had enough points in service to leave the Army, junior engineering officer Rudy Palihnich of the USAMP *Spurgin* could not depart, since officers were needed to man

USAMP Spurgin awaits sailing orders at Sausalito dock, October 14, 1945. (R. Palihnich)

the ships that pulled up the mines. But the Army discharged enlisted crewmen in such numbers that the mineplanters could not put to sea. "Most of the time we didn't have enough crew to go out into the minefield," Palihnich recalled ironically, "yet I was kept back in order to get the mines up." Whenever enough of a ship's crew was gotten together, the *Spurgin* went out; otherwise, the vessel stayed at the Sausalito dock.

Since large numbers of servicemen remained in San Francisco, clubs established for their welfare continued to operate. City guide books published in the first months of peace still listed numerous servicemen's centers. The Hospitality House, which opened to such fanfare in 1941, remained in business at the Civic Center. "Ship dances arranged and hostesses provided," was their watchword. The USO maintained several clubs in the area, including one on Geary and Buchanan Streets for black service personnel. Most USO clubs featured recording machines so every serviceman could send home a "letter on a record." "Out of the muck of waterfront taverns" on Clay Street off the Embarcadero, the Golden Gate Group of American Writers turned a former loft into the Harbor Club for Men in Service. This was a unique servicemen's dormitory, possibly the most cultural in the Bay Area. In the club's big lounge with open fireplace, well-known local writers like Oscar Lewis and Gertrude Atherton dropped by to meet the GI's. Hotel rooms at reduced rates for servicemen and their families were featured at the King George Hotel on lower Mason Street, run by the National Lutheran Council Service Commission. And the

Merchant Marine operated a recreation center on Market Street near the waterfront. Even enlisted personnel of the British Navy had their own club in the city---the Union Jack Club on Pine Street near Market for "enlisted men, merchant and navy men of the British Empire."

On November 15, 1945, Headquarters of the Army Service Forces approved a massive study submitted by HDSF proposing postwar harbor defense plans for the Golden Gate. The detailed report specified the existing armament to be kept, together with recommendations for their improvement. The proposed tactical plan counted among its batteries the modern 6-inch and 16-inch emplacements uncompleted at the end of the war. The 6-inch battery on Baker Beach and the 3-inch fixed antiaircraft batteries, all deactivated since 1944, would be resurrected. The study recommended retaining the minefields, the AMTB defenses including the Fort Point 3-inch batteries, as well as the Navy submarine net and underwater listening devices. The proposals were only suggestions. As HDSF awaited Army decisions concerning the future of seacoast defenses at San Francisco, coast artillery officers speculated that mine defenses, and not the big seacoast guns, stood the best chance of being retained in a budget-conscious postwar Army.

As 1945 ended, the Harbor Defenses returned to the easier pace of a peacetime Army post. A garrison force maintained the armament just as earlier harbor defensemen had done before the war. Though some officers saw a future role for the Coast Artillery, the generals who ran the postwar Army were not coast artillerymen by training. Most of them came from the Pacific and European war theatres, where amphibious landings overcame enemy fixed fortifications. There would now be little sympathy for maintaining harbor defenses like those at San Francisco.

Chapter 11:

Operation Blowtorch

The Harbor Defenses of San Francisco did not end abruptly after World War II despite the Army's waning support for coast artillery. On April 1, 1946, the War Department announced the move of Army Ground Forces to Fort Monroe; thus the Coast Artillery School at that historic location, which trained officers and enlisted specialists for leadership roles in seacoast artillery units, needed a new home. The Army chose Fort Winfield Scott as the replacement site, because it considered the Golden Gate fortifications equal if not superior to the harbor defenses at Chesapeake Bay. "At Fort Scott, the School will be established in the heart of a modern Harbor Defense," wrote the *Coast Artillery Journal*. "The terrain and climactic conditions of the San Francisco area will permit more realistic instruction in that increasingly vital factor of seacoast gunnery and radar." Fort Scott, with its many sub-posts, allowed room for future expansion of the school. The Army earmarked one-half million dollars to move equipment and personnel from Fort Monroe to San Francisco and equip the Fort Scott buildings for school use. On June 1, 1946, the Coast Artillery School formally departed Fort Monroe for the Golden Gate.

A beachcomber wandering the San Francisco shore just west of the Golden Gate Bridge on June 5th, discovered a rusty torpedo lodged in the rocks. The hiker reported the discovery to the Coast Guard, which in turn called the Presidio for help. Finally, the Navy arrived on the beach to dispose of the twenty-one foot torpedo which newspapers described as "broken in two and badly rusted." Navy demolitions men blew up the torpedo with three shaped charges. The *San Francisco Chronicle* speculated that a Japanese submarine, "hiding on the Marin side of the Gate," must have fired the torpedo sometime during the war. A June 7th editorial in the *Chronicle* offered a more reasonable explanation. The errant torpedo could have come from anywhere between San Francisco and the Asian coast, suggested the editorial. "The history of the sea include some verified drifts that would be too marvelous for fiction." Jack Lehmkuhl, General Stockton's former aide, now back in the Bay Area as a civilian, read the newspaper account with more than passing interest. His memories went back to the H-Station on the night of December 8, 1941 when an underwater contact was lost in the city's first blackout. Lehmkuhl wondered if his unidentified submarine had anything to do with the battered, rust-covered torpedo discovered on the beach five years later.

July 1, 1946 marked the official opening of the Coast Artillery School at Fort Scott. "The new 'mecca' of the CAC is located on a hill overlooking the city of San Francisco," said the *Coast Artillery Journal*. The school's first commandant was Major General Robert T. Frederick, a coast artillery officer who gained fame in World War II as founder and commander of the Army's 1st Special Service Force. (Many years later, a movie called "The Devil's Brigade" was made about General Frederick and this elite unit.) Also on July 1st, the Harbor Defenses activated a headquarters detachment. This caretaking detachment maintained the mothballed armament and guarded outlying stations. A month later on August 1st, several reserve training units were activated for Bay Area coast artillery reservists.

The Coast Artillery School began classes at the end of summer 1946. Officers new to coast artillery started with a thirteen-week basic course. Then each department offered eighteen-week courses in their specialties. The Department of Gunnery and Tactics instructed officers and enlisted specialists in seacoast gunnery, mobile weapons, and harbor defense techniques. Simulated range exercises took place indoors on a large plastic surface representing the ocean. Students took readings through an actual depression range finder at scale ship models pulled across the table. In the Department of Engineering, officers and men studied electronics, and learned to repair and maintain seacoast armament. The submarine mine warfare course instructed students with an elaborate 225-foot scale model of the San Francisco harbor entrance complete with flashing navigation buoys. Rows of inert lights

across the surface represented the minefields. Showing through the clear plastic table-top, a miniature submarine on strings headed toward the Golden Gate, its movement accompanied by recorded narration and underwater propeller sounds. As the submarine crossed the minefield, appropriate panel lights illuminated in a full-sized replica of the mine casemate. Then as the miniature vessel passed over a "mine" activated by the student operators, the satisfying sound of a recorded underwater explosion erupted over the loudspeaker.

At the real harbor entrance, Army mineplanters had dismantled all minefields by July 1946. The lack of trained mine crews due to mass release of men from the Army after the war delayed the work. The planters brought mines and cable back to their regular storage buildings at Forts Scott and Baker. Excess cable went to the Coast Guard Depot on the southwest shore of Yerba Buena Island.

"Contrary to public opinion, our present seacoast materiel is not obsolete," wrote an officer in the *Coast Artillery Journal*, "but is perfectly capable of destroying any of the present water borne vessels of modern warfare." In words expressed often in the postwar 1940's whenever coast artillerymen spoke of the future, the writer felt that "practically all of this materiel will be replaced by guided missiles." Another Army officer, Major General LeRoy Lutes was prophetic in mid-1946 when he envisaged "a perimeter rocket defense" of the United States and industrial areas by short-range ground fired rockets. "We believe this will be an AA mission," Lutes concluded, predicting accurately the Nike missile defenses of the 1950's.

In May 1947, Army

MG Robert T. Frederick, commandant of Coast Artillery School, with volunteer at founding of "Teen-Age Club" at Fort Scott, March 27, 1947. (San Francisco Archives, S.F. Public Library)

Ground Forces informed continental commands that scrapping of older coast artillery installations would begin the coming autumn. HDSF abandoned all armament except the minefields, the two modern 6-inch batteries which covered them, and the two 16-inch casemated batteries. The Army had not decided whether minefields and modern seacoast guns had a future mission, so their termination was deferred. The long-range 16-inch guns had been a bulwark of the Harbor Defenses since before the war. But the newest 6-inch rapid fire emplacements, Battery 243 south of San Francisco and Battery 244 at Fort Miley were still unarmed, though gun mounts had been ready to receive the barrels five years ago. Not until the scrap drive began in November 1947, did the barrels finally arrive to arm the modern 6-inch batteries.

Students and instructors of Naval School of Harbor Defense at Fort Scott, November 29, 1947. (San Francisco Archives, S.F. Public Library)

The 1948 session at the Seacoast Branch of the Artillery School (which the Fort Scott harbor defense school was now named) saw the institution of a new course in harbor entrance control techniques. The program taught Army and Navy officers the joint-operations of the harbor entrance control post "as developed in the Continental United States and in the island campaigns of the Pacific during World War II," stated the *Army Almanac*. Though HECP's did not operate in peacetime, the specialized field of harbor entrance control was kept alive through a reservoir of trained Army and Navy officers. Navy men also attended the school's submarine mine warfare courses. The USAMP *Spurgin* served as a "floating laboratory" for field exercises in mine planting and cable laying. "It has become a common sight now," wrote the *Coast Artillery Journal*, "to see as many Navy hands as soldiers aboard the Spurgin as she works in the San Francisco harbor entrance."

In the spring of 1948, the *Spurgin* pulled a target in the last firing of a 16-inch seacoast battery at the Golden Gate. Brigadier General William S. Lawton, school commandant, reported that instructors and students of the Department of Engineering would "anticipate with interest" the firing of Battery Townsley. Many of the coast artillery students had never before witnessed the thunderous eruption from a 16-inch rifle. Firing the long-range battery would test the accuracy of

Army and Navy harbor defense students study mineplanting operations at the Golden Gate in 1949. USAMP Spurgin in background. (San Francisco Archives, S.F. Public Library)

Battery Townsley at Fort Cronkhite on day of last target practice on March 22, 1948. (Presidio Army Museum)

radar and electronic fire-control systems. "Coast Artillery To Practice Today," proclaimed a small headline in the *San Francisco Chronicle* on March 22, 1948 in the obligatory statement to bay mariners issued whenever the big guns fired. Without giving the exact location of the guns, the announcement specified a danger zone between Tennessee Point and Point Bonita at a maximum range of thirty-five thousand yards and a maximum altitude of twenty thousand feet.

At Fort Cronkhite, General Lawton inspected the 16-inch guns, then along with a dozen newspaper reporters, stood back to observe the action. A colonel from the Seacoast Service Test Section of Army Ground Forces took command of the firing. On this first day of the practice, two-thirds the normal powder charge propelled the armor-piercing rounds. After the practice, the Public Information Office at the Presidio released a press statement saying these World War II guns still posed a deterrent to would-be aggressors. The 16-inch rifles were more powerful than ever, the press release stressed, because they were equipped with "the magic eye of radar to find their targets, regardless of weather conditions, and electronic brains to calculate instantly the data for their firing."

On July 14, 1948, Colonel Bedford W. Boyes, commanding the 319th Harbor Defense Battalion of the Officers' Reserve Corps, wrote a letter to his superiors at 6th Army, urging retention of the Harbor Defenses of San Francisco and its remaining unit, the Headquarters Battery; "It is believed that the inactivation of these 'going concerns' will prove detrimental to the best interests of the Army," Colonel Boyes wrote, noting the headquarters detachment contained trained coast artillerymen. Without them, no personnel would be manning the defenses on a daily basis, Boyes continued, and "in case of a National emergency, the existing harbor defenses should be manned immediately." The colonel then urged activation of reserve battalions for minefields, 155mm guns,

Battery Townsley thunders for the last time. (San Francisco Archives, S.F. Public Library)

and 6-inch guns. Boyes also proposed inclusion of a guided missile battery in a future harbor defense.

Colonel Boyes' superior at the Presidio, Brigadier General F.B. Butler, Senior Instructor of the California-Nevada Officers' Reserve Corps, forwarded the letter through channels with his indorsement; "The interest and standards developed in local Organized Reserve Harbor Defense Units is high, and it is recommended . . . a large number of Harbor Defense Units be retained in this area." General Butler also recommended keeping the Seacoast Branch of the Artillery School, because it offered unique training for harbor defense reservists. The Boyes letter with indorsement eventually reached the 6th Army commander at the Presidio, General Mark W. Clark, who replied through his adjutant that a policy statement was forthcoming from the Department of the Army on the future of harbor defenses. "You will be kept informed of developments," the reply added.

By the end of 1948, the Army decided to scrap all 16-inch guns. At the Golden Gate, the Army awarded a salvage contract to the Pierce Industrial Engineer Company. "Operation Blowtorch," which the San Francisco Chronicle called the scrapping, began with Battery Davis at Fort Funston. In December 1948, Pierce company workmen cut the 16-inch gun barrels into manageable five-foot sections, each piece weighing twenty-three tons. Trucks hauled the barrel sections and dismantled gun mounts to the Pacific States Steel Company in the East Bay,

where the surplus metal was put into furnaces and resmelted. The scrapping of the Funston battery took five weeks to accomplish. The Chronicle announced that a one thousand-bed veterans' hospital for neuropsychiatric patients would be erected on the site of the emplacement. "Although the location of the guns is no secret now," confided the newspaper, "the defensive measures to be employed in future Bay Area defenses are strictly hush-hush. Security-wise Army officials speak only in generalities on the types of defensive weapons to come." The only armament of the once elaborate Golden Gate defenses to be spared the blowtorch at this time were 6-inch Batteries 243 at Milagra Knob and 244 at Fort Miley. These guns were kept to protect the submarine minefields which the Army thought might be replanted some day.

In 1948, an Army staff study on the future of submarine mine warfare concluded that American harbor defense minefields of World War II were inefficient because no enemy vessels had been destroyed by them. By the same token, minefields were considered effective because no ship protected by mines had been destroyed. Declassified enemy documents showed that German submariners were aware that extensive minefields protected U.S. eastern ports and dared not challenge them. But since the war, all minefields had been dismantled; and the Army had not the budget to spend 26.9 million dollars in main-

At Fort Funston, 16-inch gun barrel of Battery Davis is measured for cutting by workmen as M.P. watches. (San Francisco Archives, S.F. Public Library)

Blowtorch cuts 16-inch barrel into sections for hauling to smelter, Fort Funston, December 3, 1948. (San Francisco Archives, S.F. Public Library)

taining the mine materiel still held in storage. On November 30, 1949, the Army transferred San Francisco mine materiel and the two 6-inch gun batteries to the Navy. In the 1950 Army reorganization, the Coast Artillery Corps went out of existence when it joined with the Field Artillery to form a single Artillery branch. Some former coast artillery units and personnel adapted themselves to guided missiles and later emerged in a new branch known as the Air Defense Artillery.

In the first half of the 20th Century, during the vogue of seacoast artillery, protective guns at the Golden Gate signified regional status and strategic importance as the Bay Area established a thriving military economy. After the Pearl Harbor attack, when the enemy seemed to be just over the Pacific horizon, seacoast artillery represented San Francisco's first and last line of defense. The Army kept the big guns secret and unseen in their defensive mission at the Golden Gate. When technology overtook the seacoast artillery, the harbor defenses faded into history without public fanfare.

The economic prosperity and regional importance Bay Area commercial interests hoped to gain in clamoring for Navy bases and military defenses in the 20's and 30's saw fruition in World War II. "Postwar San Francisco would never be the San Francisco of 1941," wrote Herb Caen around the time the Army scrapped the seacoast guns. The war had brought 200,000 newcomers to the bay; they were the servicemen and war workers "who discovered San Francisco and its hoarded delights and had decided to stay."

120mm antiaircraft guns at Toll Plaza of Golden Gate Bridge in the early 1950's--- the days of the Cold War. (Presidio Army Museum)

Bibliography

American Naval Fighting Ships. 11 vols. Washington D.C.: Navy Department, Office of the Chief of Naval Operations, Naval History Division, 1963.

Anger, Kenneth. *Hollywood Babylon.* New York: Dell Publishing Company, Inc., 1981.

Armed Forces Information School. *The Army Almanac: A Book of Facts Concerning the Army of the United States.* Carlisle Barracks, Pa.: U.S. Government Printing Office, 1950.

Arne, Sigrid. *United Nations Primer.* New York: Farrar & Rhinehart, Inc., 1945.

Averbuch, Bernard. *Crab is King.* San Francisco: Mabuhay Publishing Co., 1973.

Banning, Kendall. *Our Army Today.* New York: Funk & Wagnall's Company, 1943.

Bogart, Charles H. *Controlled Mines: A History of Their Use by the United States.* Bennington, Vt: Weapons and Warfare Press, 1986.

Brack, Mark L., and James P. Delgado. *Presidio of San Francisco National Historic Landmark District: Historic American Buildings Survey Report.* San Francisco: U.S. Department of the Interior, National Park Service, Western Region, and U.S. Department of Defense, Department of the Army, Presidio of San Francisco, 1985.

Brown, Allen. *Golden Gate: Biography of a Bridge.* Garden City, N.Y.: Doubleday and Co., Inc., 1965.

Caen, Herb. *Baghdad by the Bay.* Garden City, N.Y.: Doubleday and Co., Inc., 1949.

----------. *Don't Call It Frisco.* Garden City, N.Y.: Doubleday and Co., Inc., 1953.

Cherny, Robert W., and William Issel. *San Francisco: Presidio, Port and Pacific Metropolis.* San Francisco: Boyd & Fraser Publishing Company, 1981.

Chinn, Thomas W. *Bridging the Pacific: San Francisco Chinatown and Its People.* San Francisco: Chinese Historical Society of America, 1989.

Cohen, Stan. *V for Victory: America's Homefront during World War II.* Missoula, Montana: Pictorial Histories Publishing Company, Inc., 1991.

Command Decisions. Washington D.C.: Office of the Chief of Military History, Department of the Army, 1960.

Conn, Stetson, Rose C. Engelman, and Byron Fairchild. *U.S. Army in World War Two, The Western Hemisphere: Guarding the United States and Its Outposts.* Washington D.C.: Office of the Chief of Military History, Department of the Army, 1964.

Delgado, James P. and Stephen A. Haller. *Shipwrecks at the Golden Gate: A History of Vessel Losses from Duxbury Reef to Mussel Rock.* California: Lexikos, 1989.

Delkin, James Ladd. *Flavor of San Francisco.* California: Stanford University, 1946.

Glines, Carroll V. *The Doolittle Raid: America's daring first strike against Japan.* New York: Orion Books, 1988.

Green, Constance M., Harry C. Thomson, and Peter C. Roots. *United States Army in World War II, The Technical Services,The Ordnance Department: Planning Munitions for War.* Washington D.C.: Office of the Chief of Military History, Department of the Army, 1955.

Grover, David H. *U.S. Army Ships and Watercraft of World War II.* Annapolis, Maryland: Naval Institute Press, 1987.

Hagwood, Joseph Jr. *Engineers at the Golden Gate.* San Francisco: U.S. Army Corps of Engineers, San Francisco District, 1980.

Hamilton, James W., and William J. Bolce. *Gateway to Victory: The Wartime Story of the San Francisco Army Port of Embarkation.* California: Stanford University Press, 1946.

Historical and Pictorial Review of the Harbor Defenses of San Francisco. Baton Rouge, La.: The Army and Navy Publishing Co., Inc., 1941.

Hogan, William and William German, eds. *The San Francisco Chronicle Reader*. New York: McGraw-Hill Book Company, Inc., 1962.

Hogg, Ian V. *The Illustrated Encyclopedia of Artillery: An A-Z guide to artillery techniques and equipment throughout the world*. Secaucus, N.J.: Chartwell Books, Inc., 1987.

Kennett, Lee. *For the Duration: The United States Goes to War*. New York: Charles Scribner's Sons, 1985.

Lapham, Helen Abbot. *Roving With Roger*. San Francisco: Cameron & Co., 1971.

Lea, Homer. *The Valor of Ignorance*. New York and London: Harper & Brothers, 1909.

Leek, Jerome B. *Corregidor G.I.* Culver City, Ca.: Highland Press, 1948.

Lewis, Oscar. *San Francisco: Mission to Metropolis*. San Diego: Howell-North Books, 1980.

Lott, Arnold S. *Most Dangerous Sea: A History of Mine Warfare, and an Account of U.S. Navy Mine Warfare Operations in World War II and Korea*. Annapolis, Md.: U.S. Naval Institute, 1959.

Martini, John A. *Fortress Alcatraz: Guardian of the Golden Gate*. Kailua, Hi.: Pacific Monograph, 1991.

Nash, Gerald D., ed. *The Urban West*. Manhattan, Kansas: Sunflower University Press, 1979.

Orita, Zenji with Joseph D. Harrington. *I-Boat Captain*. Canoga Park, Ca.: Major Books, 1976.

Phillips, Cabell. *The Truman Presidency: The History of a Triumphant Succession*. N.Y.: The Macmillan Company, 1966.

Rosskam, Edwin. *San Francisco: West Coast Metropolis*. New York: Alliance Book Corporation, 1939.

Sawicki, James A. *Antiaircraft Artillery Battalions of the U.S. Army*. 2 vols. Dumfries, Va.: Wyvern Publications, 1991.

Stanton, Shelby L. *Order of Battle, U.S. Army, World War II*. Novato, Ca.: Presidio Press, 1984.

Steinberg, Alfred. *The Man from Missouri: The Life and Times of Harry S. Truman*. New York: G.P. Putnam;s Sons, 1962.

Stilwell, Joseph W. *The Stilwell Papers*. Arranged and edited by Theodore H. White. New York: William Sloane Associates, Inc., 1948.

Sullivan, Charles J. *Army Posts and Towns: The Baedeker of the Army*. 4th ed. Los Angeles: Haynes Corporation, Publishers, 1942.

Thompson, Erwin N. *Historic Resource Study, GGNRA, California Forts Baker, Barry, and Cronkhite*. Washington D.C.: National Park Service, U.S. Department of the Interior, 1979.

-----------------. *Historic Research Study, Seacoast Fortifications, San Francisco Harbor*. Denver: Denver Service Center Historic Preservation Team, National Park Service, U.S. Department of the Interior, 1979.

Thompson, George R. *United States Army in World War II, The Technical Services, The Signal Corps: The Test*. Washington D.C.: Office of the Chief of Military History, Department of the Army, 1957.

Walters, Vernon A. *Silent Missions*. New York: Doubleday & Co., Inc., 1978.

Webber, Bert. *Silent Siege: Japanese Attacks against North America in World War II*. Fairfield, Washington: Ye Galleon Press, 1984.

Weinert, Richard P. Jr. and Colonel Arthur Robert. *Defender of the Chesapeake: The Story of Fort Monroe*. Annapolis, Md.: Leeward Publications, Inc., 1978.

INDEX

Air Force, 4th: 58, 62, 156; Bombardment Cmd., 4th: 51; Interceptor Cmd., 4th: 58, 63, 64, 68, 70, 71; Bomb Sqd., 41st: 54; Observation Sqd., 115th: 51
Alameda, 31, 105, 157; Naval Air Station, 93
Albers, George, 129
Alcatraz, 2, 3, 30, 64, 86
American Federation of Labor, 31, 33
Angel Island, 2, 3, 41, 130
Antiaircraft Artillery Brigade, 101st: 57, 58
Antiaircraft Artillery Group, San Francisco, 148, 151, 152
Aquatic Park, 41, 58, 65, 148
Armed Forces Entertainment Committee, 132
Army, 4th U.S., 11, 41, 66, 126
Army, 6th U.S., 162
Army and Navy Club, 72
Army Ground Forces, 132, 159, 160, 162
Army Service Forces, 83, 106, 158
Atherton, Gertrude, 158

Bachman, Melvin O., 40
Baker Beach, 3, 27, 32, 43, 57, 65, 101, 110, 116, 117, 124, 139, 140, 158
Baldwin, Karl F., 95
Baldwin, Lawrence C., 96
Barnhart, Dale, 30, 34, 35, 73, 87, 88
Batteries, HDSF: Alexander, 3; Bluff, 90; Boutelle, 2; Chamberlin, 3, 27, 117; Chester, 3, 60, 61, 90, 119; Cranston, 2; Crosby, 3; Davis, 8, 9, 13, 21, 60, 90, 97, 163; Duncan, 3; Gate, 110; Godfrey, 2; Howe-Wagner, 2; Kirby, 3; Lancaster, 2, 86; Lobos, 118, 156; Mendell, 3, 27, 28, 32, 60, 123; Miller, 2; Battery 129; 45, 46, 120, 143; O'Rorke, 3, 142; Point, 110; Rathbone-McIndoe, 3, 143, 156; Saffold, 2, 32; Smith-Guthrie, 3, 143, 156; Spencer, 3; Springer-Livingston, 3; Stotsenburg-McKinnon, 3; Townsley, 8, 9, 13, 14, 35, 39, 56, 60, 75, 76, 91, 96, 161; Battery 243; 119, 161, 163; Battery 244; 161, 163; Wagner, 3; Wallace, 4, 6, 60, 95, 121, 143; Walter Howe, 4, 17, 90, 97; Yates, 3
Bay Cities Metal Trades Council, 31
Bay Cities Naval Affairs Committee, 6
Bell, Charles L., 22-24, 69
Bell Laboratories, 112, 136
Benecia, 106
Berkeley, 1, 28, 58
Berry, M.L., 110
Bethlehem Steel, 31, 106, 115
Biddle, Francis, 83
Blaugrund, Charles, 150
Bohemian Club, 119
Bolinas Bay, 62, 117
Bonesteel, Charles H., 139
Boyes, Bedford W., 162, 163
Bradley, LaVerne, 109
Brunson, Gilbert C., 130
Burgin, Henry T., 12, 16, 30, 40, 95
Burr, George D., 45, 91
Burton, Clark D., 120
Butler, F.B., 163

Caen, Herb, 30, 52, 61, 146, 147, 150, 164
California National Guard, 11, 42, 64; State Guard, 86, 129
Camps, Army: Callan, 34, 49; Haan, 26, 57, 58; McQuaide, 140; Spurr, 29; Stoneman, 106, 156
Cannady, Preston B., 16, 46, 48, 59, 76
Captain Tilson, 91
Carlsen, Richard T., 20, 69, 113, 133
Carquinez Straits, 106
Castillo de San Joaquin, 2
Cavalry Group, 107th: 131

Channels, S.F. harbor entrance: Main, 67, 68, 79-82, 90, 99, 102, 112; North, 49, 69, 79, 99, 112; Potato Patch, 49, 69, 79, 80, 134; South, 79, 80, 99
Chickering, Roger W., 99
Chin, Calvin, 29, 42
China Basin, 83
Chinatown, 29, 61, 122, 139, 145; China War Relief Association, 139; Chinese Chamber of Commerce, 38; Chinese Six Companies, 38; Chinese Sky Room, 146; Club Shanghai, 146; Twin Dragon, 146; St. Mary's Square, 108
City Hall, 56, 64, 156
City of Paris (department store,) 121, 122
Civic Auditorium, 38, 122
Civic Center, 6, 104, 108, 148, 149, 158
Civilian Aircraft Warning Service, 58
Civilian Conservation Corps, 19, 28, 29
Clark, Mark W., 87, 163
Cliff House, 30, 107; Seal Rocks, 107
Club Alabam, 146
Coast Artillery Battalion, 6th: 139, 140, 141, 143, 154;130th CA BN, (AA): 92, 100, 104, 131, 132; Btry. B, 93;172nd CA BN: 139, 150; Btry. B, 141, 142; 173rd CA BN: 140; Btry. B, 154; 174th CA BN: 139
Coast Artillery Corps, 2, 51, 77, 78, 116, 155, 164
Coast Artillery District, 9th: 12, 16, 30, 40, 41, 44, 55, 56, 95, 98
Coast Artillery Journal, 32, 33, 89, 99, 134, 137, 140, 154, 160
Coast Artillery Mineplanter Battery, 4th: 157
Coast Artillery Regiment, 6th: 7, 11, 36, 51, 95, 99, 104, 118, 132, 139; Band, 22, 28, 38, 40, 56, 91, 100, 121, 140; HQ Btry., 13, 26; HQ Btry, 1st BN, 13; Mine Command, 29; 3rd BN, 34, 130; 4th BN, 26; Btry. A, 13, 19, 20, 23, 29, 37, 69, 79, 81, 130; Btry. B, 13, 15, 17-19, 31, 34, 45, 57, 66, 101, 133; Btry. C, 12, 13, 15, 20-22, 39, 40, 57, 85, 96, 97, 115-117, 128, 131; Btry. D, 27, 28, 31, 57, 117; Btry. E, 13, 15, 16, 46-49, 59-65, 74, 91, 124; Btry. F, 16, 22, 27, 29, 30, 33, 69, 77, 81; Btry. G, 34, 71, 92, 109; Btry. H, 34, 109; Btry. I, 34, 49, 50, 59, 72, 92, 124; Btry. K, 13, 16, 31, 121, 125; Btry. L, 27, 133; Btry. M, 27, 71; Btry. N, 27, 128
Coast Artillery Regiments: 18th CA, 2nd BN: 28, 30, 33, 36, 40, 51, 117, 128; HQ Btry., 26, 27; Btry. D, 26, 27, 32, 57, 58, 60, 130, 131; Btry. E, 26, 27, 32, 43, 57, 97, 98; Btry. F, 26, 27, 32, 57, 59, 118; 54th CA: 88, 94; 56th CA: 34, 40, 51, 53, 55, 68, 88, 102: HQ Btry., 35, 36; Btry. B, 62, 73, 87; 65th CA: 11, 22, 26; 211th CA (AA): 65; 216th CA (AA): 71, 72, 86, 92; Btry. E, 58; Btry. F, 58, 60, 73, 86; 217th CA (AA): 58, 71; 250th CA: 11
Coast Defenses of San Francisco, 3, 7
Collier's, 87
Concord, 88
Connolly, Thomas, A., 139
Cook, Daniel G., 16, 22-24, 27, 30, 49, 50, 92, 109
Cooper, Kenneth, 16, 96, 97, 102, 115, 117, 118, 128, 132
Corps of Engineers, S.F. District, 7, 8, 14, 45
Courtney, Ralph, 23
Coutoure, Aurel, 138
Cox, Fannie, 143
Crockett, Charles, 38
Crowe, George F., 7
Curran Theatre, 101, 138

Daly City, 102
Davis, Richmond P., 15
Delkin, James, 144
DeMoisy, Ralph G., 35, 36, 59, 68, 74, 87, 88
Devils Slide, 46, 62, 93, 117
DeWitt, John L., 11, 64, 72, 76, 92, 108, 119, 120

DiMaggio, Joe, 37
Doney, Carl S., 59, 99
Dos Passos, John, 105, 106
Dragon's Lair, 132
Drake, Frank, 34-36, 56
Drakes Bay, 8, 61, 62, 65, 73, 74, 87
Dutra, Eurico Gaspar, 119-121

East, Joe C., 95
Elk Valley, 8
Embarcadero, 5, 33, 72, 86, 106, 108, 145, 156
Emeryville, 105
Emmons, Delos C., 119
Endicott Board, 2
Engineer Battalion, 113th, Co. A: 51
entertainer celebrities: Allen, Gracie, 125; Arbuckle, Roscoe,
    5; Arnold, Edward, 38; Ball, Lucille, 122; Baxter, Anne,
    125; Burns, George, 125; Cagney, James, 122; Cantor,
    Eddie, 38; Carlisle, Kitty, 101; Darnell, Linda, 38; Garland,
    Judy, 50, 122; Garson, Greer, 122, 148; Grayson, Kathryn,
    122; Hope, Bob, 125; Horne, Lena, 148; Hutton, Betty,
    122; Jenkins, Allen, 125; Marx, Harpo, 122; O'Brien, Pat,
    125; Romero, Caesar, 148; Rooney, Mickey, 125;
    Rutherford, Ann, 38; Silvers, Phil, 125; Sims, Ginny, 125;
    Stern, Isaac, 125; Withers, Jane,125
Etolin, 62, 87, 88, 102

Fairmont Hotel, 122,151, 153; Cirque Room, 147, 148;
    Tonga Room, 147
Farallon Islands, 13, 14, 54, 70, 72, 86, 102, 133, 134
Father O'Malley, 147
Ferry Building, 145
Field Artillery Regiment, 147th: 51, 53
Fisherman's Wharf, 82, 83, 86, 104, 148
Five Power Naval Treaty, 7
Fleishhaker Zoo, 44; Pool, 130
Fonvielle, John H., 49, 56, 66
Ford Motor Company, 28
Fort Baker, 3, 13, 16, 19, 22, 23, 27, 29, 30, 37, 45, 49, 50,
    56, 63, 81, 84, 91, 101, 110, 120, 125, 136, 140, 160;
    BOQ, 24; Marine Repair Shop, 83, 113, 114, 135; Station
    Hospital, 46, 83, 87, 143, 150
Fort Barry, 3, 4, 9, 27, 29, 31-34, 45, 46, 49, 50, 53, 56, 60,
    67, 71, 72, 76, 81, 92, 101, 109, 117, 125, 140-142, 150;
    Land Mine School, 130; Mendell Service Club, 125; Mine
    Casemate, 79, 143; Orientation School, 143
Fort Cronkhite, 8, 9, 13, 34-36, 39, 46, 48, 52, 53, 56, 59,
    63, 66, 71, 74, 87, 89, 91, 104, 117, 137, 143, 154;
    Commando School, 129
Fort Funston, 4-8, 12, 13, 16-19, 31, 39, 43-45, 52, 53,
    59-61, 65, 71, 85, 96, 101-103, 114-118, 120, 125, 130,
    131, 137, 146, 163
Fort Mason, 2, 71, 106; Construction QM, 46; Port of
    Embarkation, 65, 87, 105, 106, 156
Fort Miley, 3-5, 53, 57, 60, 117-121, 128, 133, 161, 163;
    Veterans Administration Hospital, 61
Fort Ord, 29, 42, 61, 65, 94
Fort Monroe, VA:16, 110, 118, 128; Coast Artillery Board,
    137, 141; Coast Artillery School, 13, 110, 116, 159
Fort Point, 2, 19, 60, 110, 140, 158
Fort Scott, 1-3, 6, 12, 13, 16, 17, 19, 27-34, 37, 39, 40, 52,
    53, 56, 60, 68, 70, 78, 81, 95, 99, 101, 104, 117, 118,
    124, 125, 127, 132, 135, 137, 138, 142, 143, 151, 155,
    156; Coast Artillery School, 159-161, 163; Mine Casemate,
    80, 120; PX, 100; BOQ, 129; Post QM, 114
49-Mile Drive, 38, 107
Frederick, Robert T., 159
Freeman, Harry, 29, 58, 60, 73, 86, 93, 94

General Electric "House of Magic," 132
Gilmore Oil Company, 30
Golden Gate Bridge, 12, 35, 40-42, 49, 50, 52, 57, 60, 63,
    68, 85, 87, 94, 98, 102, 110, 150, 152, 155, 157, 159; Toll

Plaza, 58, 61, 67, 71, 86, 93
Golden Gate Guardian, 84, 104, 121-123
Golden Gate Park, 148; Conservatory, 148; Polo Grounds, 30
Granada, 62
Great Highway, 17, 53, 61
Green, Joseph A., 25
Greenslade, John W., 55, 87
Gyn, Rose, 147, 148

Haight, Stanley M., 20, 42
Haines, Ralph E., 102, 104, 108, 112, 114, 117-120,
    123-127, 130, 138, 139, 143, 155
Half Moon Bay, 28, 61, 62
Hall of Justice, 36
Halsey, William F., 157
Hamilton Field, 51, 52, 54, 150, 152, 156
Harbor Club for Men in Service, 158
Harbor Defense Battalion, 319th: 162
Harbor Defense Officers' Club, 37, 84, 88, 91, 95, 120, 124,
    155
Harbor Defenses of San Francisco (HDSF,) 7; HQ, 92, 100,
    117, 140, 162; HECP, 67, 68, 82, 118, 123, 124, 136,
    156, 161; H-Station, 55, 56, 62-68, 80, 89, 90, 94-98,
    118, 120, 123, 126, 133, 140, 159; hydroacoustic listening
    post, 63, 81, 82; Standing Operating Procedure, 67, 80,
    89, 90, 92, 99; Special Services, 100, 101, 114, 125, 132,
    137; Mine Battalion, 68, 69, 81, 83, 91, 99, 112; Flotilla,
    77, 81-83, 120, 134, 135; Josie Lena, 85; JR-boats, 110,
    140, 141; Lincoln, 83; Mercury, 83; Redwood, 141; AA
    Groupment, 55; Funston Grpmt., 55, 90, 97; Mine Grpmt.,
    55, 62, 81-83, 90, 112, 113, 117, 142; Separate Grpmt.,
    55; Group 1; 90
Hawkins, Benjamin, 92, 104
Hayward, 63
Henneberg, Robert C., 40
Henry Bergh, 133, 134
Hershenow, William K., 121, 122
Hill 640; 60, 62, 117
Holden, F.H., 28, 33, 36
Hollywood All-Stars, 37
Hoppe, Willie, 104
Horseshoe Cove, 3, 19, 77, 83, 140
Hornet, 93, 94, 102
Hospitality House, 38, 108, 158
Huff, J.E., 51
Hunters Point, 5, 31, 58, 106
Hutson, J.C., 117, 118

Infantry Division, 7th: 29, 42; 40th: 42
Infantry Regiment, 17th: 65; 30th: 11, 38, 51, 53; 53rd: 65,
    108; 159th: 11
Insinger, Frederick, 114
International Settlement, 29, 68, 146; Barbary Coast, 30;
    Goman's "Gay 90's," 146; Hurricane Club, 132, 146

Jacott, Frank, 157
Japanese submarines: I-15: 70, 72; I-17: 88; I-25: 98; I-26: 62
Junior Chamber of Commerce, 11, 30, 41

Kanof, Lee, 115, 116
Kelly, Peter K., 137
Kilcourse, William, 98
King George Hotel, 158
Kirby Beach, 3, 49, 50, 81, 110, 124, 143
Knox, Frank, 31
Kobbe Avenue, 22, 101
Kramer, Arthur, 13, 14, 26, 39, 40, 60, 85, 96-98, 127, 140,
    141, 152
Kuskie, Glen, 143

L-8 Navy airship, 102, 103
LaFrenz, William F., 27, 31, 40, 96, 98, 114, 118, 119, 127,
    128, 137, 138, 140-143, 151, 154, 155

Lake Merced, 4
Land, Emory S., 31
Lands End, 3, 53, 57, 94, 95, 110
Lapham, Helen A., 149-151, 157
Lapham, Roger, 144, 156, 157
Lawton, William S., 161, 162
Lehmkuhl, Jack R., 55, 59, 63, 64, 67, 68, 76, 94, 95, 102, 159
Letterman General Hospital, 46, 156
Lewis, Oscar, 158
Lime Point, 3, 49
lion cub, 50, 59, 92, 124, 141
Liwski, Frank A., 19, 20, 60, 69, 79, 81, 82, 91, 92, 99, 112, 113, 136
Lockheed Aircraft Company, 75
Lutes, LeRoy, 155, 160

Mack, Walter S., 108
Madame Chiang Kai-shek, 108
Mahoney, Frank, 78, 118, 130-132
Maiden Lane, 72
Mardikian, George, 146
Mare Island, 8, 31, 65, 106
Marietta Manufacturing, 111
Marin, 36, 61, 150
Marina, The, 41, 42, 157
Marina District, 65, 68, 114
Market Street, 5, 13, 56, 144, 145, 148, 156
Mark Hopkins Hotel, 29
Marshall, George C., 117
May, John B., 133
McCloy, John D., 65
McIntyre, Hal, 132
McKinley, Howard, 38
McQuiston, Denver, 85
McReynolds, Samuel M., 95
Medical Battalion, 7th: 51
Milagra Knob, 61, 117, 119, 121, 163
Mile Rock, 79, 95, 99
Milo, Nino, 125
Mineplanter Service, U.S. Army, 77
Mineplanters, HDSF: California Bear, 82, 98; El Aquario, 13, 69, 77; L-74: 69; Samuel M. Mills, 111, 113, 135, 156; Ellery W. Niles, 19, 20, 69, 77, 78, 112, 113, 136, 156, 157; Horace F. Spurgin, 111-113, 120, 133-136, 156, 157, 161;
Minnesota National Guard, 58, 104
Mission District, 5
Mister Rhine, 100
Mitty, John J., 139, 157
Moffett Field, 95, 102, 103
Molotov, V., 151, 152
Montara, 102, 157
Moorman, Richard R., 17, 19, 43-45, 71, 92, 93, 117, 125, 132
Morley, John J., 139
Mount Tamalpais, 74, 115
Muir Woods, 149
Muni Pier, 41
Murphy, Leo, 114, 126, 128, 138
Music Box, 125

National Geographic, 109
Naval District, 12th: 41, 54, 55, 66, 87
Newsweek, 77, 78
Nob Hill, 122, 146, 147
North Beach, 68

Oakland, 13, 58,114; Army Base, 105; Scavenger Company, 86, 87
Ocean Beach, 1, 4, 17, 53, 61, 79, 81, 94, 107
Office of Strategic Services (OSS,) 128, 129
Olema, 74, 75

Olson, Culbert, 72, 83
Olympic Club, 102, 138
Omar Khyyam's, 146
Ordnance Department, 4, 21, 39, 75, 96, 137
Orita, Zenji, 70, 72
Osterhaus, H.W., 54, 55
Ottinger, Charles, 117

Pacific, 136, 137
Pacific States Steel Company, 163
Pacific Telephone and Telegraph, 136
Palace Hotel, 108
Palace of the Legion of Honor, 151
Palihnich, Rudy, 111-113, 133-135, 157
Palo Alto, 131
Pan American Airways, 65
Paolini, Mario, 141, 142
Payne, Harrison, 16, 17, 34, 44, 45, 71, 74, 95, 110, 124, 136, 137
Pepsi Cola Center, 108
Pfeiffer, J.O., 30
Pierce Industrial Engineer Company, 163
Pillar Point, 55, 117
Playland, 107
Plummer, Harry, 83, 114
Point Bonita, 52, 67, 79, 81, 110, 117, 130, 142, 162; Cavallo, 110; Diablo, 98; Lobos, 55, 118, 140; Reyes, 55, 62, 67, 102; San Jose, 2; San Pedro, 4
Port Chicago, 31
Potrero District, 5
Pratt, Henry Conger, 143, 156, 157
Presidio of S.F., 2, 3, 11, 12, 29, 41, 46, 51, 52, 55, 63, 65, 83, 84, 119, 124, 143, 157, 159, 162; Crissy Field, 11, 26, 40, 94, 95, 136; National Military Cemetery, 43; Marine Hospital, 53; YMCA, 37
Pulley, Boyd, 101, 124

Quartermaster Corps, 13, 69, 77, 83

Reconaissance Troop, 122nd: 154
Red Cross, 91, 122, 125, 126, 132, 133; Cookie Brigade, 100, 104
Redwood City, 36
Reserve Officers Training Corps (ROTC,) 7, 15, 16, 28, 34, 56, 118, 128
Rice, Charles, 20, 41
Richmond, 105, 106; Kaiser Shipyard, 106
Richmond District, 5, 28, 53, 128
Rodeo Beach, 59, 65, 79, 81, 130; Lagoon, 34, 50
Romulo, Carlos P., 148
Roosevelt, Franklin D., 6, 25, 33, 37-39, 66, 121, 144, 147
Roosevelt, James, 147
Rossi, Angelo J., 6, 38, 56, 108, 122
Rosskam, Edwin, 10, 29, 144
Rowntree, Kenneth, 154
Ruddell, J.C., 97

SCR-296 radar, 116, 117
St. Francis Hotel, 5, 119, 121, 147
St. Francis Yacht Club, 41, 42
San Francisco newspapers: Call-Bulletin, 143; Chronicle, 5, 6, 30, 31, 37, 38, 40, 52, 56, 57, 86-89, 98, 159, 163; Examiner, 5
San Francisco-Oakland Bay Bridge, 1, 33, 60, 61
S.F. Police Department Pistol Range, 12, 116
San Francisco Seals, 37, 38; Seals Stadium, 37
S.F. Stock Exchange, 70
San Joaquin River, 106
San Mateo, 130
San Pablo Bay, 106
San Rafael, 54
Santa Clara, 42
Santa Cruz, 87, 94

Santa Rosa, 63, 65, 154
Saroyan, William, 29, 107
Sausalito, 41, 42, 49, 59, 77, 106, 133, 135, 158; Four
    Winds, 23, 24; Hazel's Sweet Shop, 24; Marinship, 106;
    Perry's Market, 23
Scally, Tom, 28, 32, 50, 65, 70, 76
Schatz, Meyer, 40
Schonher, John, 28, 36, 60-63, 65, 66, 74-76, 84, 91, 95,
    118, 150, 152-155
Sea Cliff, 107
Selective Service Bill, 22
Sergeant Williams, 22-24
Service Command, 9th: 156
Shipment 9098-B, 87
Sequoia, 136
Signal Corps, 116, 136
signal stations, 67, 93, 94, 118
Sir Francis Drake, 147
Spitzer, Willis E., 46-48, 60-62, 74
Special Service Force, 1st: 160
Special Training Program, 99
Stettinius, Edward, 149, 151, 153
Stewart, Harley A., 130
Stilwell, Joseph W., 66
Stinson Beach, 8, 60, 62, 117
Stockton, Edward A., 1, 22, 26, 28, 39, 45, 50-56, 59, 60,
    64-67, 73, 76, 92, 94, 97, 102, 103, 159
Stroh, D.A., 41
Sullivan, Charles, 28, 36, 58, 69, 96, 116, 117
Sunnyvale, 31
Sunset District, 5
Sutro Baths, 63; Sutro Heights, 17

Taheny, John, 128, 129
Tahoe, 86, 87
Tait's at the Beach, 44, 45
Telegraph Hill, 105
Tennessee Cove, 65, 69; Tennessee Point, 8, 82, 162
Tenderloin, 61
Terry, Thomas A., 12, 15, 22
Teuscher, Ivan M., 59
Thomason Act, 15-17
Thurston, George, 50
Tiburon Net Depot, 20, 31, 41, 42
Tilton, Rollin L., 22
Time, 108
Training Memorandum No. 6: 28, 31
Transportation Corps, 106

Treasure Island, 13, 15, 31, 65, 78, 102, 117, 134, 135, 150;
    Golden Gate International Exposition, 13, 31
Truman, Harry S., 149, 152, 153
Twin Peaks, 5, 64

Union Jack Club, 158
Union Square, 5
United Airlines, 37
United Service Organization (USO,) 37, 38, 57, 100, 125,
    132, 138, 158
U.S.-Brazilian Defense Commission, 119
U.S. Congress, 2, 6, 7, 15, 25, 38, 87, 103
U.S. Maritime Commission, 31
University of Alabama, 16; U. of California, Berkeley, 15, 16,
    102; UC Hospital, 60; U. of San Francisco, 15, 16, 28, 34,
    118, 128; U. of Santa Clara, 15
Usis, Felix, M., 1, 28, 29, 33, 60, 69, 81-84, 96, 98, 100,
    104, 109, 110, 111, 117

Vallejo, 31, 65
Vartnaw, William, 86

Wainwright, Jonathan M., 156
Walters, Vernon A., 119
War Department (Dept. of the Army,) 2, 4, 46, 55, 56, 66, 87,
    98, 110, 113, 116, 119, 131, 135, 137, 139, 159, 163;
    Operations Division, 103, 104; War Plans Division, 6, 25
War Memorial Opera House and Veterans' Building, 6, 149,
    152, 153
Warren, Earl, 108, 149
Washington Naval Treaty, 6
Webster, George B., 12, 13, 15, 21, 22, 148, 151
Western Defense Command, 60, 63-66, 72, 74, 76, 84-87,
    90, 92, 98, 99, 113, 119,122, 126, 136, 137, 143, 156;
    Pacific Coastal Defense Sector, 55; Northern California
    Sub-sector, 55, 70, 94, 119, 129, 131, 138, 143, 152, 155
West Pointers, 12, 16, 17, 22, 28, 39, 109
White House (department store,) 122
Wildcat, 62, 117
Wilson, Walter K., 41, 55, 56, 94, 95, 119
Winter, William, 143
Wise, Jack, 75
Wolf Ridge, 8, 46, 66, 68, 71, 73, 93, 100, 117, 124, 149,
    150
Womens' Army Corps, 132, 133, 156
Wright, Harry, 117

Yerba Buena Island, 3, 160

ABOUT THE AUTHOR

Brian Burr Chin, born and raised in San Francisco, received a Master's Degree in history from the University of California at Santa Barbara. But his drawing and model-building skills allowed him to blend history and art in creating exhibits at the Presidio Army Museum in the late 1970's. Chin later worked on Hollywood motion picture special effects on such films as *Escape from New York*, *Star Trek: The Wrath of Khan*, *Battle Beyond the Stars*, and *Pumpkinhead*. For the last ten years, Chin has worked in television animation on such shows as *Batman: The Animated Series*. The author also painted the cover for this book, *Artillery at the Golden Gate*, his first non-fiction work.